Goldsmith
Interviews and Recollections

GOLDSMITH

Interviews and Recollections

Edited by

E. H. MIKHAIL
University of Lethbridge
Alberta, Canada

St. Martin's Press

First published in Great Britain 1993 by
THE MACMILLAN PRESS LTD
Houndmills, Basingstoke, Hampshire RG21 2XS
and London
Companies and representatives
throughout the world

This book is published in Macmillan's *Interviews and Recollections* series

A catalogue record for this book is available
from the British Library.

ISBN 0–333–45614–9

Printed in Great Britain by
Antony Rowe Ltd
Chippenham, Wiltshire

First published in the United States of America 1993 by
Scholarly and Reference Division,
ST. MARTIN'S PRESS, INC.,
175 Fifth Avenue,
New York, N.Y. 10010

ISBN 0–312–10193–7

Library of Congress Cataloging-in-Publication Data
Goldsmith : interviews and recollections / edited by E. H. Mikhail.
p. cm.
Includes bibliographical references and index.
ISBN 0–312–10193–7
1. Goldsmith, Oliver, 1728–1774—Interviews. 2. Goldsmith,
Oliver, 1728–1774—Friends and associates. 3. Authors, Irish—18th
century—Biography. I. Mikhail, E. H.
PR3493.G55 1993
828'.609—dc20
[B]   93–13921
                                                          CIP

Contents

v

Acknowledgements

My gratitude is due to the following for assistance, support, encouragement, information, editorial material or notification of certain items that appear in this book: Ms Lorraine Bailes, Mr Robert Chapman, Ms Rosemary Howard, Mr Keith Jarvis, Dr David Latham, Mr Robert Nicholson, Mr Ralph Payne, Mr Kenneth Robinson and Dr Brent Shaw. The book has benefited greatly from comments and suggestions made by Dr Richard Arnold. I am greatly indebted to Ms Cindy Cole for research assistance, and to Ms Bea Ramtej for her kindness and patience in the final preparation of the manuscript.

Several publications have been of immense help to me, particularly: G. S. Rousseau (ed.) *Goldsmith: The Critical Heritage* (London and Boston: Routledge & Kegan Paul, 1974); and Samuel H. Woods, Jr, *Oliver Goldsmith: A Reference Guide* (Boston: G. K. Hall, 1982).

Thanks are due to the University of Lethbridge for granting me a sabbatical leave, without which this book could not have come into existence.

It is also a pleasant duty to record my appreciation to the staff of the University of Lethbridge Library; the National Library of Ireland; Trinity College Dublin Library; the British Library; the Newspaper Library, Colindale; and the New York Public Library.

E. H. MIKHAIL

Introduction

'Oliver Goldsmith was a man who, whatever he wrote, did it better than any other man could do', said Dr Samuel Johnson. This, indeed, is the sentiment which he subsequently translated into Latin for the famous epitaph in Westminster Abbey, and which, translated back into English, comes out as: 'He left scarcely any style of writing untouched and touched nothing that he did not adorn.' Goldsmith was pronounced the greatest poet of his time by Sir Walter Scott; 'the most beloved of English writers' by Thackeray; and the 'author of the best novel of the eighteenth century' by Goethe. A host of others – including Schiller and Byron – gave their assent to these critical judgements, which have been affirmed by posterity. Goldsmith's reputation has stood the test of time, and his cumulative achievements in the novel, poetry, drama, criticism, the essay, biography, and history entitle him to be honoured as the most versatile genius of all English literature.

Goldsmith has not only exhibited great variety, but has earned the unusual distinction of being equally admired in prose, in poetry, and in drama. In each of these categories of literature, so rarely united in a high degree of merit in the same writer, Goldsmith attained eminence. As a prose writer, he combined – with the graces of a style that charms by its elegance, its simplicity, and its purity – sentiments refined without false delicacy, pathos that was never overwrought, and humour that was never forced; a moralist without hypocrisy, a teacher without pedantry, a reformer without intolerance, and a satirist without bitterness. His prose carried on the manner of Addison and Swift. As a poet, he enjoys a higher place still – perhaps the highest in that class which one might almost say he had created in England. In power of description, whether it be the delineation of nature or of humanity, Goldsmith is a master; his paintings are all portraits – true, vigorous, characteristic, and finished. There is no poet who holds a wider or a firmer grasp of the sympathies, the affections, and the intellect of every class of readers. No eighteenth-century poem, except Gray's *Elegy*, meant so much to mankind as *The Traveller* and *The Deserted Village*, both of which scored signal and instantaneous popularity, and which led many to pronounce Goldsmith the leading poet of his time. It must be admitted that, as a dramatist, he produced one of the most successful comedies of his day, abounding in happy strokes of wit, sprightly dialogue, admirable delineation of character, and humour that is never gross. *She Stoops to Conquer* still holds the stage after two centuries; in that era no one other than Sheridan can claim as much. Yet still we have not taken into account Goldsmith's essays that were and still remain the delight of every household; his biographies which are fascinating in diction, purity, and simplicity of style; or his natural history that was the most delightful and instructive in the English language up to his day.

No master has been less adequately assessed. It is a remarkable circumstance that the greatest genius of his age, who as a writer was equalled historically only by Voltaire, should have been overlooked by his contemporaries and allowed to depend on the sympathy and love of an after-generation for the perpetuation of his memory. He had no Boswell, and references by his contemporaries are rarely dated. The place of his birth has been disputed: four Irish counties claim him as their own. Even Dr Johnson, in the celebrated epitaph in Westminster Abbey, places the year of Goldsmith's birth as 1731 when it was actually 1728, and names Elphin as his birthplace, whereas it was Pallas. Goldsmith did not have a biographer until fifty years after his death, when Sir James Prior, his countryman and admirer, favoured the world with his first full-length life of Goldsmith,[1] the material of which was gleaned from many obscure and imperfect sources. Amid the various reprints and editions of Goldsmith's works which appeared in the first twenty-five years after his death, most curious is the absence of any serious biography. Glover's *Life of Goldsmith* was not a Life,[2] but a selection of anecdotes and extracts. Percy, who had undertaken to write a biography, seems to have felt that the notes he had collected hardly sufficed for such a work. He handed over the task to Dr Johnson, who produced nothing.[3] It was not until 1801 that Percy published his *Life* as a preface to an edition of the *Miscellaneous Works*.[4] This was the first carefully written life of Goldsmith, based on Bishop Percy's close friendship with him. However, as John Montague has pointed out,[5] the usual biographical portrait of Goldsmith is a sad travesty:

> there must be few cases where biographical irrelevances have distorted the qualities of a writer as much. It is partly the fault of

the Johnsonian idolators; by the time Percy's long delayed *Memoir* of Goldsmith appeared in 1801, Goldsmith had already been cast in his role of foil for Dr Johnson by Hester (Thrale) Piozzi, Sir John Hawkins and Boswell. And not merely foil but fool as well: anecdotes illustrating Goldsmith's absurdity, his voluble simplemindedness abound in memoirs of the period.

Goldsmith's ill-luck is particularly noticeable in the period immediately after his death, those years in which memoirs, collected editions and biographies begin to create the basis of a writer's subsequent reputation. He was excluded from the major critical survey of the century, Johnson's *Lives of the Poets*, on technical grounds: *The Lives* ends with Lyttleton, who died in 1773, the year before Goldsmith. The efforts by nineteenth-century writers like Thackeray, Macaulay and Scott to redress the balance in favour of Goldsmith are equally unsatisfactory. The first full-scale critical biography of Goldsmith, that by Ralph Wardle,[6] did not appear until the mid-twentieth century. It is curious, then, that a writer of Goldsmith's stature should have remained so long without textual and biographical analysis.

Critics have been trying to understand a man whose character so often appears in contradiction with his writings. Goldsmith's was a particularly elusive character: it did not lend itself to easy generalisations. The highest regions of intellectual society were open to him; but he was not prepared to move in them with confidence and success. He had brought from Ireland, as he said, nothing but his 'brogue and his blunders', and they had never left him. He had been a tutor, an apothecary's drudge, a petty physician of the suburbs, a bookseller's hack, slaving for daily bread. He was near 40 years of age when he published *The Traveller* and was lifted by it into celebrity; but he bore upon him the scars of his twelve years' conflict. He had a clownish appearance, a persistent stammer, and a face pitted with smallpox. Socially he had no advantage either; and both appearance and ancestral background were important in eighteenth-century England. Goldsmith's character seemed permanently marked by powerful feelings of inferiority, for which he tried to compensate by acts of brashness. He gambled recklessly, borrowed irresponsibly, drank excessively, and envied other writers inordinately. He made an awkward figure in the elegant drawing-rooms which were now open to him. In the Literary Club, he was something of a misfit and never wholly at his ease there, and outside the Club his very celebrity brought him into continual comparison with Johnson.

Goldsmith's contemporaries did tend to transfer something of their judgement of his character to his work. 'No man', said Johnson, 'was more foolish when had not a pen in his hand, or more wise when he had.' And Boswell echoed this: 'Goldsmith's incessant desire of being conspicuous in company, was the occasion of his sometimes appearing to such disadvantage as one should hardly have supposed possible in a man of his genius.' This is the figure of Goldsmith that moves through the pages of the *Life of Johnson* and with which the majority of readers are most familiar.[7] Mrs (Thrale) Piozzi's picture of Goldsmith is among the cruellest of the contemporary sketches.[8]

There were some, however, who found in Goldsmith a somewhat different person from the one depicted by Johnson, Boswell, or Mrs (Thrale) Piozzi. These others knew him under essentially different conditions, when he was under no strain to prove himself. Among the portraits of Goldsmith that should be placed beside the figure given us by Boswell in his *Life of Johnson* is that by Sir Joshua Reynolds, who wrote his character sketch about two years after Goldsmith's death. However, it was not published at that time; somehow the manuscript came into Boswell's possession and ended up in Malahide Castle, Ireland, where it lay forgotten until its discovery in 1940. The first printing occurred in 1952,[9] when it appeared in the series of *Yale Editions of the Private Papers of James Boswell*.

The present volume is a composite biography made from the collected views of most of those who were associated with Goldsmith. The exigencies of space, however, limit the number of writers who can be included. I have aimed mostly at selecting those recollections that have not been reprinted, as well as those that are not readily available. The pieces, arranged chronologically, cover almost all the stages of Goldsmith's life, so as to present as many facets as possible.

NOTES

1.   Sir James Prior, *The Life of Oliver Goldsmith, MB, from a Variety of Original Sources*, 2 vols (London: John Murray, 1773).

2.   Samuel Glover, 'Anecdotes of the Late Dr Goldsmith', *Annual Register*, 17 (July 1774) pp. 29–34. Reprinted as *The Life of Dr Goldsmith* (London: R. & J. Doddsley, 1777).

3.   See Arthur Lytton Sells, *Oliver Goldsmith: His Life and Works* (London: Allen & Unwin; New York: Barnes & Noble, 1974) p. 190; and R. W. Chapman, *Johnsonian and Other Essays and Reviews* (Oxford: Clarendon Press, 1953) pp. 171–3.

4.   Thomas Percy, 'The Life of Dr Oliver Goldsmith', in *The Miscellaneous Works of Oliver Goldsmith, MB* (London: J. Johnson *et al.*, 1801) vol. 1, pp. 1–118.

5.   John Montague, 'Tragic Picaresque: Oliver Goldsmith, the Biographical Aspect', *Studies: An Irish Quarterly Review*, 49 (Spring 1960) pp. 45–53.

6.   Ralph Wardle, *Oliver Goldsmith* (Lawrence: University of Kansas Press, 1957).

7.   On Goldsmith's character see Ricardo Quintana, *Oliver Goldsmith: A Georgian Study* (New York: Macmillan, 1967) pp. 88–97; Wardle, *Oliver Goldsmith*, pp. 290–3; and Montague, 'Tragic Picaresque', pp. 45–53.

8.   Hester Lynch (Thrale) Piozzi, *Anecdotes of the Late Samuel Johnson* (London: T. Cadell, 1785); and *Autobiography, Letters and Literary Remains*, ed. A. Hayward, 2 vols (London: Longman, 1861).

9.   Sir Joshua Reynolds, *Portraits*, ed. Frederick W. Hilles (London: William Heinemann, 1952).

A Note on the Text

In the extracts given, spelling errors in the originals have been silently corrected, American and archaic spelling and punctuation have been anglicised and brought to date, and the spellings of names have been rendered consistent throughout.

Chronological Table

1728	10 Nov: Oliver Goldsmith born at Pallas, County Longford, Ireland. His father was the Reverend Charles Goldsmith, Rector of Kilkenny West, Ireland. Goldsmith's childhood home was in Lissoy (since renamed Auburn), County Westmeath. He had two sisters: Catherine and Jane; and four brothers: Henry (priest), Maurice (carpenter), Charles, and John.
1737–44	Attends school in Elphin, Athlone, and Edgeworthstown. Contracts smallpox at 7.
1745	11 June: Enters Trinity College Dublin as a sizer, since his father is no longer able to place him there as a pensioner, as he has done his eldest son Henry.
1747	His father dies. 25 May: Gets involved in a College riot and is punished by a public admonition. Leaves College temporarily. 15 June: Elected one of the exhibitioners on the foundation of Erasmus Smyth.
1749	27 Feb: Receives the degree of Bachelor of Arts.
1750–2	Idles at home. Prepares to take holy orders. Rejected by the Bishop of Elphin. Leaves Ireland permanently.
1752–3	Autumn: Arrives in Edinburgh to study medicine. After spending two winters there, prepares to finish his medical studies on the Continent.
1753	13 Jan: Becomes a member of the Medical Society of Edinburgh.
1754	April or May: Imprisoned briefly. Takes ship for Leyden to study medicine.
1755	Feb: Leaves Leyden for unknown reasons. Probably studies medicine at Padua for six months. Travels on foot through Northern Italy, Switzerland, France, and perhaps Germany.
1756	1 Feb: Lands at Dover, England. Becomes apothecary assistant in London; then an usher at Peckham School.
1757	Feb: Does editorial work on the *Monthly Review* under

Ralph Griffiths and his wife, with whom he lives in Paternoster Row.

Sept: Breaks off his agreement with the publisher (by mutual consent) and moves to lodgings in the vicinity of Salisbury Square, near Fleet Street.

1758   Feb: Publishes a translation of *The Memoirs of a Protestant, Condemned to the Galleys of France for His Religion*, by Jean Marteilhe. Moves to Green Arbour Court, off Ludgate Hill.

21 Dec: Undergoes his examination at College of Surgeons' Hall. The examiners find him 'not qualified' as 'mate to an hospital'.

end of Dec: Begins to contribute to the *Critical Review*.

1759   21 Feb: Spends the evening at his friend, Dr Grainger's, where he is introduced to Reverend Thomas Percy.

3 Mar: Thomas Percy, later Bishop of Dromore, calls on Goldsmith at 12 Green Arbour Court.

3 Apr: Publishes *An Inquiry into the Present State of Polite Learning in Europe*.

6 Oct–24 Nov: *The Bee* (nos I–VIII) appears. Tobias Smollett enlists Goldsmith for the *British Magazine*; John Newbery employs him for the *Public Ledger*.

1760–1   Publishes the 'Chinese Letters' in the *Public Ledger*. Moves to 6 Wine Office Court, Fleet Street. Edits *Lady's Magazine*, for which he writes *Memoirs of M. de Voltaire*.

1761   31 May: Thomas Percy introduces him to Dr Samuel Johnson, who makes his appearance as a guest at a literary supper given by Goldsmith to a numerous party at his new lodgings in Wine Office Court.

1762   1 May: *The Citizen of the World* published.

14 Oct: *The Life of Richard Nash, Esq.* published.

28 Oct: Sells a third share of *The Vicar of Wakefield*.

1763   *Plutarch's Lives*, 5 vols published. Moves to Garden Court, the Temple. Joins the Literary Club.

Aug–Nov: Lives in the village of Islington.

1764   Apr–June: Again lives in Islington.

26 June: *An History of England in a Series of Letters of a Nobleman to His Son*, 2 vols published.

19 Dec: *The Traveller* published. It was the first time that Goldsmith had announced his name in connection with anything he had written.

1765   3 June: *Essays by Mr Goldsmith published.*
        Private edition of *Edwin and Angelina* for the Countess of
        Cumberland published.
1766   27 Mar: *The Vicar of Wakefield* published.
        Translation of *History of Philosophy and Philosophers*, by
        M. Formey, published. *Poems for Young Ladies* published.
        Writes *The Good-Natur'd Man.*
1768   29 Jan: *The Good Natur'd Man* opens at Covent Garden.
        Moves to 2 Brick Court, Middle Temple.
        Rents cottage on Edgeware Road with Edward Bott.
        May: His elder brother Henry dies.
1769   18 May: *The Roman History*, 2 vols published
        13 June: Agrees to write for Davies within two years a
        history of England in four volumes.
        Dec: Appointed Professor of Ancient History to the Royal
        Academy.
1770   *Life of Bolingbroke* and *Life of Parnell* published.
        26 May: *The Deserted Village* published.
        Autumn: Visits France for six weeks.
        His mother dies.
1771   Writes *The Haunch of Venison* and *She Stoops to Conquer.*
        Lives with Farmer Selby 'near the six-mile stone, on
        Edgeware Road'.
        6 Aug: *History of England* published.
1772   20 Feb: *Threnodia Augustalis* published.
        Dec: *The Roman History*, an abridgement for schools, pub-
        lished.
        Begins *An History of the Earth, and Animated Nature.*
1773   24 Feb: Johnson writes to Boswell remarking that Gold-
        smith's new comedy is to be produced in the spring, add-
        ing that no title has yet been given to it.
        4 Mar: Johnson informs a correspondent that the play is in
        rehearsal.
        15 Mar: *She Stoops to Conquer* opens at Covent Garden.
        26 Mar: *She Stoops to Conquer* is brought out as a book.
        29 Mar: Boswell writes Goldsmith a congratulatory letter,
        noting with pride that his wife had given birth to a daugh-
        ter on the very evening that *She Stoops to Conquer* had
        opened.

12 Apr: Boswell has a chance to form an independent estimate of Goldsmith's abilities when he goes to Covent Garden to see the new play.

15 Apr: Boswell, Johnson, and Goldsmith dine at the home of General Paoli, the exiled Corsican patriot whom Boswell had met during his travels abroad.

21 Apr: (morning): Goldsmith has breakfast with Thomas Percy, and it is probably then that Percy agrees to serve as his biographer.

21 Apr: (evening): Boswell, Johnson, and Goldsmith dine at the Thrales' house.

25 Apr: Boswell visits Goldsmith at the Temple and makes notes in his Journal on their conversation.

29 Apr: Johnson gives the play unqualified approval: 'I know of no comedy for many years that has so much exhilarated an audience, that has answered so much the great end of comedy – making an audience merry.'

1774   25 Mar: His fever becomes exceedingly violent.

4 Apr: Dies at 2 Brick Court.

9 Apr: Buried privately in the Temple Churchyard.

19 Apr: 'Retaliation' published.

15 June: *The Grecian History*, 2 vols and *An History of The Earth and Animated Nature*, 8 vols published.

11 Jul: The furniture of Goldsmith's rooms and his substantial library are catalogued and sold at auction.

1776   A monument erected in Westminster Abbey, with the Latin inscription by Johnson.

1864   Jan: A full-length statue by Foley, the Academician, is placed in front of Trinity College, Dublin.

Oliver Goldsmith*

ROBERT ANDERSON

Oliver Goldsmith was the third son of the Rev. Charles Goldsmith, and was born at Elphin, in the county of Roscommon, (according to his epitaph in Westminster Abbey, at Pallas, in the county of Longford) in Ireland, in 1729.[1] He was instructed in classical learning at the school of Mr Hughes, from whence he was removed to Trinity College, Dublin, where he was admitted an usher the 11th of June 1744. At the University, he exhibited no specimen of that genius which distinguished him in his maturer years. On the 27th of February 1749, O. S.[2] two years after the regular time, he obtained the degree of Bachelor of Arts. Intending to devote himself to the study of physic, he left Dublin, and proceeded to Edinburgh, in 1751, where he continued till the beginning of the 1754, when, having imprudently engaged to pay a considerable sum of money for a fellow-student, he was obliged precipitately to quit the place. He made his escape as far as Sunderland; but there was overtaken by the emissaries of the law, and arrested. From this situation, he was released by the friendship of Mr Laughlin Maclane and Dr [J. F.] Sleigh, who were then in the College. On his being set at liberty, he took his passage on board a Dutch ship for Rotterdam; from whence, after a short stay, he proceeded to Brussels. He then visited [a] great part of Flanders; and, after passing some time at Strasbourg and Louvain, where he obtained the degree of Bachelor in Physic, he accompanied an English gentleman to Geneva.

This tour was made for the most part on foot. He had left England with little money, and being of a thoughtless disposition, and at that time possessing a body capable of sustaining any fatigue, he proceeded resolutely in gratifying his curiosity, by the sight of different countries.

* In *A Complete Edition of the Poets of Great Britain*, vol. 10 (London: Bell & Bradfule, 1795) pp. 809–14.

He had some knowledge of the French language and of music; he played tolerably well on the German flute, which now at times became the means of his subsistence. His learning procured him an hospitable reception at most of the religious houses that he visited, and his music made him welcome to the peasants of Flanders and Germany . . .

On his return he found himself so poor, that it was with difficulty he was enabled to reach London with a few halfpence only in his pocket. He was an entire stranger, and without any recommendation. He offered himself to several apothecaries, in the character of a journeyman, but had the mortification to find every application without success.

At length he was admitted into the house of a chemist near Fish Street Hill, and was employed in his laboratory, until he discovered the residence of his friend Dr Sleigh, who patronised and supported him.

'It was Sunday', said Goldsmith, 'when I paid him a visit, and it is to be supposed, in my best clothes. Sleigh scarcely knew me. - *Such is the tax the unfortunate pay to poverty.* However, when he did recollect me, I found his heart as warm as ever; and he shared his purse and his friendship with me, during his continuance in London.'

By the recommendation of the chemist, who saw in Goldsmith talents above his condition, he soon after became an assistant to Dr Milner, who kept an academy at Peckham. He remained not long in this situation; but being introduced to some booksellers, he returned to London, took a lodging in Green Arbour Court, near the Old Bailey, and commenced author.

Mr Griffiths, the proprietor of the *Monthly Review*, gave him a department in his Journal, and Mr Newbery, the philanthropic bookseller in St Paul's Church-Yard, gave him a department in the *Public Ledger*, where he wrote those periodical papers, called *Chinese Letters*, which now appear in his works, under the title of *The Citizen of the World*.

His first works were *The Bee*, a weekly pamphlet, and *An Inquiry into the Present State of Polite Learning in Europe*, published before the close of the year 1759.

Soon after his acquaintance with Mr Newbery, for whom he held the 'pen of a ready writer,' he removed to lodgings in Wine Office Court, Fleet Street, where he finished the *Vicar of Wakefield*, which by the friendly interference of Dr Johnson, was sold for sixty pounds, to discharge his rent. 'A sufficient price when it was sold,' as he informed Mr Boswell; for then the fame of Goldsmith had not been elevated, as it afterwards was by his *Traveller*; and the bookseller had so faint hopes of profit by his bargain, that he kept the manuscript by him a long time, and did not publish it till after *The Traveller* had appeared. Then to be sure, it was accidentally worth more money.

In 1765, he published *The Traveller; or, a Prospect of Society*, 4to, of which Dr Johnson said, 'There has not been so fine a poem since Pope's time.' Part of his poem, as he says in his dedication to his brother, the Rev. Henry Goldsmith, was formerly written to him from Switzerland, and contained about two hundred lines. The manuscript lay by him some years without any determined idea of publishing, till persuaded to it by Dr Johnson, who gave him some general hints towards enlarging it; and in particular, as Mr Boswell informs us, furnished line 240,

> To stop too fearful, and too faint to go.

and the concluding ten lines, except the last couplet but one.

> The lifted ax, the agonizing wheel,
> Luke's iron crown, and Damien's bed of steel.

Luke, in the last line, is mentioned by mistake for *George*. In the *Respublica Hungarica*, there is an account of a desperate rebellion in 1514, headed by two brothers of the name of *Zeck*, George and Luke. When it was quelled, *George*, not *Luke* was punished, by his head being encircled with a red hot iron . . .

This poem established his reputation among the booksellers, and introduced him to the acquaintance of several men of rank and abilities, Lord Nugent, Mr [Edmund] Burke, Sir Joshua Reynolds, Dr [Robert] Nugent, Topham Beauclerc, Mr [Samuel] Dyer, &c. who took pleasure in his conversation, and by turns laughed at his blunders, and admired the simplicity of the man, and the elegance of his poetical talents.

The same year he published a collection of *Essays*, which had been printed in the newspapers, magazines, and other periodical publications.

He now made his appearance in a professional manner, in a scarlet great coat, buttoned close under the chin, a physical wig and cane, as was the fashion of the times, and declined visiting many of those public places, which formerly were so convenient to him in point of expense, and which contributed so much to his amusement. 'In truth,' said he, 'one sacrifices something for the sake of good company; for here I am shut out of several places where I used to play the fool very agreeably.'

In 1766, *The Vicar of Wakefield* appeared, and completely established his literary reputation.

Soon after the publication of *The Traveller*, he removed from Wine Office Court to the Library Staircase, Inner Temple, and at the same time took a country house, in conjunction with Mr [Edward] Bott, an intimate literary friend, on the Edgware Road, at the back of Cannons. This place he jocularly called the Shoemaker's Paradise, being originally built, in a fantastic taste, by one of the craft.

Here he wrote his *History of England, in a series of letters from a nobleman to his son*, 2 vols 12mo, a work generally attributed to Lyttleton, and, which is rather singular, never contradicted either directly or indirectly by that nobleman or any of his friends. This book had a very rapid sale, and continues to be esteemed one of the most useful introductions of that sort to the study of our history.

His manner of compiling this history is thus described by an intelligent writer,[3] who lived in the closest habits of intimacy with him for the last ten years of his life, in the *European Magazine* for 1793 . . .

In 1768, he brought on the stage at Covent Garden his *Good-natur'd Man*,[4] a comedy; which, though evidently written by a scholar and a man of observation, did not please equal to its merits. Many parts of it exhibit the strongest indications of his comic talents. There is, perhaps, no character on the stage more happily imagined and more highly finished than Croaker's. His reading of the incendiary letter in the fourth act,[5] was received with a roar of approbation. Goldsmith himself was so charmed with the performance of Shuter in that character, that he thanked him before all the performers, telling him, 'he had exceeded his own idea of the character, and that the fine comic richness of his colouring made it almost appear as new to him as to any other person in the house.' The prologue was furnished by Dr Johnson.

The unjustifiable severity with which this play was treated by the town, irritated his feelings much, and what added to the irritation, was the very great success of Kelly's *False Delicacy*,[6] which appeared at the other house, just at the same time.

Such was the taste of the town for sentimental writing, in which this comedy abounds, that it was played every night to crowded audiences; ten thousand copies of the play were sold that season, and the booksellers concerned in the profits of it, not only presented Kelly with a piece of plate, value £20, but gave him a public breakfast at the Chapter coffeehouse.

The success of *False Delicacy* dissolved the intimacy between Kelly and Goldsmith; who, though the type of his own *Good-natur'd Man*, in every other respect, yet in point of authorship, and particularly in poetry,

Could bear no rival near his throne.

Had Kelly been content to keep in the background, Goldsmith would have shared his last guinea with him, and in doing it would have felt all the fine influences of his good-nature; but to contend for the bow of Ulysses, 'this was a fault; that way envy lay'.

Goldsmith cannot be acquitted of all manner of blame in his enmity to Kelly, who was a very deserving man, and, by the publication of his *Thespis, Babbler*, some novels, and *False Delicacy*, had raised himself much into public notice; and what justly increased it, was the consideration of his doing all this from an humble beginning, and a very narrow education. He had a growing family too, which he supported with decency and reputation.

Though the fame of his *Good-natur'd Man* did not bear him triumphantly through; yet, by the profits of his nine nights, and the sale of the copy, he cleared five hundred pounds. With this, and the savings made by his compilations of a *Roman History*, in 2 vols 8vo, and a *History of England*, in 4 vols 8vo. which he used to call 'building a book' he descended from his attic story in the Staircase, Inner Temple, and purchased chambers in Brooke Court, Middle Temple, for which he gave four hundred pounds. These he furnished rather in an elegant manner, fitted up and enlarged his library, and commenced quite a man of 'lettered ease' and consequence.

About this time he was concerned in a fortnightly publication, called *The Gentleman's Journal*, in conjunction with Dr Kenrick, Bickerstaff, &c. which was soon discontinued. When a friend was observing what an extraordinary sudden death it had, 'Not at all, Sir,' says Goldsmith, 'a very common case, it died of too many doctors.'

His next original publication was *The Deserted Village*, which came out in the spring of 1770, and had a very rapid sale. He received a hundred pounds for the copy from Mr [T.] Griffin his bookseller, which he returned, under an idea of its being too much; and his way of computation was this: 'That it was near five shillings a couplet, which was more than any bookseller could afford, or indeed more than any modern poetry was worth.' He, however, lost nothing by his generosity, as the bookseller paid him the hundred pounds, which the rapid sale of the poem soon enabled him to do. He was, by his own confession, four or five years collecting materials in all his country excursions for this poem, and was actually engaged in the construction of it above two years. Dr Johnson furnished the four last lines.

The year following, he prefixed *A Life of Parnell*, to a new edition of his *Poems on Several Occasions* [published] by T. Davies, 8vo.; a performance worthy of Parnell's genius and amiable disposition.

His next original work was his comedy of *She Stoops to Conquer, or, the Mistakes of a Night*, which was acted at Covent Garden, in 1772;[7] and, notwithstanding the opinion of Mr Colman and some others, that there were parts in it too farcical, it met with great success, and restored the public taste to his good opinion. One of the most ludicrous circumstances it contains, that of the robbery, is borrowed from *Albumazar*.[8] The first night of its performance, instead of being at the theatre, he was found sauntering between seven and eight o'clock in St. James's Park; and it was on the remonstrance of a friend, who told him how 'useful his presence might be in making some sudden alterations which might be found necessary in the piece,' that he was prevailed upon to go to the theatre. He entered the stage-door, just in the middle of the 5th act, when there was a hiss at the improbability of *Mrs Hardcastle* supposing herself fifty miles off, though in her own ground, and near her own house. 'What's that?' says he, terrified at the sound. 'Pshaw, Doctor,' says Colman, who was standing by the side of the scene, 'don't be fearful of *squibs*, when we have been sitting almost these two hours upon a barrel of gunpowder.' He never forgave Colman this reply to the last hour of his life.

He cleared eight hundred pounds by this comedy: but though this year was very successful to him, by the *History of Greece*, 2 vols, the *Life of Bolingbroke*, prefixed to a new edition of *The Patriot King*, and other publications; what with his liberality to poor authors . . . and a ridiculous habit of gaming, he found himself, at the end of it, considerably in debt. This he lamented in secret, but took no effectual means for the cure of it.

This period is further remarkable for his dismissing the title of

Doctor from his address, and calling himself *Mr* Goldsmith. Whether he had only then decided never to practise the profession he was bred to, or that he thought *Mr* a more familiar manner of launching himself into the fashionable world, which he was then vain enough to affect to be fond of, is not ascertained; this, however, was the fact, that the world would not *let him lose his degree*, but called him *Doctor* (though he was only Bachelor of Physic) to the end of his life.

Besides his *Histories of England, of Greece,* and *of Rome,* he submitted to the drudgery of compiling *An History of the Earth and Animated Nature,* 8 vols, 8 vo, 1774, which procured for him more money than fame. Just before his death, he had formed a design for executing *An Universal Dictionary of Arts and Sciences;* a plan which met with no encouragement.

The poem, *Retaliation,* was his last performance, which he did not live to finish. It was written in answer to certain illiberal attacks, which had been made on his person, writings, and dialect, in a club of literary friends, where wit is said to have sometimes sparkled at the expense of good-nature. When he had gone as far as the character of Sir Joshua Reynolds, he read it in full club, where, though *some* praised it, and others *seemed* highly delighted with it, they still thought the publication of it not altogether so proper. He now found that a little sparkling of *fear* was not altogether an unnecessary ingredient in the friendship of the world, and though he meant not immediately, at least, to publish *Retaliation,* he kept it, as he expressed himself to a friend, 'as a rod in pickle upon any future occasion'; but this occasion never presented itself: A more awful period was now approaching, 'when kings as well as poets cease from their labours'.

He had been for some years afflicted with a strangury, which, with the derangement of his worldly affairs, brought on a kind of habitual despondency, in which he used to express 'his great indifference about life'. At length, in March 1774, being seized with a nervous fever, he, against the advice of his physician, took so large a portion of James's powder, that it was supposed to have contributed to his dissolution, on the 4th of April 1774, after an illness of ten days, in the 45th year of his age. He was buried in the Temple Churchyard, the 9th of the same month. A pompous funeral was intended; but most of his friends sent excuses, and a few coffeehouse acquaintances, rather suddenly collected together, attended his remains to the grave. A monument has since been erected to his memory, in Westminster Abbey, at the expense of the literary club to which he belonged . . .

His *Miscellaneous Essays* in prose and verse were collected into one volume, 8vo, 1775. His Poetical and Dramatic Works were collected, and printed in 2 vols, 8vo, 1780. An edition of his *Miscellaneous Works* was printed at Perth, 3 vols, 8vo, 1793. His *Traveller* and *Deserted Village* have been frequently reprinted, and with his *Retaliation* and other pieces, were received into the edition of the *English Poets*, 1790.

With some awkward impediments and peculiarities in his address, person, and temper, Goldsmith attained a share of literary eminence and emolument, which, with common prudence, might have protected the remainder of his life from the irritating uncertainties of want. In the course of fourteen years, the produce of his pen is said to have amounted to more than eight thousand pounds. But all this was rendered useless by an improvident liberality, which prevented him from distinguishing properly the objects of his generosity, and an unhappy attachment to gaming, with the arts of which he was very little acquainted. He was so humane in his disposition, that his last guinea was the general boundary of his munificence. He had two or three poor authors always as pensioners, besides several widows and poor housekeepers; and when he had no money to give the latter, he always sent them away with shirts or old clothes, and sometimes with the whole contents of his breakfast-table, saying, with a smile of satisfaction, after they were gone, 'Now let me suppose, I have ate a heartier breakfast than usual, and am nothing out of pocket.' He was always very ready to do service to his friends and acquaintance, by recommendations, &c.; and as he lived latterly much with the great world, and was much respected, he very often succeeded, and felt his best reward, in the gratification of doing good. Dr Johnson knew him early, and always spoke as respectfully of his heart as of his talents. Goldsmith, in some respect, conciliated his good opinion, by almost never contradicting him; and Dr Johnson, in return, laughed at his oddities, which only served as little foils to his talents and moral character.

'His person,' says Mr Boswell, in his *Life of Dr Johnson*, 'was short, his countenance coarse and vulgar, his deportment that of a scholar, awkwardly affecting the complete gentleman. No man had the art of displaying with more advantage as a writer, whatever literary acquisitions he made. His mind resembled a fertile but thin soil; there was a quick, but not a strong vegetation of whatever chanced to be thrown upon it. No deep root could be struck. The oak of the forest did not grow there; but the elegant shrubbery, and the fragrant parterre appeared in gay succession. It has been generally circulated

and believed, that he was a mere fool in conversation. In allusion to
this, Mr Horace Walpole, who admired his writings, said, he was 'an
inspired idiot;' and Garrick described him as one

—for shortness call'd *Noll,*
Who wrote like an angel, and talk'd like poor *Poll.*[9]

But in truth this has been greatly exaggerated. He had, no doubt, a
more than common share of that hurry of ideas, which we often find
in his countrymen, and which sometimes produces a laughable confusion in expressing them. He was very much what the French call
un étourdie;[10] and from vanity, and an eager desire of being conspicuous wherever he was, he frequently talked carelessly, without any
knowledge of the subject, or even without thought. Those who were
in any way distinguished, excited envy in him to so ridiculous an
excess, that the instances of it are hardly credible. He, I am told, had
no settled system of any sort, so that his conduct must not be too
strictly criticised; but his affections were social and generous, and
when he had money, he gave it away liberally. His desire of imaginary consequence predominated over his attention to truth.'

NOTES

Robert Anderson (1750–1830), a physician with literary interests. The text is
an extract from his 'Biographical and Critical Preface.'
 1. Goldsmith was born on 10 November 1728. See Katharine C. Balderston,
'The Birth of Goldsmith', *Times Literary Supplement* (London) 7 March 1929,
pp. 185–6.
 2. Old style.
 3. William Cooke. See his 'Table Talk', *European Magazine,* 24 (August
1793) pp. 91–5; (September 1793) pp. 170–4; (October 1793) pp. 258–64.
 4. *The Good-Natur'd Man* opened at Covent Garden on 29 January 1768.
 5. See *The Good-Natur'd Man,* Act IV, lines 210–36.
 6. Hugh Kelly (1739–1777), Irish playwright and editor.
 7. *She Stoops to Conquer* opened at Covent Garden on 15 March 1773, not
1772.
 8. By Thomas Tomkis (fl. 1604–15), Fellow of Trinity College, Cambridge.
The reference is to Act III, lines 84–220 of *She Stoops to Conquer,* supposedly
adapted from Act III of Tomkis's play, which was acted in 1615 before James
I at Cambridge.
 9. From David Garrick's imaginary epitaph on Goldsmith which inspired
Retaliation (1774).
 10. A giddy type of fool; a thoughtless, heedless person.

Mrs Hodson's Narrative*

CATHERINE HODSON

the Docter was born Novr ye^l 10 1729[2] at Pallace in the County of Longfoord near the seat of the Present Lord Annaly he was the Son of the Revd Chas Goldsmith Rector of Kilkenny West in the County Westmeath & Ann Jones Daughter to the Revd Oliver Jones Rector of Elphin.

as to the Charactor of his father none c^d. draw it better then himself in the Village Preacher in his Deserted Village which is none to be a just Picture of that Worthy man, he had seven Children viz 5 sons & 2 Daughters his Eldest the Revd Henry Goldsmith to whom the Docter Dedicates his treveler remarkable for his polite Learning on whom the father formed his most sanguine hopes but he marrying at nineteen a Lady he liked left the College & retired to the Country and at his fathers Death possessed his Living.

The Docter the second son in his infancy was remarkably humorous but it was uncommon mostly to serious & reserved but when in Spirrits none more agreeably so he was taken a most perticular notice of by all the friends of his family who were all in the Church & found in him an Early Genius for Learning & the muses, for at the age of seven & eight he had a natural turn to Ryhming that often amused his father and freinds at that time he c^d hardly write legibly & yet he was allways writting & allways burning what he wrote, & to make these little annecdotes of his life more regular I shall give any little occurance I can recollect as the happen'd.

there was company at his fathers at that time he was turnd of seven they were attended at tea by a little boy who was desired to hand the Kettle—but the handle being to hot the boy took up the skirt of his coate to put between him & it but unfortunately the Ladys perceived some thing which made them Laugh immodarately whether from the akwardness of the turn or any thing that might be

* In *The Collected Letters of Oliver Goldsmith*, ed. Katharine C. Balderston (Cambridge: University Press, 1928) pp. 162–77. All notes are Balderston's.

seen there I cant say but the Docter immeadietly perceived there
cause of Laughter & informed his father who promised him a reward of Gingerbread to write some thing on it and as it was one of
his earliest productions that can be recollected tho perhaps not fit for
the Publick I shall insert it here

Theseus did see as Poets say
Dark Hell & its abysses
But had not half so Sharp an Eye
As our young Charming Misses
For they c^d through boys breeches peep
And view what ere he had there
It seemed to Blush & they all Laughd
Because the face was all Bare
They laughed at that
Which some times Else
Might give them greatest pleasure
How quickly the c^d see the thing
Which was their darling treasure

the Docter at this time was at School with the villiage Master
whom he describes in his Poem he first gave him a taste for travail
which he ever after lik^d., this man was a Quarter Master in Lord
Galway's Regiment and serving many Champaigns with the Duke
of Marlburrough came home & after a number of missfortunes was
rewarded, with what, why was made a Country school master to a
Country Parson this man read tolarably well for an Irish man & was
employd by the Docters father for the early instruction of his children & those of all the Gentlemen in the neighbourhood tho he was
severe on the D^r yet he was his greatest favourite & from him I realy
beleive he first Learnd to despise fortune & feel more for every
creature he saw in distress then for him self.

at this time his fathers family increased by the Byrth of a third Son
unexpected as his mother was for seven years without bearing a
Child, this made the Father propose him for business in the Mercan-
tile way as he thought his fortune to small to breed him & his Brother
in the College & a younger family coming on his Brother was then at
School with the Rev^d Mr Nelagin at Longford & the year following
Entered Trinity College Dublin, however the D, being his mother
greatest favourite she proposed giving him a liberal Education for a
tradesman & as Mr Nelagin then retired to the Country the D was

sent at eight to the Publick school of Elphin under the inspection & care of his uncle John Goldsmith Esq' who lived near the Town he there saw many of his freinds & was by them greatly Carressd who at that time thought him a Prodigy for his age nor was there any subject worth Olivers wit but he was obliged to exorcise it on.

one evening for a large Company of young people at his Uncles a young Gentleman playd the fiddle who thought him self a greater wit & humourist than any one Else did the Company insisted upon the Dr danceing a horn pipe which he refuse a long time but on the commands of his uncle he exibited he was then 9 years old & had lately had the small pox which left very deep red marks & he realy cut an ugly figure how ever he was a very good subject for the wit of our fiddleing Gentleman who Cryd out in rapture there was Esop how like Esop he was the very man by G, the D still danced for more then an hour till he fatagued our wit sufficiently who still kept on the Comparison of Esop with a very hearty Laught at so bright a thought when the D stopt short & repeated these lines

The Herald proclaimed out then saying
See Esop Dancing & his Monkey playing

the Laugh turn^d against our Wit & the D was Embreaced by his uncle & got some sweetmeats which was always his reward by this time he made as great a progress in his school learning as one of his age c^d & it was then recommended to his father to have him fitted the College by all his freinds but in perticular by the Revd Thos Contarine his Fathers Brother in Law as none c^d be a better judge then this Gentleman being a man of most remarkable sence & universal Learing his father Chose rather to distress his younger Children & encourage his Genius by sending him to the College

He was therefore brought from Elphin & sent to Athlone which was within five miles of his fathers to Mr Campell who had set up in that Town & was reckonned a most ingenious Gentle man with him he continued two years till the employment not agreeing with Mr Campells health he was obliged to retire to the Country & the D was sent to the Revd Pat: Hughes Glergyman of Edgworths Town in the County of Longford here he was fitted for the College, & from his last journey from his fathers to this pleace he has I beleive taken the plot of his Play of the mistakes of a night, for in his journy to this Town some freind gave him a Guinea the Town was twenty Miles from his fathers and he diverted the day vewing the Gentlemens

seats on the road & night fell at a Village Call^d Ardagh, upon his
coming to the Village he enquired for the best house in Town which
he was shew'd upon his riding to the door he Call^d for the Hostler
who appear^d he desired his horse might rubd waterd and beated &
very great care taken of him & rushd in himself to a handsom
Parlour where as he thought sat the Landlord before a good fire after
the usual salutes he beleived a bottle of wine c^d not be bad that cold
night & let him also know he had been fasting all day & to get some
thing comfortably good in a hurry for that he was very hungry the
man flew to obey his orders & immedietly a waiter with bottle &
Glases appear^d & he & his host sat to their bottle while it was
drinking the Man was inquisitive about his father his pleace of
Abode his name & famally upon his information the man seem^d to
be accquainted with them & to treat him with great complisance an
Elegant Supper was immedietly served the Company was the Host
his wife & two Daughters who were all pressing on Master Goldsmith to sup he call^d affter two bottles more & insisted on the Ladys
telling their Choice for while the Guinea lasted the Docter knew not
how to spare he was shew^d a very good Chamber where he slept but
before he parted desired Breakfast might be Early ready & the best in
the house & bespoke a hot cake, which was all prepared before left
his room, after breakfast he went to the Stable & had his horse dressd
& oated & then went to the Land Lord & call^d for his Bill but how
much was he confounded when the Gentleman told him he never
kept an Inn a Mr Fanh F: & he was proud to have it in his power to
enterain Mr Goldsmith son his dear Old freind & neighbour.

The June following 1743^3 the D was sent to the College & Entered
under Mr Wilder, his temper was rather warm so was the D Wilder
was the son of a neighbouring Gentleman and Mr Goldsmith requested a perticular care from him over his sons morals & behaviour
as he was then but thirteen & a half, the D, then began to have a taste
for the Sosiciety & as he was very pleasing he was invited by many
he gave his accquaintance a dance & supper at his Chamber but
unfortunately his Tutor heard of it who went imeadietly to his room
& abused him most Greely & the Altercation ended in his Tutors
giving him a box on the ear which he ever after resented

his first step was to dispose of the best of his Cloaths & he then left
the College but spent a few days in the Citty till he spent the best part
of what mony he had & I have often heard him say he left Dublin
with only a shilling in his Pocket he thought he c^d get Bread any
where was fully resolved to go to Cork & take Shiping for he knew

not where but he soon found his error for when his stock was spent which he husbanded for three days he was then obliged to sell his shirts waist coat and any other little things he had about him for a support his shoes were worn out & he was then eighty miles from Dublin & about forty from his fathers house without Cloaths Shoes or a penny in his Pockett, he then to Late began to think of what he had done & as the Prodgal son returnd to his father after suffering all that nakedness & famine c^d endure & he has told me a handfull of Grey pease he got from a Girl at a weak as he passed through the Country was the most Comfortable repast he ever made after fasting 24 hours, within a few miles of his fathers house he wrote to his Brother who fitted him out again & brought him to Dublin & at least outwardly reconciled him to his Tutor from this the D wod fall into many little extravagances when ever he got a remtance from the country he liv'd well but still was calld a good Idle Scholar but never pleased his Tutor who imagined was rather convinced he c^d do much more then he did how ever he got all the Honnours of the College for his standing.

I now must request the reader will read himself in the Character of the Man in Black in the Citizen of the world he there gives an account of his Fathers Death which I w^d wish to ommit & many other incidents of his life as I am sertain that Charector is his own.

after his Fathers Death he was taken a perticular notice of by his Uncle Contrine who w^d have him persue his studdys & brought him to him self where he asisted[4] till he took his degree he then w^d have him read for orders & w^d have given him Bread, but this he never liked for his inclination led him to Travail but Condescending to his Uncles desire he did read for Orders and waited on Bishop Sing at Elphin & answerd Examinaton the Bishop asked his age which he told was twenty and his Lord Ship said he must wait till he was of a proper age for it was thought his Lordship designd his uncles living for another as he was that time an old man his Uncle got him at that time a Tuition at a Gentlemans family in the Neighbourhood where he lived a year but he never liked confinement at the end of this year he made an excursion to Munster & brought with him a handsome horse and about thirty pound in his pocket he stay'd about six weeks away and all his freinds concluded he had left the Kingdom but he returnd to his mothers without a penny upon a little horse worth about eighteen shillings which he call^d Fiddle Back his Mother was much concern^d at his folly & c^d not be readily reconcild to him, but his Brother & Sisters so contrived to meet at his Mothers to bring on a reconciliaton & after many cool repremands on her side She insisted on where he had been where he had spent his money horse linnen &c. as he brought nothing home but what was on his back,

he then told his mother if she c^d cooly sit down & listen he wd resolve the many Questions askd he informd us he had been in Cork that he had sold his horse & paid for his passage to a Captian of an American Ship but the winds did not answer for three weeks during which time he saw every thing curious in & about the City of Cork that he had met some accquaintance & that he did not know how to starve with mony in his Pockett that unfortunatly the day the wind served he hapened to be on a party in the Country with some freinds & his friend the Captian never enquired after him he stayd in Cork while he c^d stay till the last two Guineas forty shillings of which he gave for Fiddle Back & then had but a Crown⁵ to bring him home, which was rather little for himself & horse for a hundred & twenty mile but on his laveing the City he recollected a fathfull freind & accquaintance he had in the College & who often most earnestly press^d him to go & spend a Summer with him at his Seate within eight mile of Cork that they w^d have the pleasures of the city & that Dr Oliver sh^d command his house & purse which was ever at his service, he had but two half crowns & on his being two miles from Town he met a poor Woman with eight little clean Children She was all in Tears & told him a long melocholy tale that her husband was that morning seiged for a Debt he had not to pay & that he was draged to Jayle & that the Labour of his hands was the only suport she had for them eight Children, the Docter redily devided his stock with her for he had his freind to apply to from whom he c^d get money ennough to carry him home at length he arrived at his freinds house all the marks of snugness about it not forgeting a large mastiff who had like to tear him to peices upon his going in but was releived by an old Grim looking woman whom he askd for his freind & sent in his name his freind flew to embreace & hoped he was then come to perform the many promises he had made of spending the sumer with him the D tould he sh^d know more of that shortly, his freind was only recovering from a severe fit of Illness in his night Gown cap & slippers & gave the D a long detail of his disorder, but how happy was he then to have the man he most loved on Earth to help his recoery asked him whether he had then come from Dublin or his mothers happy was my poor D to have so faithfull a freind to lay open his distresses to & informd him òf every thing that had happen^d him since he left his freinds that he was now returning with but half a Crown in his Pocket, but upon his recolecting him, his dear freind, it made him quiet easy he returnd no answer but walkd about & rubd his hands in short the time of dineng was come the D grew hungry & impeatiaently waited for dinner which he saw no prospect of till six oClock when the old woman appeard with 2 pleates & a spoon & Cloath which She laid on a table which renewd the D spirrits & up She brought a very small bowl of Segoe a small poranger of bad sower milk & a peice of bad brown bread he invited the D to eat & highly recomended a milk Diet for his part he was Confined to such Slops as this thrusting a spoonfull into the D mouth the D lookd but sower at his entertainment but had he ennough of even what he got he wd have been pleased, at eight a Clock his freind recomended a regular life that for his part to lye with the lamb & rise with the Lark was what he wd recommend to his freinds the D stomack was greater for another peice of his bread & milk but he was obliged to acquese & go to bed.

in the morning he was resolved to borrow a Guinea & go of for his freinds living he did not like but when he mentioned his going of, why truly to be sure he had given his mother & freinds high offence at his foolish ramble that the longar he stayd from them the greater their anger must be, and that he would advize him by all means to go home with all expedition, but S^r says the D you know my ability to travial on half a Crown more then a hundred miles now if you lend me a Guinea I will remit it to you & return you many thanks & you know S^r tis what I often done for, why look you Mr Goldsmith that is neither here nor there, all the money I have ever borrowd from you you know I have paid you & this dam^d. sickness of mine it has taken a way all my Cash, but I have found out an easie method for your going home, how pray S^r says the D why sell your horse & I will lend you one and pray S^r says the D shew me the horse you intend to lend me with that he brought him to his bed Chamber which the D thought a strange pleace for a horse & from under his bed he brought him out an oak stick & said that was it, the D took it in his hand look^d earnestly at it & then at him & had it just redy drawn to give him a great beating when a loud wrap at the street door made the freind fly to it & introduce into the parlour a Gentleman dressd in mourning of a most pleasing aspect whom he introduced to the D, a Councelor F. G. & the D to him as his worthy & ingenious freind M^r. Goldsmith of whom he had so often heard him spake with rapture, the D all this while walked about the room rubbing his hands biteing his lips & giving his freind many angry looks till the subject was cheanged by the polite Conversation of the Councelor, after spending an hour the Councelor invited the D & his freind to Dine with him at his sate which the D declined for some time but he was pressd by both that he waited on the Councelor for two reasons first because he liked the councelor & secondly he wanted a dinner as he had not eat nothing but bread & Milk[6] since he left Cork, at the Counselors he found every thing neat and elegan a Most beautifull place there ware two lovely Daughters which the Counselor introduc^d. to the D^r. the spent a Most agreeable evening his Friend desir^d. him to prepare for home, the counselor who had observd the many sower looks the D^r. had given him insisted on Mr Goldsmiths spending a few days with him he prest so earnestly that the D^r. was at last oblig^d. to declare he wod not stir a step with the dam^d. paltroon and desird him to goe home and be sure the next day you goe abroad dont forget ye Horse our Gentleman went of with a Sneer and left the D^r. to inform the Counselor of his tratement of him, who laught hartily and at the same time told Mr Goldsmith he believ^d. M^r. H. was a verry grate scounderle, the Ladies brought the D^r. to the Gardens where the amus^d. themselvs playing a bouls and at Night they playd the Harpsicord and sung, the Dr Observ^d. the Counselor drown^d in Tears on hearing Ladys sing and p[lay] which he beg^d. Mr Goldsmith wod excuse; since it had been their first time to play or sing since the Death of their Mother & of his Wife, but that he wish^d. in any respect they cod be pleasing to him, the next day the D^r attempted to go but the Conselor wod by no means hear of it and told him he sho^d. have a good Hors and servant at his Service, the D^r. spent three days with him and at his goeing the Counselor offerd him his purse and Insisted he sh^d take what he wanted also a Horse and Servant however he took three half Guineas but posotivly refus^d. the Counselors Horse

And now D^r. Mother says he since I have struggeld so hard to come home to you why are you not better pleas^d. to see me, and pray says the Mother have you ever wrote a letter of thanks to that dear good man since you came home, no says the D^r. I have not then says the Mother you are an ungratefull Savage a Monster in short the whole boddy of his Friends which ware present up braid^d. him for which he for a full half houre sat listning to with grate composure and after they had vented their Passion he beg^d. they wod sit down and compos themselv^s. for what he told them was only to amuse them and that there was not one word in it; how ever he afterward assur^d me of its veracity

After this he did not know well what to do with himself for to return to his Tuition he wod not, he liv^d. som time with his Sister Hodson before he wod attempt to see his Uncle Contrine but soon a reconciliation was brough on Mr. and Mr^s. Lawder his Uncles daughter who was verry fond of him and a particular Friend

His Uncle and Friends then Concluded to send him to the Temple and had his name enter^d. they then acquipt him handsomly he accordingly set of for Dublin on his way to London but unfortunatly met a Mr. S. at a Coffie house they both fell into play and los every shill^g. of fivty Pound so once more return^d to his Mother a hart broken dejected being twas then he began to [repen]t of his past misconduct and if he was once more taken notice of [promised to] behave with more circumspection for the future, they then desir^d. him he migh prepair for the studdy of physick and once More his Good Uncle was reconsil^d. to him at len^th. he was sent to Edinburg and in 1753 enter^d that College From this date I am a Stranger to what happn^d. him he wrote several letters to his Friends from Switzerland Germany and Italy for six years [   ].^7

NOTES

Catherine Hodson, wife of Daniel Hodson, was Goldsmith's elder sister.

1. The spelling and punctuation exactly reproduce the original, which forms part of the Goldsmith collection in the possession of Miss Constance Meade.

2. '9' has been heavily corrected to '8' in ink of a darker colour. In a contemporary copy which accompanies the MS. the date reads '1729'.

3. '1743' is written between the lines in Mrs Hodson's hand, without a caret or other mark of punctuation.

4. Here is scratched out, 'him with his Mother'.

5. A note to this appears at the foot: '1 guinea is 21. 5s. 6d. Irish.' Two guineas is obviously meant.

6. Here the handwriting changes to Maurice's, who evidently wrote the remainder at Mrs Hodson's dictation.

7. The last line, beginning with 'six', is scored out. Only the first two words are decipherable.

Continued Struggle*

JOHN WATKINSON

But this county [Co. Westmeath] boasts of a still greater honour, the birth of the much lamented Oliver Goldsmith. I have learned a very curious anecdote of this extraordinary man, from the widow of a Doctor Radcliffe, who had been his Tutor in Trinity College, Dublin. She mentioned to me a very long letter from him, which she had often heard her husband read to his friends, upon the commencement of Goldsmith's celebrity. But this, with other things of more value, was unfortunately lost by accidental fire, since her husband's death.

It appears that the beginning of his career was one continued struggle against the waves of adversity. Upon his first going to England he was in such distress, that he would have gladly become an usher to a country school; but so destitute was he of friends to recommend him, that he could not, without difficulty, obtain even this low department. The master of the school scrupled to employ him, without some testimonial of his past life. Goldsmith referred him to his tutor, at college, for a character; but, all this while, he went under a feigned name. From this resource, therefore, one would think, that little in his favour could be even hoped for. But he only wanted to serve a present exigency – an ushership was not his object.

In this strait, he writes a letter to Dr Radcliffe, imploring him, as he tendered the welfare of an old pupil, not to answer a letter which he would probably receive, the same post with his own, from the schoolmaster. He added, that he had good reasons for concealing, both from him and the rest of the world, his name, and the real state of his case: every circumstance of which he promised to communicate upon some future occasion. His tutor, embarrassed enough before to know what answer he should give, resolved at last to give none. And thus was poor Goldsmith snatched from between the

---

* *A Philosophical Survey of the South of Ireland* (London: Printed by W. Strahan, 1777) pp. 286–8. Editor's title.

horns of his present dilemma, and suffered to drag on a miserable life for a few probationary months.

It was not till after his return to London, from his rambles over [a] great part of the world, and after having got some sure footing on this slippery globe, that he at length wrote to Dr Radcliffe, to thank him for not answering the schoolmaster's letter, and to fulfil his promise of giving the history of the whole transaction. It contained a comical narrative of his adventures from his leaving Ireland to that time: His musical talents having procured him a welcome reception wherever he went.

Goldsmith and William*

HESTER MILNER

There was a servant in the family who waited at table, cleaned shoes, &c. whose name was *William*; a weak but good-tempered young man. Goldsmith would now and then make himself merry at his expense, and poor *William* generally enjoyed the joke without any diminution of his own self-satisfaction.

William used to think, that in *his* way he was not to be outdone, and Goldsmith thought, one day, that he would make trial of him. Accordingly, having procured a piece of *uncoloured Cheshire cheese*, he rolled it up in the form of a candle, about an inch in length, and twisting a bit of white paper to the size of a wick, he thrust it into one of the ends, having blackened the extremity that it might have more the appearance of reality. He then put it in a candlestick over the fire-place in the kitchen, taking care that a bit of *real candle*, of equal size, should be placed by the side of it in another candlestick. The apparatus being thus prepared, in came *William* from his daily task; when Goldsmith immediately taking down the bit of candle of his own manufacture, challenged *William* in the following terms: – '*William*, if you will eat yonder piece of candle' (pointing to what remained on the shelf), 'I will eat *this* in my hand – but it must be done together, and I will begin!' – The challenge was accepted in the presence of the

* *European Magazine*, 53 (May 1808) pp. 373–4.

other servants in the kitchen, and Goldsmith immediately began gnawing his candle, making sad wry faces, but not flinching from his task. *William* beheld with astonishment the progress he was making in devouring it, however nauseous, but having no heart or stomach to touch his own. At last, when *William* saw that Goldsmith had devoured all but the last morsel, he, not willing to be outdone, opened his mouth, and flung his own piece down his throat in a moment. This sudden triumph over his antagonist made the kitchen ring with laughter. Some little time after, *poor William* could not help expressing his surprise to Goldsmith that he had not done as he did, swallowing so disagreeable a morsel all at once. – 'Truly,' replied Goldsmith, with great gravity, 'my bit of candle was no other than a bit of *very nice Cheshire cheese*, and therefore, *William*, I was unwilling to lose the relish of it!'

Another time, Goldsmith, wishing to have a little innocent merriment with *William*, hit on the following scheme, which he accomplished.

William had fallen in love with a young woman who lived in the neighbourhood as servant, and they for some time kept each other's company. The young woman soon after left her situation, and went back into Yorkshire, her native county. But she promised to write to *William*; though, for some reason or another, that promise was never fulfilled. This circumstance gave him no little uneasiness; and having so often inquired of the postman to no purpose, he had nearly sunk into despair. Goldsmith, availing himself of *poor William*'s condition, took upon him to imitate a bad hand, and to indite a *letter*, which, for sentiment and expression, might be taken for a real epistle out of Yorkshire. This being done with exactness Goldsmith gave it to one of the young gentlemen, with the request that he would deliver it next morning, immediately after the postman had called at the house. The young gentlemen were in the habit of running towards the door whenever the postman made his appearance; of course, one of the group returned from the door with this said letter, gave it directly to *William*, who, snatching it with eagerness, thrust it into his bosom, and withdrew, to make himself acquainted with the contents. The substance of the epistle was, that '*she* had, for various reasons, delayed writing; but had to inform him, that a young man, by trade a glass-grinder, had paid his addresses to her; that she had not given him much encouragement, though her relations were for the match; that she, however, often thought of *William*, and he was not long out of her mind, for she did not forget the pleasant mo-

ments they had passed together on former occasions.' She concluded by saying, 'that something must now be done one way or
another,' &c. This gratified *William*, though not without a mixture of
the painful passion of jealousy; which, however, was not so great as
to destroy the pleasure arising from this fresh token of her attachment to him. When, in the evening, he came into the kitchen, with
features expressive of an accession to his happiness, Goldsmith accosted him in these words: 'So, *William*, you have had a letter from
Yorkshire – What does she say to you? – Come, tell me all about it.'
'Yes,' returned *William*, nodding his head, 'I have had a letter from
Yorkshire, but I shan't tell you, Mr Goldsmith, any thing about it: no,
no, that will never do.' 'Well, then,' said Goldsmith, after having put
a few more questions, which were all negatived, 'suppose, *William*,
I tell you what the contents of the letter are?' When looking upon a
newspaper which he had in his hand, he adds, 'Come, I will read
you *your letter* just as I find it here:' when he read aloud the several
words of which the letter was composed, with a steady countenance,
and without the least faltering or hesitation. *William* was thunder-
struck, became very angry, and exclaimed, 'You use me very ill, Mr
Goldsmith! you have opened my letter!' Upon this Goldsmith immediately unravelled the difficulty, by telling him, that he himself had,
the preceding evening, written *the letter*, and thus made *poor William*
believe that it was his wisest way never to expect any epistle from his
Dulcinea, who had evidently forsaken him, and ought not, therefore,
to be suffered, for the time to come, to disturb his repose!

NOTE

The Reverend Thomas Milner, a dissenting clergyman and author of Latin
and Greek grammars used in their day, ran an Academy for Boys. In 1756 Dr
Milner's health was failing and he was in an immediate need of an assistant.
Goldsmith accepted the post on the understanding that he was not committing himself to more than a temporary appointment, and by the end of the
year he was working as a schoolmaster in Peckham. At the close of the
century, Dr Milner's daughter, Hester, wrote this account of two anecdotes
of Goldsmith's humour and cheerfulness.

Goldsmith and Religion*

JOHN EVANS

At that period of life when Dr G. lived under the roof of Dr Milner, at Peckham, he seemed much impressed with a sense of religion. Not that he was bigotedly attached to any particular system of faith, or to any particular mode of worship. He joined himself to no one peculiar sect or denomination of the christian world – but admired every character amongst them in whom devotion and benevolence were united. So far from resembling too many men of genius in that infidelity and scepticism by which our age is unhappily distinguished, he recognised with joy the existence and perfections of a Deity. For the christian revelation also, he was always understood to have a profound respect – knowing that it was the source of our best hopes and noblest expectations.

One of Dr Milner's daughters, an excellent young lady, died while he was at Peckham: one morning, on his coming down to breakfast, he enquired after her with his usual solicitude; and being told she had expired in the night, he lifted up his hands and eyes, exclaiming with a solemn emphasis – *'She is now with God!'* The manner after which he uttered these expressions, struck the family with a deep impression of his piety. Indeed there are passages in his works which bear testimony to his belief of a *future state*, as well as to his sense of the *wise* and *superintending providence* of the Deity.

* 'Prefatory Address to *The Traveller*', in *The Poetical Works of Oliver Goldsmith* (London: Thomas Hurst, 1804) pages unnumbered. Editor's title.

Goldsmith Visits Me*

DR FARR

From the time of Goldsmith's leaving Edinburgh, in the year 1754, I never saw him till 1756, when I was in London, attending the hospitals and lectures; early in January [1756 is an evident mistake for 1757] he called upon me one morning before I was up, and on my entering the room, I recognised my old acquaintance, dressed in a rusty full-trimmed black suit, with his pockets full of papers, which instantly reminded me of the poet in Garrick's farce of *Lethe*. After we had finished our breakfast, he drew from his pocket a part of a tragedy; which he said he had brought for my correction; in vain I pleaded inability, when he began to read, and every part on which I expressed a doubt as to the propriety, was immediately blotted out. I then more earnestly pressed him not to trust to my judgment, but to the opinion of persons better qualified to decide on dramatic compositions, on which he told me he had submitted his production, so far as he had written, to Mr Richardson, the author of *Clarissa*, on which I peremptorily declined offering another criticism on the performance. The name and subject of the tragedy have unfortunately escaped my memory, neither do I recollect with exactness how much he had written, though I am inclined to believe that he had not completed the third act; I never heard whether he afterwards finished it. In this visit I remember his relating a strange Quixotic scheme he had in contemplation of going to decipher the inscriptions on the *written mountains*, though he was altogether ignorant of Arabic, or the language in which they might be supposed to be written. The salary of 300*l*. per annum, which had been left for the purpose, was the temptation!

NOTE

Dr Farr was one of Goldsmith's fellow-students at Edinburgh.

* In John Forster, *The Life and Times of Oliver Goldsmith* (London: Bradbury *et al.*, 1854) p. 51. Editor's title.

Worldly Wisdom*

OLIVER GOLDSMITH

[c. 13 January 1759]

Dear Sir,

Your punctuality in answering a man whose trade is writing, is more than I had reason to expect; and yet you see me generally fill a whole sheet, which is all the recompense I can make for being so frequently troublesome. The behaviour of Mr Mills[1] and Mr Lawder[2] is a little extraordinary.[3] However, their answering neither you nor me is a sufficient indication of their disliking the employment which I assigned them. As their conduct is different from what I had expected, so I have made an alteration in mine. I shall, the beginning of next month, send over two hundred and fifty books,[4] which are all that I fancy can be well sold among you, and I would have you make some distinction in the persons who have subscribed. The money, which will amount to sixty pounds, may be left with Mr Bradley as soon as possible.[5] I am not certain but I shall quickly have occasion for it.

I have met with no disappointment with respect to my East India voyage, nor are my resolutions altered; though, at the same time, I must confess, it gives me some pain to think I am almost beginning the world at the age of thirty-one. Though I never had a day's sickness since I saw you, yet I am not that strong, active man you once knew me. You scarcely can conceive how much eight years of disappointment, anguish, and study have worn me down. If I remember right, you are seven or eight years older than me, yet I dare venture to say, that, if a stranger saw us both, he would pay me the honours of seniority. Imagine to yourself a pale, melancholy visage, with two great wrinkles between the eyebrows, with an eye disgustingly severe, and a big wig, and you may have a perfect picture of

---

* In *The Collected Letters of Oliver Goldsmith*, ed. Katharine C. Balderston (Cambridge: University Press, 1928) pp. 56–66. Editor's title.

my present appearance. On the other hand, I conceive you as perfectly sleek and healthy, passing many a happy day among your
own children, or those who knew you a child.

Since I knew what it was to be a man, this is a pleasure I have not
known. I have passed my days among a parcel of cool, designing
beings, and have contracted all their suspicious manner in my own
behaviour. I should actually be as unfit for the society of my friends
at home, as I detest that which I am obliged to partake of here. I can
now neither partake of the pleasure of a revel, or contribute to raise
its jollity. I can neither laugh nor drink; have contracted a hesitating,
disagreeable manner of speaking, and a visage that looks ill-nature
itself; in short, I have thought myself into a settled melancholy, and
an utter disgust of all that life brings with it. Whence this romantic
turn that all our family are possessed with? Whence this love for
every place and every country but that in which we reside – for
every occupation but our own? this desire of fortune, and yet this
eagerness to dissipate? I perceive, my dear sir, that I am at intervals
for indulging this splenetic manner, and following my own taste,
regardless of yours.

The reasons you have given me for breeding up your son a scholar
are judicious and convincing; I should, however, be glad to know for
what particular profession he is designed. If he be assiduous and
divested of strong passions (for passions in youth always lead to
pleasure), he may do very well in your college; for it must be owned
that the industrious poor have good encouragement there, perhaps
better than in any other in Europe. But if he has ambition, strong
passions, and an exquisite sensibility of contempt, do not send him
there, unless you have no other trade for him but your own. It is
impossible to conceive how much may be done by proper education
at home. A boy, for instance, who understands perfectly well Latin,
French, arithmetic, and the principles of the civil law, and can write
a fine hand, has an education that may qualify him for any undertaking; and these parts of learning should be carefully inculcated, let
him be designed for whatever calling he will.

Above all things, let him never touch a romance or novel: these
paint beauty in colours more charming than nature, and describe
happiness that man never tastes. How delusive, how destructive are
those pictures of consummate bliss! They teach the youthful mind to
sigh after beauty and happiness that never existed; to despise the
little good which fortune has mixed in our cup, by expecting more
than she ever gave; and , in general, take the word of a man who has

seen the world, and who has studied human nature more by experience than precept; take my word for it, I say, that books teach us very little of the world. The greatest merit in a state of poverty would only serve to make the possessor ridiculous – may distress, but cannot relieve him. Frugality, and even avarice, in the lower orders of mankind, are true ambition. These afford the only ladder for the poor to rise to preferment. Teach then, my dear sir, to your son, thrift and economy. Let his poor wandering uncle's example be placed before his eyes. I had learned from books to be disinterested and generous, before I was taught from experience the necessity of being prudent. I had contracted the habits and notions of a philosopher, while I was exposing myself to the approaches of insidious cunning; and often by being, even with my narrow finances, charitable to excess, I forgot the rules of justice, and placed myself in the very situation of the wretch who thanked me for my bounty. When I am in the remotest part of the world, tell him this, and perhaps he may improve from my example. But I find myself again falling into my gloomy habits of thinking.

My mother, I am informed, is almost blind; even though I had the utmost inclination to return home, under such circumstances I could not, for to behold her in distress without a capacity of relieving her from it, would add much to my splenetic habit. Your last letter was much too short; it should have answered some queries I had made in my former. Just sit down as I do, and write forward until you have filled all your paper. It requires no thought, at least from the ease with which my own sentiments rise when they are addressed to you. For, believe me, my head has no share in all I write; my heart dictates the whole. Pray give my love to Bob Bryanton,[6] and entreat him from me not to drink. My dear sir, give me some account about poor Jenny.[7] Yet her husband loves her: if so, she cannot be unhappy.

I know not whether I should tell you – yet why should I conceal these trifles, or, indeed, anything from you? There is a book of mine will be published in a few days: the life of a very extraordinary man; no less than the great Voltaire.[8] You know already by the title that it is no more than a catchpenny. However, I spent out four weeks on the whole performance, for which I received twenty pounds. When [it is] published, I shall take some method of conveying it to you, unless you may think it dear of the postage, which may amount to four or five shillings. However, I fear you will not find an equivalent of amusement.

Your last letter, I repeat it, was too short; you should have given

me your opinion of the design of the heroi-comical poem which I
sent you. You remember I intended to introduce the hero of the
poem as lying in a paltry ale-house. You may take the following
specimen of the manner, which I flatter myself is quite original. The
room in which he lies may be described somewhat in this way:

> The window, patched with paper, lent a ray
> That feebly show'd the state in which he lay;
> The sanded floor that grits beneath the tread,
> The humid wall with paltry pictures spread;
> The game of goose was there exposed to view,
> And the twelve rules the royal martyr drew;
> The Seasons, framed with listing, found a place,
> And Prussia's monarch show'd his lamp-black face.
> The morn was cold: he views with keen desire
> A rusty grate unconscious of a fire;
> An unpaid reckoning on the frieze was scored,
> And five crack'd tea-cups dress'd the chimney-board.

And now imagine, after his soliloquy the, landlord to make his
appearance in order to dun him for the reckoning:

> Not with that face, so servile and so gay,
> That welcomes every stranger that can pay:
> With sulky eye he smoked the patient man,
> Then pull'd his breeches tight, and thus began, &c.[9]

All this is taken, you see, from nature. It is a good remark of
Montaigne's, that the wisest men often have friends with whom they
do not care how much they play the fool. Take my present follies as
instances of my regard. Poetry is a much easier and more agreeable
species of composition than prose; and, could a man live by it, it
were not unpleasant employment to be a poet. I am resolved to leave
no space, though I should fill it up only by telling you, what you
very well know already, I mean that I am your most affectionate
friend and brother,

OLIVER GOLDSMITH

NOTES

On 21 December 1758 Goldsmith underwent his examination at College of Surgeons' Hall. The examiners found him 'not qualified' as 'mate to an hospital'. While in forlorn Arbour Court, suffering under extreme depression of spirits, and his harsh collisions with the bookseller and publisher, R. Griffiths, Goldsmith wrote this letter to his elder brother, Henry.

1. Goldsmith's cousin, Edward Mills.

2. Husband of Goldsmith's cousin Jane, daughter of Uncle Contarine.

3. Goldsmith had written to a number of his relatives to obviate the peril of his new book's being pirated in Ireland and to promote its sales there so as to bring him a reasonable return.

4. *An Inquiry into the Present State of Polite Learning in Europe.* His previous remarks apply to the subscription.

5. Irish bookseller.

6. Robert Bryanton, squire of Ballymahon.

7. His sister, Mrs Johnston. Her marriage, like that of Mrs Hodson (Catherine), was private, but in pecuniary matters much less fortunate.

8. *The Life of Voltaire,* alluded to in the letter, was the literary job undertaken to satisfy the demands of Griffiths. It was to have preceded a translation of the *Herinade,* by Ned Purdon, Goldsmith's old schoolmate, now a Grub-Street writer, who starved rather than lived by the exercise of his pen, and often taxed Goldsmith's scanty means to relieve his hunger. His miserable career was summed up by our poet in the following lines written some years after the time we are treating of, on hearing that he had suddenly dropped dead in Smithfield:

> Here lies poor Ned Purdon, from misery freed,
>   Who long was a bookseller's hack;
> He led such a damnable life in this world,
>   I don't think he'll wish to come back.

9. The projected poem, of which these were specimens, appears never to have been completed.

Goldsmith's Singularities and Merits*

SIR JOHN HAWKINS

Goldsmith is well-known by his writings to have been a man of genius and of very fine parts; but of his character and general deportment, it is the hardest task anyone can undertake to give a description. I will, however, attempt it, trusting to be excused if, in the spirit of a faithful historian, I record as well his singularities as his merits.[1]

There are certain memoirs of him extant, from which we learn, that his inclination, co-operating with his fortunes, which were but scanty, led him into a course of life little differing from vagrancy, that deprived him of the benefits of regular study: it however gratified his humour, stored his mind with ideas and some knowledge, which, when he became settled, he improved by various reading; yet, to all the graces of urbanity he was a stranger. With the greatest pretensions to polished manners he was rude, and, when he most meant the contrary, absurd. He affected Johnson's style and manner of conversation, and, when he had uttered, as he often would, a laboured sentence, so tumid as to be scarce intelligible, would ask, if that was not truly Johnsonian; yet he loved not Johnson, but rather envied him for his parts; and once entreated a friend to desist from praising him, 'for in doing so,' said he, 'you harrow up my very soul.'

He had some wit, but no humour, and never told a story but he spoiled it. The following anecdotes will convey some idea of the style and manner of his conversation:

He was used to say he could play on the German flute as well as most men; at other times, as well as any man living. But, in truth, he understood not the character in which music is written, and played

---

* In *The Life of Samuel Johnson, LL.D.* (London: T. Cadell, 1787) pp. 415–19. Editor's title.

on that instrument, as many of the vulgar do, merely by ear. Roubillac the sculptor, a merry fellow, once heard him play, and minding to put a trick on him, pretended to be charmed with his performance, as also, that himself was skilled in the art, and entreated him to repeat the air, that he might write it down. Goldsmith readily consenting, Roubillac called for paper, and scored thereon a few five-lined staves, which having done, Goldsmith proceeded to play, and Roubillac to write; but his writing was only such random notes on the lines and spaces as anyone might set down who had ever inspected a page of music. When they had both done, Roubillac showed the paper to Goldsmith, who looking it over with seeming great attention, said it was very correct, and that if he had not seen him do it, he never could have believed his friend capable of writing music after him.

He would frequently preface a story thus: 'I'll now tell you a story of myself, which some people laught at, and some do not.'[2]

At the breaking up of an evening at a tavern, he entreated the company to sit down, and told them if they would call for another bottle they should hear one of his *bons mots*: they agreed, and he began thus: 'I was once told that Sheridan the player,[3] in order to improve himself in stage gestures, had looking glasses, to the number of ten, hung about his room, and that he practised before them; upon which I said, then there were ten ugly fellows together.' The company were all silent: he asked why they did not laugh, which they not doing, he, without tasting the wine, left the room in anger.

In a large company he once said, 'Yesterday I heard an excellent story, and I would relate it now if I thought any of you able to understand it.' The company laughed, and one of them said, 'Doctor, you are very rude'; but he made no apology.

He once complained to a friend in these words: 'Mr Martinelli is a rude man: I said in his hearing, that there were no good writers among the Italians, and he said to one that sat near him, that I was very ignorant.'

'People,' said he, 'are greatly mistaken in me: a notion goes about, that when I am silent I mean to be impudent; but I assure you, gentlemen, my silence arises from bashfulness.'

Having one day a call to wait on the late Duke, then Earl of Northumberland, I found Goldsmith waiting for an audience in an outer room; I asked him what had brought him there: he told me an invitation from his lordship. I made my business as short as I could, and, as a reason, mentioned, that Dr Goldsmith was waiting without. The earl asked me if I was acquainted with him: I told him I was, adding what I thought likely to recommend him. I retired, and stayed in the outer room to take him home. Upon his coming out, I asked him the result of his conversation: 'His lordship,' says he, 'told me he had read my poem,' meaning *The Traveller*, 'and was much delighted with it; that he was going [to be] Lord Lieutenant of Ireland, and that, hearing that I was a native of that country, he should be glad to do me any kindness.' And what did you answer, asked I, to this gracious offer? 'Why,' said he, 'I could say nothing but that I had a brother there, a clergyman, that stood in need of help: as for myself, I have no dependence on the promises of great men: I look to the booksellers for support; they are my best friends, and I am not inclined to forsake them for others.'

Thus did this idiot in the affairs of the world, trifle with his fortunes, and put back the hand that was held out to assist him! Other offers of a like kind he either rejected or failed to improve, contenting himself with the patronage of one nobleman,[4] whose mansion afforded him the delights of a splendid table, and a retreat for a few days from the metropolis.

While I was writing the *History of Music*, he, at the club, communicated to me some curious matter: I desired he would reduce it to writing; he promised me he would, and desired to see me at his chambers: I called on him there; he stepped into a closet, and tore out of a printed book six leaves that contained what he had mentioned to me.

As he wrote for the booksellers, we, at the club, looked on him as a mere literary drudge, equal to the task of compiling and translating, but little capable of original, and still less of poetical composition: he had, nevertheless, unknown to us, written and addressed to the Countess, afterwards Duchess, of Northumberland, one of the finest poems of the lyric kind that our language has to boast of, the ballad *Turn Gentle Hermit of the Dale*; and surprised us with *The Traveller*, a poem that contains some particulars of his own history. Johnson was supposed to have assisted him in it; but he contributed to the perfection of it only four lines: his opinion of it was, that it was the best written poem since the time of Pope.

Of the booksellers whom he styled his friends, Mr Newbery was one. This person had apartments in Canonbury House, where Goldsmith often lay concealed from his creditors. Under a pressing necessity he there wrote his *Vicar of Wakefield*, and for it received of Newbery forty pounds.[5]

Of a man named Griffin, a bookseller in Catherine Street in the Strand, he had borrowed by two and three guineas at a time, money to the amount of two hundred pounds; to discharge this debt, he wrote the *Deserted Village*, but was two years about it. Soon after its publication, Griffin declared, it had discharged the whole of his debt.

His poems are replete with fine moral sentiments, and bespeak a great dignity of mind; yet he had no sense of the shame, nor dread of the evils, of poverty. In the latter he was at one time so involved, that for the clamours of a woman, to whom he was indebted for lodging, and for bailiffs that waited to arrest him, he was equally unable, till he had made himself drunk, to stay within doors, or go abroad to hawk among the booksellers a piece of his writing, the title whereof my author does not remember.[6] In this distress he sent for Johnson, who immediately went to one of them, and brought back money for his relief.

In his dealings with the booksellers, he is said to have acted very dishonestly, never fulfilling his engagements. In one year he got of them, and by his plays, the sum of £1800 which he dissipated by gaming and extravagance, and died poor in 1774.

He that can account for the inconsistencies of character above-noted, otherwise than by showing, that wit and wisdom are seldom found to meet in the same mind, will do more than any of Goldsmith's friends were ever able to do. He was buried in the Temple Churchyard. A monument was erected for him in the poets' corner in Westminster Abbey, by a subscription of his friends, and is placed over the entrance into St Blase's Chapel. The inscription thereon was written by Johnson. This I am able to say with certainty, for he showed it to me in manuscript.

NOTES

Sir John Hawkins (1719–89), English magistrate and writer; friend of Dr Johnson and member of the Literary Club; drafted Johnson's will and served as one of his executors.

1. From this account of Goldsmith only a brief passage from *The Traveller* is omitted.

2. A parody of one of Goldsmith's stories prefaced in this way is contained in Sir Joshua Reynolds's *Portraits*, published in 1952.

3. Thomas Sheridan, father of playwright Richard Brinsley Sheridan.

4. Nugent, Lord Clare.

5. Johnson told Boswell that he wrote eight of the last ten lines of *The Traveller* and that he obtained £60 for Goldsmith for the manuscript of *The Vicar of Wakefield*.

6. This was *The Vicar of Wakefield*. For Johnson's account of the incident, see Boswell's *Life of Johnson*, vol. I, p. 416.

In Great Distress*

SAMUEL JOHNSON

I received one morning a message from poor Goldsmith that he was in great distress, and as it was not in his power to come to me, begging that I would come to him as soon as possible. I sent him a guinea, and promised to come to him directly. I accordingly went as soon as I was drest, and found that his landlady had arrested him for his rent, at which he was in a violent passion. I perceived that he had already changed my guinea, and had got a bottle of Madeira and a glass before him. I put the cork into the bottle, desired he would be calm, and began to talk to him of the means by which he might be extricated. He then told me that he had a novel ready for the press,[1] which he produced to me. I looked into it, and saw its merit; told the landlady I should soon return, and having gone to a bookseller, sold it for sixty pounds. I brought Goldsmith the money, and he discharged his rent, not without rating his landlady in a high tone for having used him so ill.[2]

NOTES

In 1763 Newbery the publisher took in hand to provide for Goldsmith's well-being. A lodging was hired where a landlady agreed for £50 a year to provide the subsistence necessary for a journeyman of letters. However, the literary hack was in trouble with his creditors when Johnson came to the rescue. This is Boswell's report, taken, as he says, 'authentically' from Johnson's 'own exact narration.'

1. *The Vicar of Wakefield*.

* In James Boswell, *The Life of Samuel Johnson*, vol. 1 (London: Charles Dilly, 1791) p. 225. Editor's title.

2. This incident has been related differently by Hester Lynch (Thrale) Piozzi and with still greater variation by Richard Cumberland. See their recollections in this book.

Goldsmith and Johnson*

ARTHUR MURPHY

Johnson felt not only kindness, but zeal and ardour for his friends. He did every thing in his power to advance the reputation of Dr Goldsmith. He loved him, though he knew his failings, and particularly the leaven of envy which corroded the mind of that elegant writer, and made him impatient, without disguise, of the praises bestowed on any person whatever. Of this infirmity, which marked Goldsmith's character, Johnson gave a remarkable instance. It happened that he went with Sir Joshua Reynolds and Goldsmith to see the fantoccini, which were exhibited some years ago in or near the Haymarket. They admired the curious mechanism by which the puppets were made to walk the stage, draw a chair to the table, sit down, write a letter, and perform a variety of other actions with such dexterity, that *though Nature's journeymen made the men, they imitated humanity*[1] to the astonishment of the spectator. The entertainment being over, the three friends retired to a tavern. Johnson and Sir Joshua talked with pleasure of what they had seen; and says Johnson, in a tone of admiration, 'How the little fellow brandished his spontoon!' 'There is nothing in it,' replied Goldsmith, starting up with impatience; 'give me a spontoon; I can do it as well myself.'

NOTES

Arthur Murphy (1727–1805), a leading playwright and actor of the age.
  1. Alluding to Hamlet's instructions to the players in *Hamlet*, III, ii, 31–2.

* *Essays on the Life and Genius of Samuel Johnson, LL.D.* (London: 1792) pp. 96–7. Editor's title.

Goldsmith and Newbery*

CHARLES WELSH

In 1766 *The Vicar of Wakefield* was published by Francis Newbery, at the Crown, in Paternoster Row. There are probably few points of literary history of the last century more obscure and involved than the story of the writing, and sale of the copyright, of this book. Various and conflicting are the accounts which have been given of it, all of which – although they may have some common basis of truth – are much interlarded with conjecture. The story upon which most of them appear to have been founded is that which Boswell represents Johnson as telling. . . .[1]

Upon this, Mr Forster, in his *Life of Goldsmith*, raises a whole fabric of ingenious speculation. He says:

> Nor does this rating seem altogether undeserved, since there are certainly considerable grounds for suspecting that Mrs Fleming was the landlady. The attempt to clear her seems to me to fail in many essential points. Tracing the previous incidents minutely, it is almost impossible to disconnect her from this consummation of them, with which, at the same time, every trace of Goldsmith's residence in her house is brought to a close. As for the incident itself, it has nothing startling for the reader who is familiar with what has gone before it. It is the old story of distress, with the addition of a right to resent it which poor Goldsmith had not felt till now, and in the violent passion, the tone of indignant reproach, and the bottle of madeira, one may see that recent gleams of success and of worldly consideration have not strengthened the old habits of endurance. The arrest is plainly connected with Newbery's reluctance to make further advances. Of all Mrs Fleming's accounts found among his papers, the only one unsettled is that for the summer months preceding the arrest;[2] nor

---

* *A Bookseller of the Last Century. Being Some Account of the Life of John Newbery* (London: Griffith *et al.*, 1885) pp. 54, 55–7. Editor's title.

can I even resist altogether the suspicion, considering the intimacy between the families of the Newberys and the Flemings which Newbery's bequests in his will show to have existed,[3] that the publisher himself, for an obvious convenience of his own, may have suggested, or at least sanctioned, the harsh proceeding. The MS. of the novel (of which more hereafter) seems by both statements, in which the discrepancies are not so great but that Johnson himself may be held accountable for them, to have been produced reluctantly as a last resource; and it is possible, as Mrs Thrale intimates, that it was still regarded as 'unfinished,' but if strong adverse reasons had not existed, Johnson would surely have carried it to Newbery. He did not do this. He went with it to Francis Newbery, the nephew.

But there is no evidence in any existing papers, that we can find, to show whether the manuscript of the novel was sold either to Mr John Newbery the elder or to Francis his nephew; nor is there anything to show the date at which the incident which Johnson represents to have taken place occurred, if, indeed, it ever took place at all.

NOTES

1. See Samuel Johnson, 'In Great Distress,' in this book.
2. A fourth version, that of Sir John Hawkins, quoted by Mr Mitford in his *Life*, and strongly smacking of the knight's usual vein, appears to me to point to Islington as the locality of the arrest, though it does not directly confirm that suggestion. 'Of the booksellers whom he styled his friends, Mr Newbery was one. This person had apartments in Canonbury House, where Goldsmith often lay concealed from his creditors. Under a pressing necessity, he there wrote his *Vicar of Wakefield*, and for it received of Newbery £40.' It does not detract from the value of this evidence, such as it is, that Sir John gives afterwards his own blundering account of the attempted arrest and Johnson's relief in apparent ignorance that the piece of writing was the *Vicar of Wakefield* (Forster, *Life of Goldsmith*).
3. My friend Mr Peter Cunningham was so kind as to examine Newbery's will for me, and found in it two bequests, of fifty guineas each, to Mrs Elizabeth Fleming and Mr Thomas Fleming. Among the Newbery papers, I should here remark, there is one in the handwriting of Mrs Fleming, endorsed by Newbery, 'Dr Goldsmith's Accts.,' and hitherto unprinted, to the following effect: 'Feb. 1763. Dr Goldsmith to a bill paid by the hands of Mr Newbery, £14; May, do., £14, 11s.; Oct. 10, do., £14, 13s. 6d.; Nov. 10, do., £15, 3s. 1764. Aug. 6, do., £16, 6s.' From this it would appear that the last of

Mrs Fleming's accounts was ultimately settled by Newbery; but, though this might in itself go far to clear her from the imputation of the arrest, the suspicion above expressed in connection with Newbery himself leaves the matter still in doubt, and the Newbery payments strengthen the belief of a private understanding existing between her and the bookseller (Forster).

Kill Only Your Enemies*

MRS GWYN

He [Goldsmith] had been called in to a Mrs Sidebotham, an acquaintance, labouring under illness, and having examined and considered the case, wrote his prescription. The quality or quantity of the medicine ordered, exciting the notice of the apothecary in attendance, he demurred to administer it to the patient; an argument ensued, which had no effect in convincing either party of error, and some heat being produced by the contention, an appeal was at length made to the patient, to know by whose opinion and practice she chose to abide. She, deeming the apothecary the better judge of the two from being longer in attendance, decided for him; and Goldsmith quitted the house highly indignant, declaring to Sir Joshua he would leave off prescribing for friends. 'Do so, my dear Doctor,' replied Topham Beauclerk, when he heard the story, and afterwards jested with him on the subject: 'whenever you undertake to kill, let it be only your enemies.'

NOTE

In 1756 Goldsmith, prompted by the uncertainty of his finances, again attempted to earn a livelihood as a physician. This step is said to have been recommended by Sir Joshua Reynolds, Mrs Montagu, and other friends. We hear of one patient, whose story is told by Prior as he had received it from Mrs Gwyn [née Mary Horneck], to whom Reynolds had related it.

* In James Prior, *The Life of Oliver Goldsmith, M.B., from a Variety of Original Sources,* vol. 2 (London: John Murray, 1837) p. 105. Editor's title.

An Encounter with Goldsmith*

JAMES BOSWELL

You [Rousseau, 1712–78] met at [the] Mitre Dr Goldsmith whom you had before called upon. You both went to Mr Johnson's, who was still bad and would not come out. 'Come then,' said Goldie, 'we will not go to the Mitre tonight, since we can't have the big man with us.' But we had sent for Davies,[1] and I insisted on going. Goldsmith said, 'I think, Mr Johnson, you don't go near the theatres. You give yourself no more concern about a new play than if you had never had anything to do with the stage.'

JOHNSON. Why, Sir, our tastes alter. The lad does not care for the child's rattle, and the old man does not care for the young man's whore.

GOLDSMITH. Nay, but, Sir, your Muse was not a whore.

JOHNSON. Sir, I don't think she was. But as we advance in the journey of life, we drop some of the things which have pleased us; whether it be that we are fatigued and don't choose to carry so many things any farther, or that we find other things which we like better.

BOSWELL. But, Sir, why don't you give us something in some other way?

GOLDSMITH. Ay, Sir, we have a claim upon you.

JOHNSON. No, Sir, I am not obliged to do any more. No man is obliged to do as much as he can do. A man is to have part of his life to himself. If a soldier has fought a good many campaigns, he is not to be blamed if he retires to ease and tranquillity. Sir, a physician who has long practised in a great city may be excused if he retires to a small town and takes less practice. Sir, the good I can do by my conversation bears the same proportion to the good I can do by my writings that the practice of a physician, retired to a small town, does to his practice in a great city.

---

* *Boswell on the Grand Tour: Italy, Corsica, and France, 1765–66*, ed. Frank Brady and Frederick A. Pottle (New York: McGraw-Hill, 1955) pp. 295–7. Editor's title.

BOSWELL. But I wonder, Sir, you have not more pleasure in writing than not.
JOHNSON. Sir, you *may* wonder.

In short, Goldsmith and I could make nothing against him. He talked of making verses.

JOHNSON The great matter is to know when you have made good ones. I generally have 'em in my mind, perhaps fifty at a time, walking in my room; and then write 'em, and often from laziness wrote only the half lines. Sir, I have written a hundred lines a day. I remember I wrote a hundred lines of *The Vanity of Human Wishes* in a day. Doctor, I made one line t'other day, but I made out no more.
GOLDSMITH. Let us hear it, and we'll put a bad one to it.
JOHNSON. No, Sir, I have forgot it.

We left him, and as we were going along Fleet Street, Goldsmith very gravely said, 'Don't you think that head's failed – wearing, eh?' O fine!

BOSWELL. No, Sir, I think he is rather more impatient of contradiction than he was.
GOLDSMITH. Sir, no man is proof against continual adulation.

Davies could not come to the Mitre, so Goldsmith carried me to his chambers in the King's Bench Walk, which he has furnished, and [which] is quite magnificent. We talked of writing against authors from envy; I said if I wrote against anything it would be against his chambers. He gave me a repast and we were well. I touched him by the story of 'Johnson and Goldsmith and those blockheads,' and upon his honour that he would not say anything of it, I told him 'twas Smith.[2] 'Well,' said he, 'by telling me it was he, you have given me a plaster for the sore.' Such is human nature.

We talked of French and English. You said the English were like noble standard oaks, which could be alone and well. The French, slender shrubs, that are nothing but in a copsewood. Goldsmith said, 'I have passed the summer among the great,' and forsooth affected to talk lightly of this. You brought him down with Johnsonian principles and Johnsonian force.

NOTES

James Boswell (1740–95), Scottish biographer. He was intimate with Samuel Johnson, whose conversation he recorded with such effectiveness until Johnson's death in 1784.
1. Thomas Davies.
2. Adam Smith, whose anecdote here hinted at seems not to have been recorded by Boswell.

Goldsmith's Character*

JOHN TAYLOR

Dr Oliver Goldsmith. This pleasing, if not great poet and admirable prose writer, I never knew. He may be said to have died before my time, but not before I had begun to turn my attention towards literary pursuits. I once volunteered the delivery of a letter to him in the Temple, from a friend of my father, in order to have a chance of seeing his person; but he either was not at home, or thought it prudent to deny himself even to a boy, as his circumstances were probably quite poetical. My old friend Mr Cooke,[1] the barrister, who brought letters to him from Cork, in the year 1766, used to speak of his benevolence and simplicity in the highest terms.

Goldsmith's life and character are so well-known to the world, that it would be wasting time to enter on particulars. I shall therefore content myself with relating one anecdote, as it marks his character and has not been printed. Mr Cooke had engaged to meet a party at Marylebone Gardens. He had cash enough to pay for admission, but not for the necessity of coach-hire and the casualty of a supper. He therefore applied to his friend Goldsmith for the loan of a guinea. Poor Goldsmith was in the same *Parnassian* predicament, but undertook to borrow the sum of a friend, and to bring it to Cooke before he departed for the gardens. Cooke waited in expectation to the last moment that allowed him a chance of witnessing the entertainments of the place, but no Goldsmith appeared. He therefore trusted to fortune, and sallied forth. Meeting some hospitable Irish country-

* *Records of My Life*, vol. 1 (London: Edward Bull, 1832) pp. 107–9. Editor's title.

men at the place, he partook of a good supper, and did not return to his chambers till five in the morning. Finding some difficulty in opening his door, he stooped to remove the impediment, and found it was the guinea that Goldsmith had borrowed for him, wrapped in paper, which he had attempted to thrust under the door, not observing the hole in the letter-box, obvious to everybody else. Cooke thanked him in the course of the day, but observed that he ought not to have exposed the sum to such danger in so critical a state of their finances, as the laundress, coming early in the morning, or any casual stranger, might have seized the precious deposit. At what time Goldsmith had left the money, he could not recollect; but he might naturally have thought that he brought it too late, as Cooke had left the chambers. In answer to Cooke's observation as to the danger of losing the guinea, he said, 'In truth, my dear fellow, I did not think of that.' The fact is, he probably thought of nothing but serving a friend.

Goldsmith in the midst of all his luxuriant playfulness, was easily put out of countenance. The Miss Clara Brooke, whom I have mentioned before as one of my earliest and dearest playmates, who lived some time in my father's family, being once annoyed at a masquerade by the noisy gaiety of Goldsmith, who laughed heartily at some of the jokes with which he assailed her, was induced in answer to repeat his own line in *The Deserted Village*,

And the loud laugh which spoke the *vacant* mind.

Goldsmith was quite abashed at the application, and retired, as if by the word *vacant* he rather meant barren, than free from care. Dr Johnson wrote the prologue to Goldsmith's comedy of *The Good-natur'd Man*, to which comedy the public have never done justice. In the copy of this prologue which appeared in the *Public Advertiser*, in 1769, the following couplet was inserted:

Amidst the toils of this returning year,
When senators and nobles learn to fear;

but it was omitted in the copy which accompanied the play, either from Goldsmith's or Johnson's caution, but probably the former. Johnson, mentioning the author in the prologue, had styled him 'our *little* bard,' but the pride of Goldsmith revolted at this epithet, and it was changed to '*anxious*'.

I mentioned these alterations to Mr Malone, who regretted that he had not known of them before, as he might have introduced them into a new edition of Boswell's *Life of Johnson*, to illustrate Goldsmith's character.

NOTES

1. William Cooke. See his recollections of Goldsmith in *Memoirs of Samuel Foote* (London: Richard Phillips, 1805) vol. 1, pp. 184–6; vol. 3, pp. 77–8; and in 'Table Talk', *European Magazine*, 21 (February 1792) p. 88; 24 (August 1793) pp. 91–5; (September 1793) pp. 170–4; (October 1793) pp. 258–64.

Goldsmith at the Temple*

ROBERT DAY

The Poet frequented much the Grecian Coffee-house, then the favourite resort of the Irish and Lancashire Templars; and delighted in collecting around him his friends, whom he entertained with a cordial and unostentatious hospitality. Occasionally he amused them with his flute or with whist, neither of which he played well, particularly the latter, but in losing his money, he never lost his temper. In a run of bad luck and worse play, he would fling his cards on the floor and exclaim, '*Bye-fore* George I ought for ever to renounce thee, fickle, faithless Fortune!'

In person he was short, about five feet five or six inches; strong, but not heavy in make; rather fair in complexion, with brown hair, such at least as could be distinguished from his wig. His features were plain, but not repulsive – certainly not so when lighted up by conversation. His manners were simple, natural, and perhaps on the whole we may say not polished, at least without that refinement and good breeding which the exquisite polish to his compositions would lead us to expect. He was always cheerful and animated, often indeed boisterous in his mirth; entered with spirit into convivial

* In Temple Scott, *Oliver Goldsmith, Bibliographically and Biographically Considered* (New York: Bowling Green Press; London: Maggs Brothers, 1928) pp. 274–7. Editor's title.

society; contributed largely to its enjoyments by solidity of information and the naïveté and originality of his character; talked often without premeditation and laughed loudly without restraint.

Being then a young man I felt myself much flattered by the notice of so celebrated a person. He took great delight in the conversation and society of Grattan whose brilliancy in the morning of life furnished full earnest of the unrivalled splendour which awaited his meridian; and finding us dwelling together in Essex Court near himself where he frequently visited my immortal friend, his warm heart became naturally prepossessed towards the associate of one whom he so much admired.

Just arrived as I then was from College, full freighted with Academic gleanings, our Author did not disdain to receive from me some opinions and hints toward his Greek and Roman histories, light and superficial works, not composed for fame, but compiled for the more urgent purpose of recruiting his exhausted finances. So in truth was his *Animated Nature*. His purse replenished by labours of this kind, the season of relaxation and pleasure took its turn in attending the Theatres, Ranelagh, Vauxhall, and other scenes of gaiety and amusement, which he continued to frequent as long as his supply held out. He was fond of exhibiting his muscular little person in the gayest apparel of the day, to which was added a bag wig and sword.

This favourite costume involved him one morning in a short but comical dialogue in the Strand with two coxcombs, one of whom pointing to Goldsmith called to his companion in allusion to the Poet's sword 'to look at that fly with a long pin stuck through it.' Goldsmith instantly cautioned the passengers aloud against 'that brace of disguised pickpockets', and having determined to teach those gentlemen that he wore a sword as well for defence from insolence as for ornament, he retired from the footpath into the coachway which admitted of more space and freedom of action, and half-drawing his sword beckoned to the witty gentlemen armed in like manner, to follow him; but he and his companion thinking prudence the better part of valour, declined the invitation and sneaked away amid the hootings of the spectators.

Whenever his funds were dissipated, and they fled more rapidly from being the dupe of many artful persons, male and female, who practised upon his benevolence, he returned to his literary labours, and shut himself up from society to provide fresh matter for his bookseller and fresh supplies for himself.

I was in London when the *Deserted Village* came out. Much had been expected from the author of the *Traveller*, and public expectation and impatience were not disappointed. In fact it was received with universal admiration, as one of the most fascinating and beautiful effusions of British genius.

His beautiful little *Hermit* which by some persons had been fathered upon Johnson, and reputed to have been given by him to his protégé to help the *Vicar of Wakefield* into popularity, was by this time restored to the owner by the public, who had discovered ere now that he excelled in the art of poetry even his eminent patron.

His broad Comedy *She Stoops to Conquer*, was received with scarcely less applause, though his friends Garrick and Colman had many misgivings of its success. His friends, of whom I was one, assembled in great force in the pit to protect it, but we had no difficulty to encounter, for it was received throughout with the greatest acclamations, and had afterwards a great run.

I was also among those who attended his funeral, along with my friend John Day, Hugh Kelly, and a few others who were summoned together rather hastily for the purpose. It had been intended that the ceremony should be of an imposing kind, and attended by several of the great men of the time, Burke, Reynolds, Garrick, and others. This determination was altered, I imagine, from the pecuniary embarrassments of the deceased Poet; the last offices were therefore performed in a private manner, without the attendance of his great friends. He was interred in the Temple burial ground. Hugh Kelly, with whom he had not been on terms of intercourse for some years, shed tears over his grave, which were no doubt sincere; he did not then know that he had been slightingly mentioned in *Retaliation*; nor would he have been so noticed there, could the deceased have anticipated this proof of good feeling. Slight circumstances often separate the most deserving persons; nor are they perhaps conscious of the worth of each other until accidental circumstances produce the discovery.

NOTE

Robert Day, a young Irish barrister who entered the Middle Temple in 1769, has left a picture of Goldsmith at that time which helps us to understand why the 'dear, charming nymph' of poetry was forced to quit his quarters. At the age of 80, when he was a retired judge, Day wrote down his memory of Goldsmith.

A Famous Dinner*

JAMES BOSWELL

He [Johnson] honoured me with his company at dinner on the 16th
October [1769], at my lodgings in Old Bond Street, with Sir Joshua
Reynolds, Mr Garrick, Dr Goldsmith, Mr Murphy, Mr Bickerstaff,
and Mr Thomas Davies. Garrick played round him with a fond
vivacity, taking hold of the breasts of his coat, and looking up in his
face with a lively archness, complimented him on the good health
which he seemed then to enjoy; while the sage, shaking his head,
beheld him with a gentle complacency. One of the company not
being come at the appointed hour, I proposed, as usual upon such
occasions, to order dinner to be served; adding, 'Ought six people to
be kept waiting for one?' 'Why, yes (answered Johnson, with a
delicate humanity), if the one will suffer more by your sitting down
than the six will do by waiting.' Goldsmith, to divert the tedious
minutes, strutted about bragging of his dress, and I believe was
seriously vain of it, for his mind was wonderfully prone to such
impressions. 'Come, come, (said Garrick,) talk no more of that. You
are, perhaps, the worst – eh, eh!' Goldsmith was eagerly attempting
to interrupt him, when Garrick went on, laughing ironically, 'Nay,
you will always *look* like a gentleman; but I am talking of being well
or *ill drest*.' 'Well, let me tell you, (said Goldsmith,) when my tailor
brought home my bloom-coloured coat, he said, "Sir, I have a favour
to beg of you. When anybody asks you who made your clothes, be
pleased to mention John Filby,[1] at the Harrow, in Water Lane.'
Johnson. 'Why, sir, that was because he knew the strange colour
would attract crowds to gaze at it, and thus they might hear of him,
and see how well he could make a coat even of so absurd a colour.'[2]

---

* Quoted by Austin Dobson in *Life of Oliver Goldsmith* (London: Walter Scott, 1888)
pp. 147–8. Editor's title.

NOTES

James Boswell records a famous dinner, which has always played an important part in all literary portraits of Goldsmith. The impression produced by
the extraordinary art of Johnson's biographer is so vivid that, although one
feels the malice of some of the touches, any attempt to soften them detracts
from the value of the picture. It must therefore be given in Boswell's own
words.

1. The tailor's Christian name was William, not John.
2. Dr Birkbeck Hill is somewhat exercised to find that Filby's accounts for
this date only chronicle 'bloom-coloured breeches'. But Goldsmith was plainly
referring to the historical suit of 'Tyrian bloom, satin grain', which had been
sent home just before the production of *The Good-Natur'd Man* (Dobson).

Write Often*

OLIVER GOLDSMITH

[c. 10 January 1770]

Dear Brother,

I should have answered your letter sooner, but in truth I am not
fond of thinking of the necessities of those I love, when it is so very
little in my power to help them. I am sorry to find you are still every
way unprovided for; and what adds to my uneasiness is, that I have
received a letter from my sister Johnson,[1] by which I learn that she is
pretty much in the same circumstances. As to myself, I believe I
could get both you and my poor brother-in-law something like that
which you desire, but I am determined never to ask for little things,
nor exhaust any little interest I may have until I can serve you, him
and myself more effectually. As yet no opportunity has offered, but
I believe you are pretty well convinced that I will not be remiss when
it arrives. The king has lately been pleased to make me Professor of
Ancient History in a royal Academy of Painting, which he has just
established, but there is no salary annexed; and I took it rather as a
compliment to the institution than any benefit to myself. Honours to

---

* In *The Collected Letters of Oliver Goldsmith*, ed. Katharine C. Balderston (Cambridge: University Press, 1928) pp. 83–7. Editor's title.

one in my situation are something like ruffles to a man that wants a shirt. You tell me that there are fourteen or fifteen pounds left me in the hands of my cousin Lawder,[2] and you ask me what I would have done with them. My dear brother, I would by no means give any directions to my dear worthy relations at Kilmore,[3] how to dispose of money, which is, properly speaking, more theirs than mine. All that I can say is, that I entirely, and this letter will serve to witness, give up any right and title to it; and I am sure they will dispose of it to the best advantage. To them I entirely leave it, whether they or you may think the whole necessary to fit you out, or whether our poor sister Johnson may not want the half, I leave entirely to their and your discretion. The kindness of that good couple to our poor shattered family, demands our sincerest gratitude, and though they have almost forgot me, yet, if good things at last arrive, I hope one day to return, and increase their good humour by adding to my own. I have sent my cousin Jenny a miniature picture of myself, as I believe it is the most acceptable present I can offer. I have ordered it to be left for her at George Faulkener's, folded in a letter. The face, you well know, is ugly enough, but it is finely painted. I will shortly also send my friends over the Shannon some mezzotinto prints of myself, and some more of my friends here, such as Burke, Johnson, Reynolds and Colman. I believe I have written an hundred letters to different friends in your country and never received an answer from any of them. I do not know how to account for this, or why they are unwilling to keep up for me those regards which I must ever retain for them. If then you have a mind to oblige me, you will write often whether I answer you or not. Let me particularly have the news of our family and old acquaintances. For instance, you may begin by telling me about the family where you reside, how they spend their time, and whether they ever make mention of me. Tell me about my mother, my brother Hodson,[4] and his son; my brother Harry's son and daughter, my sister Johnson, the family of Ballyoughter, what is become of them, where they live, and how they do. You talked of being my only brother, I don't understand you – Where is Charles? A sheet of paper occasionally filled with news of this kind, would make me very happy, and would keep you nearer my mind.[5] As it is, my dear brother, believe me to be yours, most affectionately,

OLIVER GOLDSMITH

NOTES

Goldsmith's youngest brother Maurice, living at home without any employment, and not provided as Oliver had been with a university degree, wrote to the famous man for assistance. This is Goldsmith's reply.

1. Jane (Jenny), wife of the struggling farmer.
2. Both Maurice and Jenny conveyed to Goldsmith at the same time the information that Mr Contarine at his death – twelve years earlier – had left Oliver a small sum, which was in the hands of Mrs Lawder, Contarine's daughter (Jenny), and her husband.
3. Kilmore is in County Roscommon.
4. Daniel Hodson, Goldsmith's brother-in-law (husband of Catherine).
5. Maurice Goldsmith finally decided to be bound to a trade (as Oliver had once expected to be bound) and fitted himself to keep a cabinet-maker's shop in Dublin. Charles settled in Jamaica. However, before long, Oliver's nephew, son of his eldest sister and Dan Hodson, arrived in London, a half-fledged medico, and proceeded to live on his uncle, though set up as apothecary in Newman Street.

His Good Nature*

M'VEAGH M'DONNELL

It was in the year 1772 that the death of my elder brother – when in London, on my way to Ireland – left me in a most forlorn situation; I was then about eighteen; I possessed neither friends nor money, nor the means of getting to Ireland, of which or of England I knew scarcely anything, from having so long resided in France. In this situation I had strolled about for two or three days, considering what to do, but unable to come to any determination, when Providence directed me to the Temple Gardens. I threw myself on a seat, and, willing to forget my miseries for a moment, drew out a book; that book was a volume of Boileau. I had not been there long when a gentleman, strolling about, passed near me, and observing, perhaps, something Irish or foreign in my garb or countenance, addressed me: 'Sir, you seem studious; I hope you find this a favourable place to pursue it.' 'Not very studious, sir; I fear it is the want of society

---

* In James Prior, *The Life of Oliver Goldsmith, MB, from a Variety of Original Sources*, vol. 2 (London: John Murray, 1837) pp. 344–7.

that brings me hither; I am solitary and unknown in this metropolis;' and a passage from Cicero – *Oratio pro Archia* – occurring to me, I quoted it: *'Hæc studia pernoctant nobiscum, peregrinautur, rusticantur.'* 'You are a scholar, too, sir, I perceive.' 'A piece of one, sir; but I ought still to have been in the college where I had the good fortune to pick up the little I know.' A good deal of conversation ensued; I told him part of my history, and he, in return, gave his address in the Temple, desiring me to call soon, from which, to my infinite surprise and gratification, I found that the person who thus seemed to take an interest in my fate was my countryman and a distinguished ornament of letters.

I did not fail to keep the appointment, and was received in the kindest manner. He told me, smilingly, that he was not rich; that he could do little for me in direct pecuniary aid, but would endeavor to put me in the way of doing something for myself; observing, that he could at least furnish me with advice not wholly useless to a young man placed in the heart of a great metropolis. 'In London,' he continued, 'nothing is to be got for nothing; you must work; and no man who chooses to be industrious need be under obligations to another, for here labour of every kind commands its reward. If you think proper to assist me occasionally as amanuensis, I shall be obliged, and you will be placed under no obligation, until something more permanent can be secured for you.' This employment, which I pursued for some time, was to translate passages from Buffon, which were abridged or altered, according to circumstances, for his *Natural History*.

It has been said he was irritable. Such may have been the case at times; nay I·believe it was so; for what with the continual pursuit of authors, printers, and booksellers, and occasional pecuniary embarrassments, few could have avoided exhibiting similar marks of impatience. But it was never so towards me. I saw him only in his bland and kind moods, with a flow, perhaps an overflow, of the milk of human kindness for all who were in any manner dependent upon him. I looked upon him with awe and veneration, and he upon me as a kind parent upon a child.

His manner and address exhibited such frankness and cordiality, particularly to those with whom he possessed any degree of intimacy. His good nature was equally apparent. You could not dislike the man, although several of his follies and foibles you might be tempted to condemn. He was generous and inconsiderate; money with him had little value.

I was abroad at the time of his death, and wept bitterly when the intelligence first reached me. A blank came over my heart as if I had lost one of my nearest relatives, and was followed for some days by a feeling of despondency. – Poor Goldsmith was himself subject to frequent fits of depression as I heard from those around him.

NOTE

During a break from his work on the *History of Animated Nature* while he was strolling in the Temple gardens, Goldsmith came across the 18-year-old M'Veagh M'Donnell studying his volume of Boileau. There was a 'great deal of conversation' in the garden and later, taking up an invitation to visit Goldsmith in his rooms, M'Donnell received both good advice and a job on the translation of Buffon's *Histoire naturelle*, which was the basis of Goldsmith's own work. M'Donnell, who was to become a well-known London doctor, recalled Goldsmith's kindness in a conversation with James Prior, who wrote the first full-length biography of Goldsmith.

For God's Sake Take the Play*

OLIVER GOLDSMITH

[January 1773]

Dear Sir,

I entreat you'll relieve me from that state of suspense in which I have been kept for a long time. Whatever objections you have made, or shall make, to my play, I will endeavour to remove and not argue about them. To bring in any new judges either of its merits or faults I can never submit to. Upon a former occasion, when my other play was before Mr Garrick, he offered to bring me before Mr Whitehead's tribunal, but I refused the proposal with indignation. I hope I shall not experience as hard treatment from you as from him. I have, as you know, a large sum of money to make up shortly; by accepting my play I can readily satisfy my creditor that way; at any rate I must

---

* In *The Collected Letters of Oliver Goldsmith*, ed. Katharine C. Balderston (Cambridge: University Press, 1928) pp. 116–17. Editor's title.

look about to some certainty to be prepared. For God's sake take the play and let us make the best of it, and let me have the same measure at least which you have given as bad plays as mine. I am your friend and servant,

OLIVER GOLDSMITH

NOTE

The manuscript of *She Stoops to Conquer* seems to have reached the hands of George Colman the Younger early in 1772; and if Goldsmith had been slow in writing, Colman was slower still in considering. All the heartbreak about *The Good-Natur'd Man* had to be gone through again. Goldsmith's letter to Colman tells its own story.

Goldsmith's Envy*

JAMES BEATTIE

Miss Reynolds[1] told me today some particulars of Goldsmith. He, it seems, not only is, but even acknowledges himself to be, envious of all contemporary authors whose works are successful, and has several times spoken with some peevishness of the attention that has been shown to me in England. 'Why should he have a pension?' (he said one day in a company where I happened to be mentioned) – 'For writing the minstrel? Then surely I have a better claim.' One of the company told him, that my claim was founded on the *Essay on Truth*, a work of public utility, and which had been attended with danger or at least no small inconvenience to the Author. Here Foote the player interposed:[2] 'I have read (said he) the *Minstrel* and think it an excellent poem; but the Author of the *Essay on Truth* is peculiarly entitled to public encouragement for writing one of the best and most ingenious books which have appeared this age.' – We came not away from Richmond till it was dark and by the way met with more than one adventure, owing to the drunkenness of the coachman; however we got safely into town about 11 o'clock: Sir

---

* *London Diary, 1773* (Aberdeen: University Press, 1946) p. 55. Editor's title.

Joshua, Messrs Ed. & Wm Burkes, Goldsmith and I in one coach; &
Mrs Burke, Miss Reynolds, Mrs Beattie and Dick Burke in another.
Rainy and dark evening.

NOTES

Dr James Beattie (1735–1803), Scottish professor, poet, and author of the
Minstrel (1771, 1774). He was awarded a pension of £200 per annum for his
Essay on Truth (1770). Goldsmith was enraged when he heard about the
pension and told Dr Johnson, 'here's such a stir about a fellow that has
written one book, and I have written many.' 'Ah, Doctor!' retorted Johnson,
'there go two-and-forty sixpences, you know, to see a guinea.' The extract is
quoted from Beattie's diary entry for 14 June 1773.

   1. Frances Reynolds, Sir Joshua Reynolds' sister.
   2. Samuel Foote (1720–70), a satirical actor and mimic.

Goldsmith in the Literary Club*

HESTER LYNCH (THRALE) PIOZZI

I have forgotten the year, but it could scarcely I think be later than
1765 or 1766, that he [Johnson] was called abruptly from our house
after dinner, and returning in about three hours, said, he had been
with an enraged author [Goldsmith], whose landlady pressed him
for payment within doors, while the bailiffs beset him without; that
he was drinking himself drunk with Madeira to drown care, and
fretting over a novel which when finished was to be his whole
fortune; but he could not get it done for distraction, nor could he step
out of doors to offer it to sale. Mr [*sic*] Johnson therefore set away the
bottle, and went to the bookseller, recommending the performance,
and desiring some immediate relief; which when he brought back to
the writer, he called the woman of the house directly to partake of
punch, and pass their time in merriment.

   It was not till ten years after, I dare say, that something in Dr
Goldsmith's behaviour struck me with an idea that he was the very

* *Anecdotes of the Late Samuel Johnson, LL.D.* (London: T. Cadell, 1786) pp. 119–22,
178–81, 245. Editor's title.

man, and then Johnson confessed that he was so; the novel was the charming *Vicar of Wakefield* . . .

Of that respectable society [the Literary Club] I have heard him speak in the highest terms, and with a magnificent panegyric on each member, when it consisted only of a dozen or fourteen friends; but as soon as the necessity of enlarging it brought in new faces, and took off from his confidence in the company, he grew less fond of the meeting, and loudly proclaimed his carelessness *who* might be admitted, when it was become a mere dinner club. I *think* the original names, when I first heard him talk with fervour of every member's peculiar powers of instructing or delighting mankind, were Sir John Hawkins, Mr Burke, Mr Langton, Mr Beauclerc, Dr Percy, Dr Nugent, Dr Goldsmith, Sir Robert Chambers, Mr Dyer, and Sir Joshua Reynolds, whom he called their Romulus, or said somebody else, of the company called him so, which was more likely: but this was, I believe, in the year 1775 or 1776 . . .

Dr Goldsmith said once to him [Johnson], we should change companions oftener, we exhaust one another, and shall soon be both of us worn out. Poor Goldsmith was to him indeed like the earthen pot to the iron one in Fontaine's fables;[1] it had been better for *him* perhaps, that they had changed companions oftener; yet no experience of his antagonist's strength hindered him from continuing the contest. He used to remind me always of that verse in Berni:[2]

> Il pover uomo che non sen' èra accorto,
> Andava combattendo – ed èra morto.[3]

Mr [sic] Johnson made him a comical answer one day, when seeming to repine at the success of Beattie's *Essay on Truth* – 'Here's such a stir (said he) about a fellow that has written one book, and I have written many.' Ah, Doctor (says his friend), there go two-and-forty sixpences you know to one guinea.

They had spent an evening with Eton Graham[4] too, I remember hearing it was at some tavern; his heart was open, and he began inviting away; told what he could do to make his college agreeable, and begged the visit might not be delayed. Goldsmith thanked him, and proposed setting out with Mr Johnson for Buckinghamshire in a fortnight; 'Nay hold, Dr *Minor*[5] (says the other), I did not invite you.'

Many such mortifications arose in the course of their intimacy to be sure, but few more laughable than when the newspapers had tacked them together as the pedant and his flatterer in *Love's Labour*

Lost. Dr Goldsmith came to his friend, fretting and foaming, and vowing vengeance against the printer, &c. till Mr Johnson, tired of the bustle, and desirous to think of something else, cried out at last, 'Why, what would'st thou have, dear Doctor! who the plague is hurt with all this nonsense? and how is a man the worse I wonder in his health, purse, or character, for being called *Holofernes*?'[6] I do not know (replies the other) how you may relish being called Holofernes, but I do not like at least to play *Goodman Dull*[7] . . .

Returning home one day from dining at the chaplain's table, he told me that Dr Goldsmith had given a very comical and unnecessarily exact recital there, of his own feelings when his play was hissed; telling the company how he went indeed to the Literary Club at night, and chatted gaily among his friends, as if nothing had happened amiss; that to impress them still more forcibly with an idea of his magnanimity, he even sang his favourite song about an old woman tossed in a blanket seventeen times as high as the moon; but all this while I was suffering horrid tortures (said he), and verily believe that if I had put a bit into my mouth it would have strangled me on the spot, I was so excessively ill . . .

NOTES

Hester Lynch Piozzi (1741–1821), later Mrs Thrale, was a friend of both Goldsmith and Johnson. These anecdotes, published shortly after Johnson's death, throw some light on why Dr Johnson wanted Goldsmith to become and to remain a member of his Literary Club.

1. The fable of the pot of iron and the pot of clay, by Jean de la Fontaine (1621–95).

2. Francesco Berni (1497–1535), Italian satirist and burlesque poet who had written a modern adaptation of *Orlando Inamorato*, by the Italian poet Lodovico Ariosto (1447–1533).

3. The poor man who had not realised he was still fighting – and who was already dead.

4. The Reverend George Graham (d. 1767), an assistant master at Eton who had written several plays.

5. A name given to Goldsmith to contrast him with Johnson, Dr 'major.' See Boswell's *Journal of a Tour to the Hebrides* for the full story; and his *Life of Johnson*, vol. 5 (Oxford: University Press, 1950) p. 97.

6. An anagram of 'Joh'nes Florio,' the first and last letters being omitted. Shakespeare, in *Love's Labour's Lost*, ridicules the lexicographer John Florio (d. 1625) as well as the general pedantry of the age.

7. Refers to Constable Dull in Shakespeare's play: a pompous official who reasons everything to absurdity via the syllogism.

The Character of Goldsmith*

RICHARD CUMBERLAND

At this time I did not know Oliver Goldsmith even by person; I think our first meeting chanced to be at the British Coffee House; when we came together, we very speedily coalesced, and I believe he forgave me for all the little fame I had got by the success of my *West Indian*, which had put him to some trouble, for it was not his nature to be unkind, and I had soon an opportunity of convincing him how incapable I was of harbouring resentment, and how zealously I took my share in what concerned his interest and reputation. That he was fantastically and whimsically vain all the world knows, but there was no settled and inherent malice in his heart. He was tenacious to a ridiculous extreme of certain pretensions, that did not, and by nature could not, belong to him, and at the same time inexcusably careless of the fame, which he had powers to command. His table-talk was, as Garrick aptly compared it, like that of a parrot, whilst he wrote like Apollo; he had gleams of eloquence, and at times a majesty of thought, but in general his tongue and his pen had two very different styles of talking. What foibles he had he took no pains to conceal, the good qualities of his heart were too frequently obscured by the carelessness of his conduct, and the frivolity of his manners. Sir Joshua Reynolds was very good to him, and would have drilled him into better trim and order for society, if he would have been amenable, for Reynolds was a perfect gentleman, had good sense, great propriety with all the social attributes, and all the graces of hospitality, equal to any man. He well knew how to appreciate men of talents, and how near akin the Muse of poetry was to that art, of which he was so eminent a master. From Goldsmith he caught the subject of his famous Ugolino; what aids he got from others, if he got any, were worthily bestowed and happily applied.

There is something in Goldsmith's prose, that to my ear is uncommonly sweet and harmonious; it is clear, simple, easy to be under-

* *Memoirs* (London: Lackington, Allen & Co., 1806) pp. 257–9, 267–74. Editor's title.

stood; we never want to read his period twice over, except for the pleasure it bestows; obscurity never calls us back to a repetition of it. That he was a poet there is no doubt, but the paucity of his verses does not allow us to rank him in that high station, where his genius might have carried him. There must be bulk,[1] variety and grandeur of design to constitute a first-rate poet. *The Deserted Village, Traveller* and *Hermit* are all specimens beautiful as such, but they are only birds' eggs on a string, and eggs of small birds too. One great magnificent *whole* must be accomplished before we can pronounce upon the *maker* to be the ὁ ποιήτης.[2] Pope himself never earned this title by a work of any magnitude but his Homer, and that being a translation only constitutes him an accomplished versifier. Distress drove Goldsmith upon undertakings, neither congenial with his studies, nor worthy of his talents. I remember him, when in his chamber in the Temple, he showed me the beginning of his *Animated Nature*; it was with a sigh, such as genius draws, when hard necessity diverts it from its bent to drudge for bread, and talk of birds and beasts and creeping things, which Pidcock's showman would have done as well. Poor fellow, he hardly knew an ass from a mule, nor a turkey from a goose, but when he saw it on the table. But publishers hate poetry, and Paternoster Row is not Parnassus. Even the mighty Doctor Hill, who was not a very delicate feeder, could not make a dinner out of the press till by a happy transformation into Hannah Glass he turned himself into a cook, and sold receipts for made-dishes to all the savoury readers in the kingdom. Then indeed the press acknowledged him second in fame only to John Bunyan; his feasts kept pace in sale with Nelson's fasts, and when his own name was fairly written out of credit, he wrote himself into immortality under an alias. Now though necessity, or I should rather say the desire of finding money for a masquerade, drove Oliver Goldsmith upon abridging histories and turning Buffon into English,[3] yet I much doubt if without that spur he would ever have put his Pegasus into action; no, if he had been rich, the world would have been poorer than it is by the loss of all the treasures of his genius and the contributions of his pen . . .

Oliver Goldsmith began at this time to write for the stage, and it is to be lamented that he did not begin at an earlier period of life to turn his genius to dramatic compositions, and much more to be lamented, that, after he had begun, the succeeding period of his life was so soon cut off. There is no doubt but his genius, when more familiarised to the business, would have inspired him to accomplish

great things. His first comedy of *The Good-natur'd Man* was read and
applauded in its manuscript by Edmund Burke, and the circle, in
which he then lived and moved: under such patronage it came with
those testimonials to the director of Covent Garden Theatre, as could
not fail to open all the avenues to the stage, and bespeak all the
favour and attention from the performers and the public, that the
applauding voice of him, whose applause was fame itself, could give
it. This comedy has enough to justify the good opinion of its literary
patron, and secure its author against any loss of reputation, for it has
the stamp of a man of talents upon it, though its popularity with the
audience did not quite keep pace with the expectations, that were
grounded on the fiat it had antecedently been honoured with. It was
a first effort however, and did not discourage its ingenious author
from invoking his Muse a second time. It was now, whilst his labours were in projection, that I first met him at the British Coffee
House, as I have already related somewhat out of place. He dined
with us as a visitor, introduced as I think by Sir Joshua Reynolds,
and we held a consultation upon the naming of his comedy, which
some of the company had read, and which he detailed to the rest
after his manner with a great deal of good humour. Somebody
suggested – *She Stoops to Conquer* – and that title was agreed upon.
When I perceived an embarrassment in his manner towards me,
which I could readily account for, I lost no time to put him at his
ease, and I flatter myself I was successful. As my heart was ever
warm towards my contemporaries, I did not counterfeit, but really
felt a cordial interest in his behalf, and I had soon the pleasure to
perceive that he credited me for my sincerity – 'You and I,' said he,
'have very different motives for resorting to the stage. I write for
money, and care little about fame' – I was touched by this melancholy confession, and from that moment busied myself assiduously
amongst all my connexions in his cause. The whole company pledged
themselves to the support of the ingenuous poet, and faithfully kept
their promise to him. In fact he needed all that could be done for
him, as Mr Colman, then manager of Covent Garden Theatre, protested against the comedy, when as yet he had not struck upon a
name for it. Johnson at length stood forth in all his terrors as cham-
pion for the piece, and backed by us his clients and retainers demanded a fair trial. Colman again protested, but, with that salvo for
his own reputation, liberally lent his stage to one of the most eccentric productions, that ever found its way to it, and *She Stoops to
Conquer* was put into rehearsal.

We were not over-sanguine of success, but perfectly determined to struggle hard for our author: we accordingly assembled our strength at the Shakespeare Tavern in a considerable body for an early dinner, where Samuel Johnson took the chair at the head of a long table, and was the life and soul of the corps: the poet took post silently by his side with the Burkes, Sir Joshua Reynolds, Fitzherbert, Caleb Whitefoord and a phalanx of North-British predetermined applauders, under the banner of Major Mills, all good men and true. Our illustrious president was in inimitable glee, and poor Goldsmith that day took all his raillery as patiently and complacently as my friend Boswell would have done any day, or every day of his life. In the meantime we did not forget our duty, and though we had a better comedy going, in which Johnson was chief actor, we betook ourselves in good time to our separate and allotted posts, and waited the awful drawing up of the curtain. As our stations were pre-concerted, so were our signals for plaudits arranged and determined upon in a manner, that gave every one his cue where to look for them, and how to follow them up.

We had amongst us a very worthy and efficient member, long since lost to his friends and the world at large, Adam Drummond, of amiable memory, who was gifted by nature with the most sonorous, and at the same time the most contagious, laugh, that ever echoed from the human lungs. The neighing of the horse of the son of Hystaspes was a whisper to it; the whole thunder of the theatre could not drown it. This kind and ingenuous friend fairly fore-warned us that he knew no more when to give his fire than the cannon did, that was planted on a battery. He desired therefore to have a flapper at his elbow, and I had the honour to be deputed to that office. I planted him in an upper box, pretty nearly over the stage, in full view of the pit and galleries, and perfectly well situated to give the echo all its play through the hollows and recesses of the theatre. The success of our manoeuvres was complete. All eyes were upon Johnson, who sat in a front row of a side box, and when he laughed everybody thought themselves warranted to roar. In the meantime my friend followed signals with a rattle so irresistibly comic, that, when he had repeated it several times, the attention of the spectators was so engrossed by his person and performances, that the progress of the play seemed likely to become a secondary object, and I found it prudent to insinuate to him that he might halt his music without any prejudice to the author; but alas, it was now too late to rein him in; he had laughed upon my signal where he found no joke, and now unluckily he fancied that he found a joke in almost everything that was said; so that nothing in nature could be more *mal-à-propos* than some of his bursts every now and then were. These were dangerous moments, for the pit began to take umbrage; but we carried our play through, and triumphed not only over Colman's judgement, but our own.

As the life of poor Oliver Goldsmith was now fast approaching to its period, I conclude my account of him with gratitude for the epitaph he bestowed on me in his poem called *Retaliation*. It was upon a proposal started by Edmund Burke, that a party of friends, who had dined together at Sir Joshua Reynolds's and my house, should meet at the St James's Coffee-House, which accordingly took place, and was occasionally repeated with much festivity and good fellowship. Dr Bernard, Dean of Derry, a very amiable and old friend of mine, Dr Douglas, since Bishop of Salisbury, Johnson, David Garrick, Sir Joshua Reynolds, Oliver Goldsmith, Edmund and Richard Burke, Hickey, with two or three others constituted our party. At one of these meetings an idea was suggested of extemporary epitaphs upon the parties present; pen and ink were called for, and Garrick offhand wrote an epitaph with a good deal of humour upon poor Goldsmith, who was the first in jest, as he proved to be in reality, that we committed to the grave. The dean also gave him an epitaph, and Sir Joshua illuminated the dean's verses with a sketch of his bust in pen and ink, inimitably caricatured. Neither Johnson, nor Burke wrote anything, and when I perceived Oliver was rather sore, and seemed to watch me with that kind of attention, which indicated his expectation of something in the same kind of burlesque with theirs, I thought it time to press the joke no further, and wrote a few couplets at a side table, which when I had finished and was called upon by the company to exhibit, Goldsmith with much agitation besought me to spare him, and I was about to tear them, when Johnson wrested them out of my hand, and in a loud voice read them at the table. I have now lost all recollection of them, and in fact they were little worth remembering, but as they were serious and complimentary, the effect they had upon Goldsmith was the more pleasing for being so entirely unexpected. The concluding line, which is the only one I can call to mind, was:

All mourn the poet, I lament the man –

This I recollect, because he repeated it several times, and seemed much gratified by it. At our next meeting he produced his epitaphs as they stand in the little posthumous poem above-mentioned, and this was the last time he ever enjoyed the company of his friends.

As he had served up the company under the similitude of various sorts of meat, I had in the meantime figured them under that of liquors, which little poem I rather think was printed, but of this I am not sure. Goldsmith sickened and died, and we had one concluding meeting at my house, when it was decided to publish his *Retaliation*, and Johnson at the same time undertook to write an epitaph for our lamented friend, to whom we proposed to erect a monument by subscription in Westminster Abbey. This epitaph Johnson executed; but in the criticism, that was attempted against it, and in the round-robin signed at Mr Beauclerc's house I had no part. I had no acquaintance with that gentleman, and was never in his house in my life.

Thus died Oliver Goldsmith in his chambers in the Temple at a period of life, when his genius was yet in its vigour, and fortune seemed disposed to smile upon him. I have heard Dr Johnson relate with infinite humour the circumstance of his rescuing him from a ridiculous dilemma by the purchase-money of his *Vicar of Wakefield*, which he sold on his behalf to Dodsley, and, as I think, for the sum of ten pounds only. He had run up a debt with his landlady for board and lodging of some few pounds, and was at his wit's-end how to wipe off the score and keep a roof over his head, except by closing with a very staggering proposal on her part, and taking his creditor to wife, whose charms were very far from alluring, whilst her demands were extremely urgent. In this crisis of his fate he was found by Johnson in the act of meditating on the melancholy alternative before him. He showed Johnson his manuscript of *The Vicar of Wakefield*, but seemed to be without any plan, or even hope, of raising money upon the disposal of it; when Johnson cast his eye upon it, he discovered something that gave him hope, and immediately took it to Dodsley, who paid down the price above-mentioned in ready money, and added an eventual condition upon its future sale. Johnson described the precautions he took in concealing the amount of the sum he had in hand, which he prudently administered to him by a guinea at a time. In the event he paid off the landlady's score, and redeemed the person of his friend from her embraces. Goldsmith had the joy of finding his ingenious work succeed beyond his hopes, and from that time began to place a confidence in the resources of his talents, which thenceforward

enabled him to keep his station in society, and cultivate the friendship of many eminent persons, who, whilst they smiled at his eccentricities, esteemed him for his genius and good qualities.

NOTES

Richard Cumberland (1732–1811), English dramatist. He first achieved recognition with *The Brothers* (1769), but his best-known play is *The West Indian*
(1771), produced with great success by Garrick, and typical of the whole
school of sentimental comedy. Cumberland, whose success made him an
important figure in the literary world of London, was extremely sensitive to
criticism.

1. It is hard to subscribe to these opinions of Cumberland; they would
exclude Pindar, Horace, Dryden, Gray and others from the list of great
poets.

2. The poet.

3. Georges Louis Leclerc, Comte de Buffon (1707–88), French naturalist.

Goldsmith as a Dramatist and a Person*

SAMUEL FOOTE

Dr Goldsmith was the first to attack this illegitimate species of writing [sentimentalism], by his successive productions of *The Good
Natur'd Man*, and *She Stoops to Conquer*. Our hero followed, with his
Piety in Pattens;[1] in which he introduces, in the true ballad style,
'How *a maiden of low degree*, by the mere effects of morality and
virtue, raised herself to riches and honours.' These two being supported by other writers, soon laid the ghost of *sentimental comedy*;
and John Bull was once more restored to his usual laugh and good
humour.

* In William Cooke, *Memoirs of Samuel Foote* (London: Richard Phillips, 1805)
vol. 1, pp. 184–6; vol. 3, pp. 77–8. Editor's title.

But it sometimes unfortunately happens in mental, as well as in corporeal diseases, that in curing one species of complaint, unskilful physicians induce another equally dangerous. This was the case in the cure of sentimental comedy. Those writers who succeeded Goldsmith and Foote in their design, but who could not follow them in their talents, perceiving the success of the ridicule against gravity, thought that by making comedy *still more laughable*, it would accommodate more the taste of the public. They, therefore, to banish the style of *The Whole Duty of Man*, and *The Economy of Human Life*,[2] took their model from Joe Miller,[3] whence it resulted, that by a profusion of stale jests clumsily fitted to modern circumstances, and pantomimic tricks which were called *dramatic situations*, the stage, in general, is even at present so contaminated, that not only our best poets on the stock list are out of fashion, but many men of real dramatic knowledge feel. the shame, as well as the risk, of writing under such a degrading and discouraging patronage . . .

Everybody who knew Goldsmith intimately, must have known that he was no less distinguished as a poet, than for the eccentricities and varieties of his character; being by turns vain and humble, coarse and refined, judicious and credulous. In one of his humiliating moments, he accidentally met with an old acquaintance at a chop-house, soon after he had finished his comedy of *She Stoops to Conquer*; and, talking to him upon the subject, requested of him as a friend, and as a critic whose judgment he relied on, that he would give him an opinion of it.

The Doctor then began to tell the particulars of his plot, in his strange, uncouth, deranged manner; which the other could only make out to be, 'that the principal part of the business turned upon one gentleman mistaking the house of another for an inn' – at which he shook his head, observing at the same time, that he was afraid the audience, under their then *sentimental impressions*, would think it too broad and farcical for comedy.

Goldsmith looked very serious at this, and paused for some time. At last, taking him by the hand, he piteously exclaimed: 'I am much obliged to you, my dear friend, for the candour of your opinion: but it is all I can do; for, alas! I find that my genius (if ever I had any) has of late totally deserted me.' One of the performers of the Haymarket Theatre was observing to Foote, 'what a *humdrum* kind of man Dr Goldsmith appeared to be in the green-room, compared with the figure he made in his poetry.' 'The reason of that,' said he, 'is, because the *muses* are better companions than the *players.*'

NOTES

Samuel Foote (1720–77), English actor and dramatist. He was an acquaintance of Goldsmith's, especially in 1772–3, when both men frequently met at
the St James's Coffeehouse. Foote was at once feared and admired by his
contemporaries, Dr Johnson being one of the few who despised him without
any wish to placate, though he said of him, 'Sir, he was irresistible.'
    1. Foote's *Piety in Pattens* was produced in 1773.
    2. Devotional books by Richard Allestree (1619–81) and Robert Dodsley
(1703–64) respectively.
    3. Joe Miller (1684–1738), English comedian.

Goldsmith and David Garrick*

THOMAS DAVIES

Dr Goldsmith having tried his genius in several modes of writing, in
essays, descriptive poetry, and history, was advised to apply himself
to that species of composition which is said to have been long the
most fruitful in the courts of Parnassus. The writer of plays has been
ever supposed to pursue the quickest road to the temple of Plutus.
    The Doctor was a perfect heteroclite, an inexplicable existence in
creation; such a compound of absurdity, envy, and malice, con-
trasted with the opposite virtues of kindness, generosity, and benevolence, that he might be said to consist of two distinct souls, and
to be influenced by the agency of a good and bad spirit.
    The first knowledge Mr Garrick had of his abilities, was from an
attack upon him by Goldsmith, when he was but a very young
author, in a book called *The Present State of Learning*. Amongst other
abuses (for the Doctor loved to dwell upon grievances) he took
notice of the behaviour of managers to authors: this must surely
have proceeded from the most generous principles of reforming
what was amiss for the benefit of others, for the Doctor at that time
had not the most distant view of commencing dramatic author.
    Little did Goldsmith imagine he should one day be obliged to ask
a favour from the director of a playhouse: however, when the office

---

* *Memoirs of the Life of David Garrick*, vol. 2 (London: Longman *et al.*, 1808) pp.
148–69. Editor's title.

of secretary to the Society of Arts and Sciences[1] became vacant, the Doctor was persuaded to offer himself as a candidate. He was told that Mr Garrick was a leading member of that learned body, and his interest and recommendation would be of consequence to enforce his pretensions.

He waited upon the manager, and, in few words, requested his vote and interest. Mr Garrick could not avoid observing to him, that it was impossible he could lay claim to any recommendation from him, as he had taken pains to deprive himself of his assistance by an unprovoked attack upon his management of the theatre, in his *State of Learning*. Goldsmith, instead of making an apology for his conduct, either from misinformation or misconception, bluntly replied, in truth he had spoken his mind, and believed what he said was very right. The manager dismissed him with civility; and Goldsmith lost the office by a very great majority, who voted in favour of Dr Templeman.

The Doctor's reputation, which was daily increasing from a variety of successful labours, was at length lifted so high, that he escaped from indigence and obscurity to competence and fame.

The first man of the age, one who, from the extensiveness of his genius and benevolence of his mind, is superior to the little envy and mean jealousy which adhere so closely to most authors, and especially to those of equivocal merit, took pleasure in introducing Dr Goldsmith to his intimate friends, persons of eminent rank and distinguished abilities. The Doctor's conversation by no means corresponded with the idea formed of him from his writings.

The Duchess of Rambouillet, who was charmed with the tragedies of Corneille, wished to have so great an author among her constant visitors, expecting infinite entertainment from the writer of the *Cid*, the *Horace*, and *Cinna*. But the poet lost himself in society; he held no rank with the *beaux esprits* who met at the hotel of this celebrated lady; his conversation was dry, unpleasant, and what the French call *distrait*.[2] So Dr Goldsmith appeared in company to have no spark of that genius which shone forth so brightly in his writings; his address was awkward, his manner uncouth, his language unpolished, his elocution was continually interrupted by disagreeable hesitation, and he was always unhappy if the conversation did not turn upon himself.

To manifest his intrepidity in argument, he would generously espouse the worst side of the question, and almost always left it weaker than he found it. His jealousy fixed a perpetual ridicule on his character, for he was emulous of everything and everybody. He went with some friends to see the entertainment of the fantoccini, whose uncommon agility and quick evolutions were much celebrated. The Doctor was asked how he liked these automatons. He replied, he was surprised at the applause bestowed on the little insignificant creatures, for he could have performed their exercises much better himself. When his great literary friend was commended in his hearing, he could not restrain his uneasiness, but exclaimed, in a kind of agony, 'No more, I desire you; you harrow up my soul!' More absurd stories may be recorded of Goldsmith than of any man: his absence of mind would not permit him to attend to time, place, or company. When at the table of a nobleman of high rank and great accomplishments, one to whom England stands indebted in many obligations, and it is hoped that he will more and more increase the debt by his continual and vigorous efforts to secure her happiness; to this great man Goldsmith observed, that he was called by the name of Malagrida; 'but I protest and vow to your Lordship, I can't conceive for what reason, *for Malagrida was an honest man!*'

When the Doctor had finished his comedy of *The Good-natur'd Man*, he was advised to offer it to Mr Garrick. The manager was fully conscious of his merit, and perhaps more ostentatious of his abilities to serve a dramatic author, than became a man of his prudence: Goldsmith was, on his side, as fully persuaded of his own importance and independent greatness. Mr Garrick, who had been so long treated with the complimentary language paid to a successful patentee and admired actor, expected that the writer would esteem the patronage of his play as a favour: Goldsmith rejected all ideas of kindness in a bargain that was intended to be of mutual advantage to both; and in this he was certainly justifiable. Mr Garrick could reasonably expect no thanks for the acting a new play, which he would have rejected, if he had not been convinced it would have amply rewarded his pains and expense. I believe the manager was willing to accept the play, but he wished to be courted to it; and the Doctor was not disposed to purchase his friendship by the resignation of his sincerity. He then applied to Mr Colman, who accepted his comedy without any hesitation.

The Good-natur'd Man bears strong marks of that happy originality which distinguishes the writings of Dr Goldsmith. Two characters in this comedy were absolutely unknown before to the English stage; a man who boasts an intimacy with persons of high rank whom he never saw, and another who is almost always lamenting misfortunes he never knew. Croaker is as strongly designed, and as highly finished a portrait of a discontented man, of one who disturbs every happiness he possesses, from apprehension of distant evil, as any character of Congreve, or any other of our English dramatists. Shuter acted Croaker with that warm glee of fancy, and genuine flow of humour, that always accompanied his best and most animated performances. The great applause and profit which attended the acting of this comedy, contributed to render the author more important in his own eyes, and in the opinion of the public. But no good fortune could make Goldsmith discreet, nor any increase of fame diminish his envy, or cure the intractability of his temper. John Home[3] was taught by experience, that his connexions with the great were of no avail with the public; and that courtly approbation was no protection from popular dislike; he therefore veiled himself in obscurity, and prevailed upon a young gentleman, his friend, to adopt his play of The Fatal Discovery; but the foster-father performed his assumed character so awkwardly at the rehearsal of this tragedy, that it was soon discovered that the child was not his own; for he submitted to have the piece altered, lopped, and corrected, with such tranquillity of temper, as the real parent could not have assumed. Of the true author Goldsmith by chance found out the knowledge; and when the play was announced to the public, it will hardly be credited, that this man of benevolence, for such he really was, endeavoured to muster a party to condemn it; alleging this cogent reason for the proceeding, that such fellows ought not to be encouraged.

No author ever spar'd a brother:
Wits are game-cocks to one another.[4]

The tragedy of The Countess of Salisbury, a play in which Mr Barry and Mrs Dancer displayed great powers of acting, was in a good degree of favour with the town. This was a crime sufficient to rouse the indignation of Goldsmith, who issued forth to see it, with a determined resolution to consign the play to perdition. He sat out four acts of The Countess of Salisbury with great calmness and seeming temper; but as the plot thickened, and his apprehension began to be terrified with the ideas of blood and slaughter, he got up in a great hurry, saying, loud enough to be heard, Brownrig! Brownrig! by G –.[5]

Goldsmith never wanted literary employment; the booksellers understood the value of his name, and did all they could to excite his industry; and it cannot be denied that they rewarded his labours generously: in a few years he wrote three Histories of England; the first in two pocket volumes in letters, and another in four volumes octavo; the first, an elegant summary of British transactions; and the other, an excellent abridgment of Hume, and other copious historians. These books are in everybody's hands. The last is a short contraction of the four volumes in one duodecimo. For writing these books he obtained 750*l*. or 800*l*.

His squabbles with booksellers and publishers were innumerable; his appetites and passions were craving and violent; he loved variety of pleasures, but could not devote himself to industry long enough to purchase them by his writings: upon every emergency half a dozen projects would present themselves to his mind; these he communicated to the men who were to advance money on the reputation of the author; but the money was generally spent long before the new work was half finished, or perhaps before it was commenced. This circumstance naturally produced reproach from one side, which was often returned with anger and vehemence on the other. After much and disagreeable altercation, one bookseller desired to refer the matter in dispute to the Doctor's learned friend, a man of known integrity, and one who would favour no cause but that of justice and truth. Goldsmith consented, and was enraged to find that one author should have so little feeling for another, as to determine a dispute to his disadvantage, in favour of a tradesman.

His love of play involved him in many perplexing difficulties, and a thousand anxieties; and yet he had not the resolution to abandon a practice for which his impatience of temper and great unskilfulness rendered him totally unqualified.

Though Mr Garrick did not act his comedy of *She Stoops to Conquer*; yet, as he was then upon very friendly terms with the author, he presented him with a very humorous prologue, well accommodated to the occasion, of reviving fancy, wit, gaiety, humour, incident, and character, in the place of sentiment and moral preachment.

Woodward[6] spoke this whimsical address in mourning, and lamented pathetically over poor dying Comedy. To her he says:

> —A mawkish drab of spurious breed,
> Who deals in *sentimentals*, will succeed.[7]

In the close of the Prologue, the Doctor is recommended as a fit person to revive poor drooping Thalia; with a compliment which hinted, I imagine, at some public transaction, of not dealing in poisonous drugs.

She Stoops to Conquer, notwithstanding many improbabilities in the economy of the plot, several farcical situations, and some characters which are rather exaggerated, is a lively and faithful representation of nature; genius presides over every scene of this play; the characters are either new, or varied improvements from other plays. Marlow has a slight resemblance of Charles in *The Fop's Fortune,* and something more of Lord Hardy in Steele's *Funeral;* and yet, with a few shades of these parts, he is discriminated from both. Tony Lumpkin is a vigorous improvement of Humphry Gubbins, and a more diverting picture of ignorance, rusticity, and obstinacy; Hardcastle, his wife, and daughter, I think, are absolutely new; the language is easy and characteristical; the manners of the times are slightly, but faithfully, represented; the satire is not ostentatiously displayed, but incidentally involved in the business of the play; and the suspense of the audience is artfully kept up to the last. This comedy was very well acted; Lewis played Marlow with the ease of a gentleman; Hardcastle and Tony Lumpkin were supported in a masterly style by Shuter and Quick; so was Miss Hardcastle by Mrs Bulkeley. Mrs Green, in Mrs Hardcastle, maintained her just title to one of the best comic actresses of the age.

Though the money gained by this play amounted to a considerable sum, more especially so to a man who had been educated in straits and trained in adversity; yet his necessities soon became as craving as ever: to relieve them, he undertook a new *History of Greece;* and a book of animals, called, *The History of Animated Nature.* The first was to him an easy task; but as he was entirely unacquainted with the world of animals, his friends were anxious for the success of his latter undertaking. Notwithstanding his utter ignorance of the subject, he has compiled one of the pleasantest and most instructive books in our language; I mean, that it is not only useful to young minds, but entertaining to those who understand the animal creation.

Everything of Goldsmith seems to bear the magical touch of an enchanter; no man took less pains, and yet produced so powerful an effect: the great beauty of his composition consists in a clear, copious, and expressive style.

Goldsmith's last work was his poem called *Retaliation,* which the historian of his life[8] says was written for his own amusement, and that of his friends, who were the subjects of it. That he did not live to finish it, is to be lamented, for it is supposed he would have introduced more characters. What he has left is so perfect in its kind, that it stands not in need of revisal.

In no part of his works has this author discovered a more nice and critical discernment, or a more perfect knowledge of human nature, than in this poem; with wonderful art he has traced all the leading features of his several portraits, and given with truth the characteristical peculiarities of each; no man is lampooned, and no man is flattered.

The occasion, we are told, to which we owe this admirable poem, was a circumstance of festivity. The literary society to which he belonged proposed to write epitaphs on the Doctor. Mr Garrick, one of the members, wrote the following fable of Jupiter and Mercury, to provoke Goldsmith to a retaliation.

Jupiter and Mercury. A Fable.
Here, Hermes! says Jove, who with nectar was
    mellow,
Go, fetch me some clay – I will make an odd fellow.
Right and wrong shall be jumbled, much gold and
    some dross;
Without cause be he pleas'd, without cause be he cross:
Be sure, as I work, to throw in contradictions;
A great lover of truth, yet a mind turn'd to fictions.
Now mix these ingredients, which, warm'd in the
    baking,
Turn to learning and gaming, religion and raking;
With the love of a wench, let his writings be chaste.
Tip his tongue with strange matter, his pen with fine
    taste;
That the rake and the poet o'er all may prevail,
Set fire to his head, and set fire to his tail.
For the joy of each sex on the world I'll bestow it,
This scholar, rake, christian, dupe, gamester, and poet.
Though a mixture so odd, he shall merit great fame,
And among brother mortals be Goldsmith his name.
When on earth this strange meteor no more shall
    appear,
You, Hermes, shall fetch him, to make us sport here.

There never was surely a finer picture, at full length, given to the world, than this warm character of the incomprehensible and heterogeneous Doctor.

And here Dr Goldsmith's portrait of Mr Garrick will be introduced with propriety:

> Here lies David Garrick, describe him who can,
> An abridgment of all that was pleasant in man:
> As an actor, confess'd without rival to shine;
> As a wit, if not first, in the very first line:
> Yet, with talents like these, and an excellent heart,
> The man had his failings – a dupe to his art.
> Like an ill-judging beauty, his colours he spread,
> And be-plastered with rouge his own natural red.
> On the stage he was natural, simple, affecting;
> 'T was only that when he was off he was acting.
> With no reason on earth to go out of his way,
> He turn'd and he varied full ten times a day:
> Though secure of our hearts, yet confoundedly sick
> If they were not his own by finessing and trick:
> He cast off his friends, as a huntsman his pack,
> For he knew, when he pleas'd, he could whistle them
>   back.
> Of praise a mere glutton, he swallow'd what came,
> And the puff of a dunce, he mistook it for fame;
> Till his relish grown callous, almost to disease,
> Who pepper'd the highest was surest to please.
> But let us be candid, and speak out our mind;
> If dunces applauded, he paid them in kind.
> Ye Kenricks, ye Kellys, and Woodfalls, so grave,
> What a commerce was yours, while you got and you
>   gave!
> How did Grub Street re-echo the shouts that you rais'd,
> While he was be-Roscius'd, and you were be-prais'd!
> But peace to his spirit, wherever it flies,
> To act as an angel, and mix with the skies;
> Those poets, who owe their best fame to his skill,
> Shall still be his flatterers, go where he will;
> Old Shakespeare receive him with praise and with love,
> And Beaumonts and Bens be his Kellys above.

The sum of all that can be said for and against Mr Garrick, some
people think, may be found in these lines of Goldsmith. That the

person upon whom they were written was displeased with some strokes of this character, may be gathered from the following *jeu d'esprit,* which Mr Garrick wrote on *The Retaliation* soon after it had been produced to the society:

> Are these the choice dishes the Doctor has sent us?
> Is this the great poet whose works so content us?
> This Goldsmith's fine feast, who has written fine
>   books?
> Heaven sends us good meat, but the devil sends cooks.

Candour must own, that Mr Garrick, in his verses on Goldsmith, was gentle in describing the subject, as well as delicate in the choice of his expressions; but that Garrick's features in *The Retaliation* are somewhat exaggerated.

Not long before his death, he had formed a design of publishing an Encyclopædia, or an *Universal Dictionary of Arts and Sciences;* a prospectus of which he printed and sent to his friends, many of whom had promised to furnish him with articles on different subjects; and, among the rest, Sir Joshua Reynolds, Dr Johnson, and Mr Garrick. His expectations from any new-conceived projects were generally very sanguine; but from so extensive a plan his hopes of gain had lifted up his thoughts to an extraordinary height.

The booksellers, notwithstanding they had a high opinion of his abilities, yet were startled at the bulk, importance, and expense of so great an undertaking, the fate of which was to depend upon the industry of a man with whose indolence of temper and method of procrastination they had long been acquainted: the coldness with which they met his proposal was lamented by the Doctor to the hour of his death, which seems to have been accelerated by a neglect of his health, occasioned by continual vexation of mind, arising from his involved circumstances. Death, I really believe, was welcome to a man of his great sensibility.

The chief materials which compose Goldsmith's character are before the reader; but, as I have with great freedom exposed his faults, I should not have dwelt so minutely upon them, if I had not been conscious, that, upon a just balance of his good and bad qualities, the former would far outweigh the latter.

Goldsmith was so sincere a man, that he could not conceal what was uppermost in his mind: so far from desiring to appear in the eye of the world to the best advantage, he took more pains to be esteemed worse than he was, than others do to appear better than they are. His envy was so childish, and so absurd,[9] that it may be very easily pardoned, for everybody laughed at it; and no man was ever very mischievous whose errors excited mirth: he never formed any scheme, or joined in any combination, to hurt any man living.

His inviting persons to condemn Mr Home's tragedy, at first sight wears an ill face; but this was a transient thought of a giddy man, who, upon the least check, would have immediately renounced it, and as heartily joined with a party to support the piece he had before devoted to destruction. It cannot be controverted, that he was but a bad economist, nor in the least acquainted with that punctuality which regular people exact. He was more generous than just; like honest Charles, in *The School for Scandal*, he could not, for the soul of him, make justice keep pace with generosity. His disposition of mind was tender and compassionate; no unhappy person ever sued to him for relief, without obtaining it, if he had anything to give; and, rather than not relieve the distressed, he would borrow. The poor woman, with whom he had lodged during his obscurity several years in Green Arbour Court, by his death lost an excellent friend; for the Doctor often supplied her with food from his table, and visited her frequently with the sole purpose to be kind to her. He had his dislike, as most men have, to particular people, but unmixed with rancour. He, least of all mankind, approved Baretti's conversation; he considered him as an insolent, overbearing foreigner; as Baretti, in his turn, thought him an unpolished man, and an absurd companion: but when this unhappy Italian was charged with murder, and afterwards sent by Sir John Fielding to Newgate, Goldsmith opened his purse, and would have given him every shilling it contained; he, at the same time, insisted upon going in the coach with him to the place of his confinement.

NOTES

Thomas Davies (?1712–85), ex-actor and bookseller who published Goldsmith's books. His shop was perhaps then the most noted rendezvous in London for poets, wits, dramatists, and literary gossips.

1. Known since 1909 as the Royal Society of Arts.
2. Listless.
3. John Home (1722–1808), minor dramatist and author.
4. John Gay, Fable X, *The Elephant and the Bookseller*, lines 75–6.
5. William Brownrigg (1711–1800), a well-known chemist.

6. Henry Woodward (1714–77), an actor at Covent Garden.

7. Lines from David Garrick's Prologue.

8. Thomas Percy. See his recollections of Goldsmith in this book.

9. At a dinner of the Royal Academicians, one of the company, by some lively jests, excited the mirth of the society: the Doctor was uneasy, and desired those who sat next to him not to laugh, for he thought in truth it would make the man vain (Davies's note).

Goldsmith and Percy*

ALICE C. C. GAUSSEN

Thomas Percy's[1] friendship for Oliver Goldsmith was of the kind that makes each meeting an event, therefore we are able to follow its course by means of his private notes. They first met on Wednesday, February 21, 1759, as the guests of Dr Grainger at the Temple Exchange Coffee House, which was used for purposes of social intercourse by many who, like Goldsmith, 'lived in a garret writing for bread, and expecting to be dunned for a milk score'. 'The gates of the Muses,' like the Kingdom of Heaven, are hard but not impossible for the rich to enter into, though 'nothing is more apt to introduce a man to them than poverty'. At the coffee house, those who, like Goldsmith, also practised the art of medicine, could be consulted by their patients, and letters might be received and written by such as were unwilling to reveal their humble dwellings. Percy met Goldsmith again at Dodsley's[2] on February 26, and on Saturday, March 3, before returning to Easton Maudit, he sat all the morning with him at his rooms in Green Arbour Court, near the Old Bailey. He found him miserably lodged in a wretched, dirty room, revising the proofs of his *Enquiry into Polite Learning in Europe*, which was at that time being printed for Dodsley and was published on April 3. He possessed but one chair, which he offered to his visitor, and sat himself in the window.

Goldsmith was at this time almost beginning the world at the age of thirty-one. Eight years of disappointment, anguish and study had

* *Percy: Prelate and Poet* (London: Smith, Elder & Co., 1908) pp. 140–50, 152–3, 157–60. Editor's title.

worn him down, and he describes his own pale, melancholy visage, with great wrinkles between the brows, an eye disgustingly severe and a big wig. He had no doubt, as he declared, contracted the suspicious manner, as well as the hesitating speech of the parcel of designing beings among whom he found himself, but we cannot believe that a man who found more pleasure in doing good-natured things than uneasiness in the doing of them was possessed of a countenance 'that looked like ill-nature itself'.

Dr Percy found that he could not spend a morning in the company of one who loved his fellow-men without witnessing some call for help. The conversation was interrupted by a poor, ragged little girl, who rapped gently at the door, and, dropping a curtsey, begged for the loan of a few coals. This visit took place a month before Dr Percy's marriage, and it is probable that his new interests diverted his mind for a while from his literary friends, for it is not until May 25, 1761, that he mentions having dined and drunk tea with Dr Goldsmith in Wine Licence Court, Fleet Street, where he was now lodged. Together they visited the exhibition in Spring Gardens, and on this occasion Percy tells us he furnished his friend with material for a magazine of which he was editor – possibly the *Monthly Review*, to which he certainly contributed about this time.

Goldsmith's circumstances as well as his surroundings must have meanwhile improved considerably, for on Sunday, May 31, when Percy supped with him, he had much company to meet Samuel Johnson. The great man was escorted by Dr Percy, who, when he called for him, was struck by the unwonted neatness of his dress. The sight of his new suit of clothes, and new wig nicely powdered, was so unexpected that Percy could not help inquiring the cause of this transformation. 'Why, sir,' said Johnson, 'I hear that Goldsmith, who is a very great sloven, justifies his disregard of cleanliness and decency by quoting my practice, and I am desirous this night to show him a better example.'

On the awkwardness of Dr Goldsmith's appearance, a supposed 'Dialogue in the Shades' between himself and Lord Chesterfield appeared in the papers:

LORD CHESTERFIELD.   Believe me, Goldsmith, if you had paid a little more court to the graces and mixed with the world, you would have passed your life more comfortably and reaped greater advantages from your abilities. How awkward must a fellow appear, stammering if he attempts to utter a syllable and seem-

ing as great a stranger to his own arms and legs as to the
company which embarrasses him. I made the graces my study
and found them of more use to me than any other acquisition.

Goldsmith here naturally inquired why, if these accomplishments
were so essential, Lord Chesterfield's own son, Mr Stanhope, had
failed in them.

'He wanted industry,' replied Lord Chesterfield.

GOLDSMITH.   You entertain too high an opinion of what human
    nature is capable. To be a genius and a fine gentleman are
    almost incompatible. Can any composition that you or
    Bolingbroke wrote compare with the works of Addison, who
    as you say was awkward; of Johnson, whom you have ridi-
    culed; or even with mine, the last of the Muses? The least a man
    of talents can expect for pleasing and instructing the world is
    lenity to his foibles, but I must beg your Lordship's pardon, for
    yonder I see Addison and Virgil in deep conversation; I prom-
    ised to meet them; they are persons I never stand upon cere-
    mony with, for they are both as ill-bred as myself.

Goldsmith sought in vain for an instance of man in his wildest
state entirely fulfilling the ideal of beauty unadorned, for he was
obliged to admit in his *Animated Nature* that 'we have a very wrong
idea of savage finery, and are apt to suppose that like the beast of the
forest they rise, and are dressed with a shake; but the reverse is true:
for no birth-night beauty takes more pains in adorning her person
than they.' When the Cherokee kings visited England, Goldsmith
waited three hours while they were dressing. They had their boxes
of oil and ochre, their fat and their perfumes, as he found to his cost;
for owing to his sympathetic manner of wearing his heart on his
sleeve, when at length they appeared, with a sudden embrace they
covered his cheeks with the oil and ochre that adorned their own.
    During the month of June 1761, Goldsmith, who was then en-
gaged in writing his *Vicar of Wakefield*, was frequently visited by
Dr Percy, who was busy collecting his *Reliques*. On June 3 he spent
the evening with him, and on the 6th, 10th and 12th he called on him.
    It was probably owing to their close intercourse during the time
their great works were preparing that, in 1765, when Dr Goldsmith
printed his beautiful ballad of *The Hermit*, he was taxed by the
inferior scribblers with having taken the idea of it from *The Friar of
Orders Grey* in Percy's *Reliques* that appeared the same year. His chief

detractor, Kenrick, who constantly denounced him as Ritson did Percy, invited the public 'to compare the insipidity of Dr Goldsmith's negus with the genuine flavour of Dr Percy's champagne.' Goldsmith declared that, if any resemblance existed, Percy's ballad was the imitation, as he had read *The Hermit* to him two years previously, when he had formed his on the same plan. Percy allowed that he had taken fragments of ancient ballads in Shakespeare's plays, whose beauty consisted in their pathetic simplicity, and together with a small quotation from Beaumont, and additional stanzas of his own, had woven them into a poem, which he called *The Friar of Orders Grey*. It was parodied by Ritson as follows:

> It was a jovial tinker,
> All of the north countrie,
> As he walk'd forth along the way
> He sang right merrily.

Goldsmith vindicated the priority of his poem in a letter that appeared in the *St James's Chronicle* in June 1767, but he allowed that the story in both of them was taken from a very ancient ballad beginning 'Gentle Herdsman.'

After Goldsmith's death Percy added the following note to his *Friar of Orders Grey*:

As the foregoing song has been thought to have suggested to our late excellent Poet, Dr Goldsmith, the plan of his beautiful ballad of *Edwin and Angelina*, it is but justice to his memory to declare that his poem was written first, and that, if there is any imitation in the case, they will be found both to be indebted to the beautiful old ballad, *Gentle Herdsman*, printed in the 2nd volume of the *Reliques* which Dr Goldsmith had much admired in MS. and has finely improved.

Finding that the Duchess (then Countess) of Northumberland had shown a taste for ballads by patronising Percy's *Reliques*, Goldsmith addressed his poem to her. He had already been invited to wait on Lord Northumberland after he returned from his period of vice-royalty in Ireland. Unfortunately Goldsmith, with his usual absent-mindedness, wasted on the Groom of the Chambers the complimentary address he had prepared for his Excellency; and when the Lord Lieutenant appeared he was so confused that he was obliged to retire without having explained the object of his visit. Lord and Lady Northumberland preferred Percy's precise, reserved and stately manner to the uncouth and genial Goldsmith, with his thick, short, clumsy figure, and a face that he himself declared to be 'ugly enough'. He came of a family 'whose hearts were always in the right place, but whose heads seemed to be doing anything but what they ought'. His own father had served as a model for the large-minded and warm-hearted Vicar of Wakefield, and the simplicity that prevailed in his family not only lent a charm to his writing but gave his own character that singleness of mind and generosity that made all the world love little Goldy, as he was familiarly called by his friends. Worldly wisdom was a lesson he never could learn, and of this Percy had a plentiful supply.

Had all men Goldsmith's gift of self-knowledge and power of expressing it, then, indeed, might we say with Dr Johnson, that a man's biography is best written by himself. No description of the poet can ever equal his own when he declared himself to be 'fond of enjoying the present, careless of the future; his sentiments, those of a man of sense; his actions, those of a fool; of fortitude able to stand unmoved at the bursting of an earthquake, yet of sensibility to be affected by the breaking of a teacup.' He had humour enough to laugh at his own foibles, and described himself as a 'philosophical vagabond'. He confessed that he was often charitable to excess, and, forgetting the rules of justice, placed himself in the very position of those who thanked him for his bounty. He was, therefore, a prey to every variety of beggar. There was the pretentious French adventurer, Colonel de Champigny, who extorted a subscription of 7½ guineas for his book, *La Nouvelle Histoire d'Angleterre*. when Goldsmith had not more than 10 guineas in the world, receiving it with all the air of conferring a favour. This worthy, who was shut up in the bailiff's house for debt, wrote to Dr Goldsmith saying that his wife's relative, Lord Westmorland, on his deathbed declared he was proud of the connection, and was glad his cousin had married into such a good family.

Then there was a helpless and dishonest beggar, W. Griffin, whom Goldsmith and Garrick had recommended as an usher at a school, whence he had taken the earliest opportunity of making good his escape after robbing the house; he wrote: 'I beg that you will be kind enough to let me know what you think I am fitt for, and whether I should prosper if I consecrated my life to the Muses? I know that a man may be indifferent in many other states of life, but that a poet must be a good one, or none at all.'

Some others tried flattery, declaring their confidence in his power to sympathise with the distressed, and his generosity in interesting himself in their concerns.

John Oakman wrote from Orange, Great Swallow Street, Carnaby Market, and addressed him as 'The Good-Natur'd Man' in compliment to his comedy:

> Oh! Doctor, assist a *poor Bard* who is ill,
> Without e'er a nurse, e'er a potion or pill,
>   From your kindness he hopes for some ease.
> Oh! would your good nature but shine forth just now,
> In a manner I'm sure your good sense will tell how,
>   Your servant Most Humble 'twould please.

In his practice of physic Goldsmith had always had plenty of patients, but he got no fees.

An actress wrote to Goldsmith asking the favour of an introduction to David Garrick, adding that it would be an insult to his benevolence to make an apology for giving him an opportunity of assisting a fellow-creature.

Even the young, who only required a frolic, obtained his assistance, as the following note, which, in his haste to oblige, breaks from the third person into the first, will show:

> Doctor Goldsmith's best respects to Mrs Percy, he requests the favour of two tickets for two young Ladies for the Masquerade on Friday night. If she can procure them for him, it will be a singular obligation, and make two young Ladies extremely happy. I have not seen Mr Percy for some time, but hope this winter we shall frequently have the happiness of being together.

> Tuesday   Brick Court, Temple

In his days of extreme poverty Goldsmith would assemble the children of his landlady and others in his room and induce them to dance to the music of his flute.

During the spring of 1763, Dr Percy visited him at Canonbury House, Middlesex, and at Islington, where he sometimes retired for the purpose of devoting himself to literature. And in November 1764 he drank tea, dined or spent the evening with Goldsmith on the 16th, 17th, 21st, 22nd, 26th, 28th and 30th, at which time he was lodged in the butler's rooms on the Library Staircase in the Temple. In 1765, the year the *Reliques* were published, Percy called on him on March 26, and on April 28 dined with him and Dr Johnson at the Feathers Tavern. It was probably about this time that Percy offered Goldsmith the use of his Vicarage. Whether the visit to Easton Maudit ever took place we do not know, but the following practical inquiries show that it was in contemplation:

To The Rev. Mr Percy, Northumberland House.
Dear Percy,
I have been thinking of your Northamptonshire offer. I beg you'll send me an answer to the following queries:
    1. In the first place are there any prying, troublesome neighbours?
    2. Can I have a chamber to myself and can I buy coals, etc.?
    3. Will I not cumber the house, and take up the room of others?
    4. How long can you spare the apartment?
    5. Is there a stage? [coach] The price? and can my books be carried down?
    6. Can I have milk, meat, and tea in the place?
And lastly, will it be in any way inconvenient to you and Mrs Percy? And when will you want to be down yourselves?
                I am, your faithful friend,
                                                OLIVER GOLDSMITH.

On Friday, January 29, 1768, Dr Percy was present at the first representation of Dr Goldsmith's play, *The Good-Natur'd Man*. The author, with his usual diffidence, considered its reception on the opening night proved it to be a failure, and with characteristic honesty confessed his mortification before a large company of friends, who were dining with Dr Percy at the chaplain's table at St James's Palace. Dr Johnson declared unfeelingly that 'no man should be expected to sympathise with the sorrows of vanity'. Fortified by the bravery of a scarlet waistcoat trimmed with gold lace, he had himself undergone a similar ordeal, and when asked how he felt on the ill-success of his play *Irene* he answered, 'Like the Monument.' Goldsmith, however, entertained his hearers with a description of his feelings when the play was hissed, and how he tried later in the evening, at a meeting of the Literary Club, to chat gaily with his friends, and, though suffering horrid tortures, to show his indifference by singing his favourite song, 'An old woman tossed in a blanket seventeen times as high as the moon.' He made more noise than usual to cover the anguish of his heart.

Dr Percy was present again at the ninth night of the play, on which, as well as the third and sixth nights, the profits, according to custom, were appropriated to the author . . .

For a short period an entire separation took place between Goldsmith and Percy in consequence of the dispute about the authenticity of the Bristol poems. Goldsmith had drawn attention at the Royal Academy dinner to the ancient manuscript discovered at Bristol, which it was supposed had been written by Rowley in the fifteenth century. He was laughed at for the enthusiasm with which he supported his belief, though all his hearers disagreed in the measure of their faith. Walpole in particular derided his credulity, and boasted that he might, if he had chosen, have had the honour of ushering the great discovery into the learned world, for the unfortunate Chatterton, by whose genius they had been forged, had first applied to him for help. But his mirth was soon dashed by hearing that their author had destroyed himself, and, cynic as he was, he heartily wished he had been the dupe of the poor young man of seventeen whose genius, had he chosen honestly to acknowledge his own writings instead of palming them off as ancient manuscripts, would have placed him among the highest rank of writers. Percy had been accused by Ritson of a similar fraud with regard to the *Reliques* and also his Chinese Novel. He opposed Goldsmith by detecting the forgery of Chatterton, and though the quarrel was entirely forgotten before 1771, the controversy continued for many years after Goldsmith's death. . . .

Before their dispute on the subject of the Bristol poems, Dr Percy had, in company with Mr Gray,[3] dined with Goldsmith on May 7 1768, in a farmhouse at Edgeware,[4] where he was writing his *History of England*. After the death of Chatterton in 1770, a reconciliation took place, and Goldsmith visited Dr Percy in his apartments at Northumberland House, and begged him to undertake his biography. He entrusted him with many valuable papers and spent a long wet afternoon dictating an account of his early life.

On April 30, 1772, Percy again visited Goldsmith in the farmhouse at Edgeware, where he was writing his Natural History, entitled *Animated Nature*, a task that he found 'was best worked at in the country.' On May 7 together with Sir Joshua Reynolds, Mr Boswell and Mr Langton,[5] Dr Percy dined with Goldsmith in the Temple, but in much better chambers than those he had before; probably this improvement was owing to the anticipated profits of his work. He had entered into an engagement, in February 1769, with his book-seller, Mr Griffin, to compile his Natural History in eight volumes at the rate of 100 guineas apiece, and was to be paid as the volumes were delivered. Before the year was out and the work was scarcely begun, he persuaded Griffin to advance him 500 guineas, and having spent the money he set about writing his *History of England*, which Davies was to pay for only on its completion. Griffin was induced to pay him the whole of the 800 guineas before two-thirds of his *Animated Nature* was completed. So he found himself somewhat in the position of Dr Johnson, who declined giving a list of the patrons of his edition of Shakespeare, saying, 'Sir, I have two very cogent reasons for not printing a list of subscribers: one that I have lost all the names; the other that I have spent all the money.'

When at length his long-anticipated book on Natural History drew near completion, Goldsmith was at Windsor, and not wishing to return to London for another fortnight, he wrote to Dr Percy and Mr Cradock begging them to revise a proof of the work, which he said they would find lying upon his table in the Temple. At the same time he wrote on a slip of paper to his servant:

> Honest John,
> Give Doctor Percy
>   My History of Animals which
>   You will find amongst my books.

Percy and Cradock met by appointment, and found his chambers in grievous disorder, expensive volumes lay scattered about the tables, and tossed on the floor. Money was lying about from which his 'occasional manservant' paid any small bills that happened to be applied for. 'What, my dear friend,' exclaimed Goldsmith, when someone had remonstrated at his implicit trust in Honest John's predecessor, Dennis, 'do you take Dennis for a thief?'

The subject with which the collaborators were expected to deal proved to be birds, and they found many of the necessary books of reference on the table.

'Do you know anything about birds?' asked Percy, smiling.

'Nothing,' replied Cradock, 'do you?'

'Not I,' rejoined Percy, 'I scarce know a goose from a swan; however, let us try what we can do.'

If his friends are to be believed, Goldsmith's own knowledge was almost as limited. When Johnson was informed that he was writing a history of *Animated Nature* he said, 'Goldsmith, sir, will give us a very fine book on the subject; but if he can distinguish a cow from a horse, that I believe may be the extent of his knowledge of Natural History.' He said that Goldsmith had trusted too much to Buffon[6] for his facts, and had transcribed into his book the statement that the cow sheds her horns every two years. Johnson wondered that Buffon, who lived in the country, should make such a mistake, but supposed that he had confounded the cow with the deer. According to Goldsmith, 'At three years old the cow sheds its horns and new ones arise in their place, which continue as long as it lives.'

But whatever might be the value of his information, Percy marvelled at the ease of Goldsmith's style. His prose flowed from him with such facility that in the whole quires of his *Animated Nature* he had seldom had occasion to alter a single word. His style was free from mannerism, and faultless in its easy simplicity and the harmony of its periods. 'Just sit down as I do,' he said to his brother, 'and write forward until you have filled your paper. It requires no thought, for my head has no share in all I write, my heart dictates the whole.' Like most great writers, Goldsmith expressed his thoughts in the smallest possible compass, and believed that if an angel wrote a book it would not be a folio. Perhaps his power of memory enabled him to form his sentences mentally, without committing them to paper, after the manner of Dr Johnson, whom Dr Percy had often heard murmuring his periods when careless observers thought he was saying his prayers. Goldsmith's poems were much more laboured, and were frequently corrected until scarce a word of the original remained. But had he been in the happy financial position of those authors whom the Muse visits not as a creditor but as a friend, he would, he declared, have confined himself to poetry, which he found 'no unpleasant employment, could a man only live by it!' He was entreated to devote some of his attention to it, for it was urged 'though the world has not obliged you, it is still your duty to oblige mankind'. At a Royal Academy dinner, when asked by a noble Lord why he forsook poetry, he answered, 'By courting the Muses, even if they smiled, I should only be rewarded by a draft of the waters of Helicon, and might go as naked as they do; but by dealing with the booksellers I drink wine, and wear good clothes, so as to be admitted to your Lordship's society and that of this good company.' His appointment by the King as historian to the Royal Academy of Painting carried no salary. It was 'like ruffles to a man who wants a shirt.'

NOTES

1. Reverend Thomas Percy (1729–1811) was Bishop of Dromore and friend of Goldsmith.
2. Dodsley brothers, publishers.
3. Thomas Gray (1716–71), English poet.
4. Believed to be The Hyde, Hendon, on the Edgeware Road.
5. Bennet Langton.
6. Georges Louis Leclerc, Comte Buffon (1707–88), French naturalist.

She Stoops to Conquer*

ALICE C. C. GAUSSEN

On Tuesday, September 21, 1772, Percy called on Goldsmith, whom he found very ill in bed, and it was on this occasion, he believes, that the poet sent for Dr James, and found such relief from his famous fever powders that he was induced to place a confidence in their efficacy that eventually cost him his life. He was at that time engaged in writing his comedy *She Stoops to Conquer*. On Sunday, October 4, Percy writes, 'I saw Goldsmith.'

On December 11 Percy attended the Club for the first time since the day of meeting had been altered to Friday. Till then it had met on Monday, ever since he became a member in 1768. He adds, 'there are still only 12 members.'

On Friday evening, January 16, 1773, Dr Goldsmith read to the members of the Club his new comedy *The Old House and New Inn*, which title was unanimously condemned; and after much labour to find a better, it was decided that it should be called *She Stoops to Conquer*.

On Saturday, March 13, Percy went with Topham Beauclerk to the rehearsal of Goldsmith's new comedy, and on Monday the 15th, the eventful day of its first representation, he went to see it, but found the theatre so crowded that he could not get in. He must doubtless have been detained by his duties at Northumberland House too late to join Goldsmith's friends, who, though not over-sanguine

---

* *Percy: Prelate and Poet* (London: Smith, Elder & Co., 1908) pp. 160–5. Editor's title.

as to the success of the piece, were determined to make a struggle on behalf of the author. Colman, the manager of Covent Garden, protested, when he lent his theatre, that *She Stoops to Conquer* was one of the most eccentric productions that had ever been put on the stage. According to Richard Cumberland, Goldsmith's supporters assembled in all their strength for an early dinner at the Shakespeare Tavern, with Dr Johnson presiding at the head of a long table. The poet silently placed himself at the president's side, and that evening took all his raillery as patiently as Boswell did habitually. The whole company betook themselves in good time to their allotted posts, and awaited the awful drawing up of the curtain. The signals for plaudits were prearranged in a manner that gave everyone his cue. When Goldsmith expressed his doubts as to how some of his best jokes would be taken by the audience, the manager replied in a reassuring tone, 'Psha, my dear Doctor, do not be fearful of squibs when we have been sitting almost two hours on a barrel of gunpowder.' A phalanx of North British applauders under the banner of Major Mills, all good men and true, followed the lead of Adam Drummond, who was gifted with the loudest and most contagious laugh that ever echoed from human lungs. The neighing of a horse was a whisper to it, and the thunder of the theatre could not drown it, but he knew no more than the cannon on a battery when to give his fire. All eyes were fixed upon Dr Johnson, who sat in a side box, and when he laughed everyone felt themselves at liberty to roar. Drummond, who was planted in an upper box above the stage, and in full view of the pit, followed the signals with so comic a rattle that he engrossed more attention than the actors. At length the pit took offence and began to hiss. Nevertheless, Goldsmith's followers congratulated themselves on having carried the play through, and triumphed not only over Colman's judgement but their own. When it was suggested that Goldsmith owed much of his success to the partiality of his friends, Johnson replied, 'No, sir, the partiality of his friends was always against him.' It required great faith on the part of anyone who knew little Goldsmith to believe that he had really written *The Traveller* himself.

Though the applause given to the new piece on the first night was suspected of being a tribute of his friends' partiality, it was far exceeded by that on the second night, when uninterrupted laughter rang incessantly throughout the play. As Goldsmith explained, 'The undertaking of a comedy, not merely sentimental, was very dangerous, and Mr Colman always thought it so. However, I ventured to trust it to the public, and I have every reason to be grateful.' Johnson knew of no comedy that had so much answered its end by making the audience merry.

After Goldsmith's death Colman paid a tribute to his memory in the prologue to *The Chapter of Accidents*, 1780:

> When Fielding, Humour's favourite child, appeared,
> *Low* was the word, a word each author fear'd!
> Till cheer'd at length by Pleasantry's bright ray
> Nature and Mirth resum'd their legal sway,
> And Goldsmith's genius bask'd in open day.

For Goldsmith it was justly claimed that he had the merit of restoring 'genuine Comedy, that for some time had been disguised in the cast-off clothes of her stately and prudish sister Tragedy, which suited neither her stature nor her complexion. Goldsmith gave her a new gown that fitted her, and made her again look charming.'

On Thursday, March 18, the fourth night of the play and the author's first benefit, Dr Percy had a place in the Duchess of Northumberland's box. On this occasion enthusiasm reached the highest pitch, and the theatre re-echoed with the loudest acclamations that had ever rung within its walls. The Duke of Gloucester had been present on the opening night, and the public, to show their sympathy with him in the matter of the Royal Marriage Act, turned to him with loud applause at the words addressed by Hastings to Miss Neville, 'We'll go to France, for there, even among slaves, the laws of marriage are respected.' Goldsmith was too independent to strike out these words, even at the risk of offending the King. However, on May 5 the play was commanded by their Majesties. Though Goldsmith had triumphed over every annoyance and difficulty that had been put in his way, he declared he was very sick of the stage, and that ease and comfort he had certainly lost while the play was in agitation. When he was advised to wait until better performers could be procured, he answered, 'I should sooner that my play were damned by bad players than merely saved by good acting.'

An attempt was made to check Goldsmith's triumph on the ninth night by a letter in the *London Packet* of March 24, 1773, which said: 'Mr Goldsmith, correct your arrogance, reduce your vanity, and believe as a man, you are of the plainest sort, and as an author, but a mortal piece of mediocrity.'

Though signed 'Tom Tickle' the letter was thought to have been written by his detractor, Kenrick, a man whom Johnson described as one of the 'many who have made themselves public without making themselves known.' Goldsmith might well have waited for the revenge that time was sure to bring by recording his name among the immortals, while that of his assailant was entirely forgotten; but, unfortunately, the fighting instinct of his race was aroused by the injudicious interference of a fellow-countryman, and he went to the editor and struck him with his cane on the back. A scuffle ensued. The real offender, Kenrick, happened to be in an adjoining room, and separated the combatants, and is believed to have written the following account of the encounter, which appeared in the *London Packet*:

Mr Evans most certainly fulfilled the title of the Doctor's Comedy, "He Stoops to Conquer"; for while the little spirited bookseller was stooping, the Doctor knocked him down; the honest Welshman sprang upon the Doctor and after mighty active strokes he conquered.

The great Johnson, some years since, knocked down the blockhead of Gray's Inn, Tommy Osborne, and because he had done so, the great Goldy thought it necessary to knock down a bookseller too. Johnson triumphed and poor Goldy fell.

I challenge the Doctor to produce a sensible man or woman that will say his piece has merit about it; and those who have read it agree, it is more contemptible in the perusal than in the acting.

When Johnson knocked down the bookseller Osborne with one of his own folios, and was asked by Mrs Thrale to describe the encounter, he answered, 'There is nothing to tell, dearest Lady, but that he was insolent, and I beat him. I have beat many a fellow, but the rest had the wit to hold their tongues.'

'What is the common price of an oak stick?' inquired Johnson, when he heard that Foote intended to produce him on the stage. 'Sixpence,' answered Davies. 'Why then, sir, give me leave to send your servant to purchase me a shilling one. I'll have a double quality; for I am told Foote means to *take me off*, and I am determined the fellow shall not do it with impunity.'

Dr Goldsmith*

JOSEPH CRADOCK

Dr Percy very kindly introduced me to dine at the Literary Club, at the bottom of St James's Street, where we met Dr Goldsmith. The table that day was crowded, and I sat next Mr Burke; but as Mr Richard Burke talked much, and the great orator said very little, I was not aware at first who was my neighbour. One of the party near us remarked, that there was an offensive smell in the room, and thought it must proceed from some dog that was under the table; but Mr Burke, with a smile, turned to me, and said, 'I rather fear it is from the beef-steak pie, that is opposite to us, the crust of which is made with some very bad butter, that comes from my country.' Just at that moment Dr Johnson sent his plate for some of it, and Burke helped him to very little, which he soon dispatched, and returned his plate for more; Burke without thought, exclaimed, 'I am glad that you are able so well to relish this beef-steak pie.' Johnson, not at all pleased that what he eat should ever be noticed, immediately retorted, 'There is a time of life, Sir, when a man requires the repairs of a table.'

Before dinner was finished, Mr Garrick came in, full-dressed, made many apologies for being so much later than he intended, but he had been unexpectedly detained at the House of Lords; and Lord Camden had absolutely insisted upon setting him down at the door of the hotel in his own carriage. Johnson said nothing, but he looked a volume.

During the afternoon some literary dispute arose; but Johnson sat silent, till the Dean of Derry, very respectfully said, 'We all wish, Sir, for your opinion on the subject.' Johnson inclined his head, and never shone more in his life, than at that period; he replied, without any pomp; he was perfectly clear and explicit, full of the subject, and left nothing undetermined. There was a pause; and he was then hailed with astonishment by all the company. The evening in gen-

---

* *Literary and Miscellaneous Memoirs*, vol. 1 (London: J. B. Nichols, 1826) pp. 228–36; vol. 4 (London: J. B. Nichols, 1828) pp. 279–88.

eral passed off very pleasantly. Some talked perhaps for amusement, and others for victory. We sat very late; and the conversation that at last ensued, was the direct cause of my friend Goldsmith's poem, called *Retaliation*.

Dr Goldsmith and I never quarrelled; for he was convinced that I had a real regard for him; but a kind of civil sparring continually took place between us. 'You are so attached,' says he, 'to Hurd, Gray, and Mason, that you think nothing good can proceed, but out of that formal school; now, I'll mend Gray's Elegy, by leaving out an idle word in every line!' 'And, for me, Doctor, completely spoil it.'

> The curfew tolls the knell of day,
> The lowing herd winds o'er the Lea;
> The plowman homeward plods his way,
> And —

'Enough, enough, I have no ear for more.'

'Cradock' (after a pause), 'I am determined to come down into the country, and make some stay with you, and I will build you an ice-house.' 'Indeed, my dear Doctor,' I replied, 'you will not; you have got the strangest notion in the world of making amends to your friends, wherever you go; I hope, if you favour me with a visit, that you will consider that your own company is the best recompence.' 'Well,' says Goldsmith, 'that is civilly enough expressed; but I should like to build you an ice-house; I have built two already; they are perfect, and this should be a pattern to all your county.'

'I dined yesterday,' says he, laying down his papers, 'in company with three of your friends, and I talked at every thing.' 'And they would spare you in nothing.' 'I cared not for that, I persisted; but I declare solemnly to you, that though I angled the whole evening I never once obtained a bite.'

'You are all of you', continued he, 'absolutely afraid of Johnson – now I attack him boldly, and without the least reserve.' 'You do, Doctor, and sometimes catch a Tartar.' 'If it were not for me, he would be insufferable; if you remember, the last time we ever supped together, he sat sulky and growling, but I resolved to fetch him out;' 'you did, and at last he told you that he would have no more of your fooleries'.[1]

It was always thought fair by some persons to make what stories they pleased of Dr Goldsmith, and the following was freely circulated in ridicule of him, 'That he attended the fantoccini in Penton

Street, and that from envy he wished to excel the dexterity of one of the puppets.' I was of the party, and remember no more, than that the Doctor, the Rev. Mr Ludlam of St John's College, and some others, went together to see the puppet-show; that we were all greatly entertained, and many idle remarks might possibly be made by all of us during the evening. Mr Ludlam afterwards laughingly declared, that he believed he must shut up all his experiments at Cambridge and Leicester in future, and take lectures only during the winter, from fantoccinis, and the expert mechanists of both the Royal Theatres.

The greatest real fault of Dr Goldsmith was, that if he had thirty pounds in his pocket, he would go into certain companies in the country, and in hopes of doubling the sum, would generally return to town without any part of it.

One of the worst affrays that Dr Goldsmith was ever engaged in, was with Evans the Bookseller, of Paternoster Row. Evans was the Editor of the *Universal Magazine,* and had suffered a most offensive article to be inserted therein, which turned to ridicule, not only the Doctor, but [also] some ladies of the highest respectability. The Doctor unfortunately went to dine with the family, in Westminster, just after they had read this insulting article, and they were all most highly indignant at it. The Doctor agonized all dinner-time; but as soon as possible afterwards, he stole away, set off in great haste for Paternoster Row, and caned Evans in his own shop. This was every way a terrible affair; and I privately consulted with Dr Johnson concerning it. He said, 'that this at any time would have been highly prejudicial to Goldsmith, but particularly now;' and he advised me, as I was intimate with both, that I should call upon Evans, and endeavour to get the matter adjusted. I followed his advice; and Evans really behaved very kindly to me on the occasion. I truly urged, 'that this publication had cut off Dr Goldsmith from the society of one of the most friendly houses that he had ever frequented, and that he could not have tortured him in a more tender point.' Evans calmly attended to me; and after much negotiation, and the interference of several discreet friends, this vexatious affair was at last finally got rid of. The name of Johnson on such an affray, will perhaps remind the reader that he himself once knocked down a very worthy bookseller in his own shop, at Gray's Inn (as related by Boswell). The story was currently reported; and caused the following *extempore*, which has never extended before beyond a private circulation:

When Johnson, with tremendous step, and slow,
Fully determin'd, deigns to fell the foe,
E'en the earth trembles, thunders roll around,
And mighty Osborne's self lies level'd with the ground.

'Lie still, Sir,' said Johnson, 'that you may not give me a second trouble!' Mr Nichols once asked Dr Johnson, 'if the story was true.' 'No, Sir, it was not in his shop, it was in my own house.'

I had not seen or heard from Dr Goldsmith for a very considerable time, till I came to town with my wife, who was to place herself under the care of Mr Parkinson, dentist, in Fleet Street, for rather a dangerous operation; and we took lodgings in Norfolk Street, that we might be in his neighbourhood. Goldsmith I found much altered, and at times very low; and I devoted almost all my mornings to his immediate service. He wished me to look over and revise some of his Works; but with a select friend or two I was most pressing that he should publish, by subscription, his two celebrated poems of *The Traveller*, and *The Deserted Village*, with notes; for he was well aware that I was no stranger to Johnson's having made some little addition to the one, and possibly had suggested some corrections at least for the other; but the real meaning was, to give some great persons an opportunity of delicately conveying pecuniary relief, of which the Doctor at that time was particularly in need. Goldsmith readily gave up to me his private copies, and said, 'Pray do what you please with them.' But, whilst he sat near me, he rather submitted to, than encouraged my zealous proceedings.

I one morning called upon him, however, and found him infinitely better than I expected, and in a kind of exulting style he exclaimed, 'Here are some of the best of my prose writings; I have been hard at work ever since midnight, and I desire you to examine them.' 'These,' said I, 'are excellent indeed.' 'They are,' replied he, 'intended as an Introduction to a body of Arts and Sciences.' 'If so, Dr Goldsmith, let me most seriously entreat, that as your name is to be prefixed, more care may be taken by those who are to compile the work, than has formerly been the case, when Knaresborough was printed for Naseby, and Yorkshire for Northamptonshire: and you know what was the consequence with Mr Cadell.'

We entered on various topics, and I left him that morning seemingly much relieved.

The day before I was to set out from town for Leicestershire, I insisted upon his dining with us. He replied, 'I will; but on one condition; that you will not ask me to eat any thing.' 'Nay,' said I, 'this answer, Goldsmith, is absolutely unkind; for I had hoped, as we are entirely served from the Crown and Anchor, that you would have named something that you might have relished.' 'Well,' says he, 'if you will but explain it to Mrs Cradock, I will certainly wait upon you.'

The Doctor found, as usual, at my apartments newspapers and pamphlets, and with a pen and ink he amused himself as well as he could. I had ordered from the tavern some fish, a roasted joint of lamb, and a tart; and the Doctor either sat down or walked about just as he liked. After dinner he took some wine with biscuits; but I was soon obliged to leave him for a while, as I had matters to settle for our next day's journey. On my return coffee was ready, and the Doctor appeared more cheerful (for Mrs Cradock was always rather a favourite with him) and in the course of the evening he endeavoured to talk and remark, as usual, but all was force. He stayed till midnight, and I insisted on seeing him safe home; and we most cordially shook hands at the Temple Gate.

Dr Goldsmith did not live long after our return into Leicestershire; and I have often since regretted, that I did not remain longer in town at every inconvenience. Yet, alas! what could I have done? With one or two select friends I might have stood by his bed-side, deeply lamenting his most unfortunate fate, till he, in a last agony, would have exclaimed

— Dear friends, adieu!
For see the hounds are full in view.

*   *   *

I am aware that what I am about to relate will somewhat subject myself to ridicule. It was the fashion of some authors frequently to retail poor Goldsmith's absurdities; but they, at times, misrepresented or exaggerated. I recollect, one evening he had launched out unboundedly, and next morning I ventured to say to him, that 'I was surprised that in that company he would lay himself so open.' His answer was, 'I believe I did; I fired at them all; I angled all the night, but I caught nothing.' When he was scheming some essay perhaps, he would force the subject on everybody, till Johnson has been quite provoked, and at last did say, 'My dear Doctor, let us have no more of your fooleries to-night.' Mr Boswell and others have given some account of these particular absurdities of Goldsmith relative to the fantoccini, then exhibiting in London; and as I was present at the greater part of what then passed I will beg to trespass with all the truth I know. Dr Goldsmith spoke most highly of the performance in Penton Street, and talked about bringing out a comedy of his own there in ridicule. When the Rev. Wm Ludlam, the great mechanic, of Leicester, came to town, I often talked about Goldsmith to him, and persuaded him to go and see the puppet-show. He was quite surprised and entertained, and declared that at the conclusion of the little comedy, the puppets acted so naturally that, though he placed himself close to the stage, he could scarce detect either string or wire. I was with Goldsmith there; but whether that night or not I cannot specify. Goldsmith merely was made known to Ludlam by me, and his low humour was not ill-adapted to Ludlam's own style of conversation; however, I will add Mr Ludlam's own remark: 'I have caught many a cold by examining the dockyards; however, in future, I believe, I must come to London, and instead of attending our mechanical societies, and rummaging for improvements afterwards, I must only visit fantoccinis, and frequent the harlequin farces. I cannot guess where the managers collect all these able mechanists.' Ludlam was likewise excessively fond of music, and I introduced Mrs Barthelemon to him at Leicester. She was a great favourite; and many of my musical friends very kindly entertained him in town with particular performances, and he was offered to take an interior view of both the great theatres. Ludlam occasionally entertained his friends at Leicester, with some Chinese Tumblers, which he had made. They were dressed puppets, with quicksilver in the veins, and surprised even at Cambridge. However, on leaving London this time, he turned to me, and slyly said, 'The first thing I shall do at my return will be to burn my Chinese tumblers.'

Polly Pattens, in the puppet-show,[2] meant Mrs Yates; but when Foote mentioned the names of Kelly, Cumberland, and Cradock on the stage, the audience would not permit him to proceed. The scene was printed in the *Bon Ton Magazine*, and illustrated by a good print, representing Foote, a strong likeness, the Devil, Polly Pattens, Harlequin, Punch, and Stevens.

Goldsmith at that time greatly wished to bring out a comedy, but he had powerful rivals to contend with, who were in full possession of the town. Goldsmith's turn was for very low humour, always dangerous; but when some authors hinted to him, that for a man to write genteel comedy it was necessary that he should be well-acquainted with high life himself; 'True,' says Goldsmith; 'and if any of you have a character of a truly elegant lady in high life, who is neither a coquette or a prude, I hope you will favour me with it.' Some one observed, that Millamant[3] was the most refined character he recollected in any comedy, neither a prude nor a coquette; and I then ventured to say, that 'however refined Millamant might be, I thought no very delicate lady would now venture upon her raillery of Mirabel, who declares, 'When I'm married to you, I'll positively get up in a morning as early as I please;' and the refined and delicate lady replies, 'Oh! to be sure; get up, idle creature!' The cry was, 'Goldsmith is envious;' but surely it was a little irritating to hear the town ring with applause of Garrick, and see him courted everywhere, and in the height of splendour, whilst he, perhaps, had only to retire *impransus*[4] to the Temple.

About the time that I think Boswell wrote a prologue in compliment to Johnson at Lichfield, a proposal was made for the play of the *Beaux Stratagem* to be acted there, by a party of friends, in honour of Johnson and Garrick. Mr Yates offered all assistance from Birmingham, where he was then manager, and, if required, to play Scrub. 'No,' says Goldsmith; 'I should of all things like to try my hand at that character.' Several smiled, thinking perhaps of his assuming such a part, who frequently, with his gold-headed cane, assumed the real character of Doctor of Physic. However, the thought amused Goldsmith at the time. It was the fashion to say, that Goldsmith's turn was merely for low humour; and that his Vicar, his Moses, and his Tony Lumpkin, were characters now obsolete. However, Goldsmith often retaliated with good effect. Dick Yates[5] at that time was much admired in Old Fondlewife,[6] and Goldsmith said he 'was surprised, in this refined age, to see Lord North and all his family in the stage-box; to be sure, Mr Yates being admonished not to sing "The soldier and the sailor" in another refined comedy, was a good sign of delicacy.' I was, however, with Mr Yates at his house just after he had received this order, and he expressed himself in violent terms against it, insomuch that I doubted whether he would play the part of Ben,[7] unless permitted as for forty years past. At last he complied.

I wrote an Epilogue, in the character of Tony Lumpkin, for *She Stoops to Conquer*, and likewise the following Song:

TALLY-HO! *A Song, intended to have been sung by Mr. Quick, in the character of Tony Lumpkin, in Goldsmith's comedy of* She Stoops to Conquer.

> Mine alone is the age,
> When all pleasures engage,
>   That horses and hounds can bestow;
> Among the great folks,
> What their whims and their jokes,
>   Compar'd with a good Tally-ho!
>
> To learn the soft airs
> Of your opera players,
>   For ever the fine ladies go;
> Ah! what are such joys
> But low trifles and toys,
>   Compar'd with a good Tally-ho!
>
> They say that in time,
> I should marry – refine,
>   If to courts and their balls I would go;
> But when tied up for life
> To a termagant wife,
>   In vain I might cry, Tally-Ho!

The Epilogue and Song were intended for Mr Quick.[8] He would, if any one, have carried them both through. The Epilogue was thought too personal, and occasioned some dissension, though not with my friend Goldsmith. That, curtailed and printed at the end of the Comedy was without either my knowledge or consent. Some of the allusions might be rather *trop libre*, but it had reference to Foote's puppet-show, which certainly was not expected to be strictly correct, nor was the character of Tony Lumpkin too refined. No comic prologue was ever more admired than Garrick's to *Barbarossa*;[9] but what is a part of it?

I particularly recollect, that when Goldsmith was near completing his *Natural History*, he sent to Dr Percy and me, to state that he wished not to return to town, from Windsor I think, for a fortnight, if we would only complete a proof that lay upon his table in the Temple. It was concerning birds, and many books lay open that he occasionally consulted for his own materials. We met by appointment; and Dr Percy, smiling, said, 'Do you know any thing about birds?' 'Not an atom,' was my reply: 'do you?' 'Not I,' says he, 'scarce know a goose from a swan: however, let us try what we can do.' We set to work, and our task was not very difficult. Sometime after the work appeared, we compared notes, but could not either of us recognise our own share.

I come now to the last day but óne I passed with poor Goldsmith, whose loss (with whatever faults he might have) I shall ever lament whilst 'memory of him holds its seat'. At his breakfast in the Temple, as usual, I offered every aid in my power as to his works; some amendments had been agreed upon in his *Traveller*, and more particularly his *Deserted Village*. Some of the bad lines in the latter I have by me marked. 'As to my *Hermit*,[10] that poem, Cradock, cannot be amended.' I knew he had been offered ten pounds for the copy; and it was introduced into the *Vicar of Wakefield*, to which he applied himself entirely for a fortnight, to pay a journey to Wakefield. 'As my business then lay there,' said he, 'that was my reason for fixing on Wakefield as the field of action. I never took more pains than in the first volume of my *Natural History*; surely that was good, and I was handsomely repaid for the whole. My *Roman History*, Johnson says, is well abridged.' Indeed, I could have added, that Johnson (when Goldsmith was absent), would frequently say, 'Why, sir, whatever that man touches he adorns;' for like Garrick, when not present, he considered him as a kind of sacred character. After a general review of papers lying before him, I took leave; when, turning to his study-table, he pointed to an article I had procured for him, and said, 'You are kindest to me.' I only replied, 'You mean more rude and saucy than some others.' However, much of the conversation took a more melancholy tone than usual, and I became very uneasy about him.

When I returned to town after his death, I had an interview with his nephew, an apothecary in Newman Street, and the two sister milliners, the Miss Gunns, who resided at a house at the corner of Temple Lane, who were always most attentive to him, and who once said to me, most feelingly, 'O, sir, sooner persuade him to let us work for him, *gratis*, than suffer him to apply to any other; we are sure that he will pay us if he can.' Circumstanced as he was, I know not what more could have been done for him. It was said, he improperly took laudanum; but all was inwardly disturbed.

Had the Doctor freely laid open all the debts he had contracted, I am certain that his zealous friends were so numerous, that they would freely have contributed to his relief. I mean here explicitly to assert only, that I believe he died miserable, and that his friends were not entirely aware of his distress.

Where the Doctor thought there was a sincere regard, he was not fastidious, but would listen with attention to the remonstrance of one whom he believed to be his friend; and when he assented to give his name for a mere trifle to a new publication, about which he never meant to give himself much trouble, I more than once spoke freely to him.

Goldsmith and I (with great satisfaction I now speak it) never had a serious dispute in our lives; we freely gave and took. He rallied me on my Cambridge pedantry, and I hinted at illegitimate education; for, to speak on my mended judgement, Johnson, he, Garrick, and some others, had convinced me 'that all literature was not confined to our own academical world'. Goldsmith truly said, I was nibbling about elegant phrases, whilst he was obliged to write half a volume. With respect to University education, even Mr Professor Mainwaring was often provoked at Hurd's fastidious opinions; and it was well that my friend Mr Russell, who afterwards possessed two good livings close to my house, did not reside in Leicestershire at an earlier period. He had lived in all companies whilst officiating for twenty years at Marylebone; and in the highest, where the subjects of discussion were old law or antiquities. He spoke in no measured terms of Hurd's refinements.

NOTES

Joseph Cradock (1742–1826), a wealthy dilettante and a friend and sometime collaborator of Goldsmith. He had written one of the unused epilogues for *She Stoops to Conquer*, and Goldsmith had supplied the prologue for his *Zobeide*.

1. Though Johnson was sometimes very rough with Goldsmith, he always made him only his own property; for when a bookseller ventured to say something rather slightingly of the Doctor, Johnson instantly retorted, 'Sir, Goldsmith never touches any subject, but he adorns it.' Once when I found the Doctor very low at his chambers, I related this circumstance to him, and it instantly proved a cordial (Cradock's note).

2. This made its first appearance at the Haymarket Theatre, 15 February 1753, under the title of the *Handsome Housemaid, or Piety in Pattens*.

3. In the comedy of *The Way of the World*, by William Congreve, acted at Drury Lane in 1700.

4. When Johnson makes use of the word *impransus*, it has been urged that he only meant that it was *before dinner*, when he wrote to Osborne that hasty note. Indeed, he very rarely complained (Cradock's note).

5. A distinguished comedian.

6. In *The Old Bachelor*, a comedy by Congreve, and originally acted by Dogget.

7. In another of Congreve's comedies, entitled *Love for Love*, and also originally acted by Dogget.
8. A distinguished comedian.
9. A tragedy by Dr Browne.
10. 'Edwin and Angelina'.

Goldsmith's Writing Career*

EDMOND MALONE

His finances were so low on his return to England, that he with difficulty got to this metropolis, his whole stock of cash amounting to no more than a few halfpence! An entire stranger in London, his mind was filled with the most gloomy reflections in consequence of his embarrassed situation! He applied to several apothecaries in hopes of being received in the capacity of a journeyman, but his broad Irish accent, and the uncouthness of his appearance, occasioned him to meet with insult from most of the medicinal tribe. The next day, however, a chemist near Fish Street, struck with his forlorn condition, and the simplicity of his manner, took him into his laboratory, where he continued till he discovered his old friend Doctor Sleigh was in London. This gentleman received him with the warmest affection, and liberally invited him to share his purse till some establishment could be procured for him. Goldsmith, unwilling to be a burden to his friend, a short time after eagerly embraced an offer which was made him to assist the late Rev. Dr Milner, in instructing the young gentlemen at the Academy at Peckham; and acquitted himself greatly to the Doctor's satisfaction for a short time; but, having obtained some reputation by the criticisms he had written in the *Monthly Review*, Mr Griffiths, the principal proprietor, engaged him in the compilation of it; and, resolving to pursue the profession of writing, he returned to London, as the mart where abilities of every kind were sure of meeting distinction and reward. Here he determined to adopt a plan of the strictest economy, and took lodgings in Green Arbour Court in the Old Bailey, where he wrote several ingenious pieces. The late Mr Newbery,[1] who at that

* In *Oliver Goldsmith: Poems and Plays* (London: B. Newbery & T. Johnson, 1780) pp. v–viii. Editor's title.

time gave great encouragement to men of literary abilities, became a kind of patron to our young Author, and introduced him as one of the writers in the *Public Ledger*, in which his *Citizen of the World* originally appeared, under the title of 'Chinese Letters.'

Fortune now seemed to take some notice of a man she had long neglected. The simplicity of his character, the integrity of his heart, and the merit of his productions, made his company very acceptable to a number of respectable persons, and he emerged from his shabby apartments near the Old Bailey to the politer air of the Temple, where he took handsome chambers, and lived in a genteel style. The publication of his *Traveller*, his *Vicar of Wakefield*, and his *Letters on the History of England*, was followed by the performance of his comedy of *The Good-natur'd Man* at Covent-Garden Theatre, and placed him in the first rank of the poets of the present age.

Our Doctor, as he was now universally called, had a constant levee of his distressed countrymen; whose wants, as far as he was able, he always relieved, and he has been often known to leave himself even without a guinea, in order to supply the necessities of others!

Another feature in his character we cannot help laying before the reader. Previous to the publication of his *Deserted Village*, the book-seller had given him a note for one hundred guineas for the copy, which the Doctor mentioned, a few hours after, to one of his friends, who observed it was a very great sum for so short a performance. 'In truth,' replied Goldsmith, 'I think so too, it is much more than the honest man can afford, or the piece is worth, I have not been easy since I received it; therefore I will go back and return him his note;' which he absolutely did, and left it entirely to the bookseller, to pay him according to the profits produced by the sale of the poem, which turned out very considerable.

During the last rehearsal of his comedy, entitled, *She Stoops to Conquer*, which Mr Colman had no opinion would succeed, on the Doctor's objecting to the repetition of one of Tony Lumpkin's speeches, being apprehensive it might injure the play, the Manager, with great keenness replied, 'Psha, my dear Doctor, do not be fearful of *squibs*, when we have been sitting almost these two hours upon a *barrel of gunpowder.*' The piece, however, contrary to Mr Colman's expectation, was received with uncommon applause by the audience; and Goldsmith's pride was so hurt by the severity of the above observation, that it entirely put an end to his friendship for the gentleman who made it.

Notwithstanding the great success of his pieces, by some of which, it is asserted, upon good authority, he cleared £1800 in one year, his circumstances were by no means in a prosperous situation, partly owing to the liberality of his disposition, and partly to an unfortunate habit he had contracted of gaming, the arts of which he knew very little of, and consequently became the prey of those who were unprincipled enough to take advantage of his ignorance.

Just before his death he had formed a design for executing an Universal Dictionary of Arts and Sciences, the prospectus of which he actually printed and distributed among his acquaintance. In this work several of his literary friends (particularly Sir Joshua Reynolds, Dr Johnson, Mr Beauclerc, and Mr Garrick) had engaged to furnish him with articles upon different subjects. He had entertained the most sanguine expectations from the success of it. The undertaking, however, did not meet with that encouragement from the booksellers which he had imagined it would undoubtedly receive; and he used to lament this circumstance almost to the last hour of his existence.

He had been for some years afflicted, at different times, with a violent strangury, which contributed not a little to embitter the latter part of his life; and which, united with the vexations he suffered upon other occasions, brought on a kind of habitual despondency. In this unhappy condition he was attacked by a nervous fever,[2] which, being improperly treated, terminated in his dissolution on the 4th day of April, 1774, in the forty-third year of his age. His friends, who were very numerous and respectable, had determined to bury him in Westminster-abbey, where a tablet was to have been erected to his memory. His pall was to have been supported by Lord Shelburne, Lord Louth, Sir Joshua Reynolds, the Hon. Mr Beauclerc, Mr Edmund Burke, and Mr Garrick; but from some unaccountable circumstances this design was dropped, and his remains were privately deposited in the Temple burial-ground.

As to his character, it is strongly illustrated by Mr Pope's line;

In wit a man, simplicity a child.[3]

The learned leisure he loved to enjoy was too often interrupted by distresses which arose from the openness of his temper, and which sometimes threw him into loud fits of passion; but this impetuosity was corrected upon a moment's reflection, and his servants have been known, upon these occasions, purposely to throw themselves in his way, that they might profit by it immediately after; for he who had the good fortune to be reproved was certain of being rewarded for it. His disappointments at other times made him peevish and sullen, and he has often left a party of convivial friends abruptly in the evening, in order to go home and brood over his misfortunes. A circumstance which contributed not a little to the increase of his malady.

The universal esteem in which his poems are held, and the repeated pleasure they give in the perusal, [are] a striking test of their merit. He was a studious and correct observer of nature, happy in the selection of his images, in the choice of his subjects, and in the harmony of his versification; and, though his embarrassed situation prevented him from putting the last hand to many of his productions, his *Hermit*, his *Traveller*, and his *Deserted Village*, bid fair to claim a place among the most finished pieces in the English language.

The writer of these Anecdotes cannot conclude without declaring, that as different accounts have been given of this ingenious man, these are all founded upon facts, and collected by one who lived with him upon the most friendly footing for a great number of years, and who never felt any sorrow more sensibly than that which was occasioned by his death.[4]

NOTES

Edmond Malone (1741–1812), literary critic, member of the Literary Club, and friend of Goldsmith.

1. John Newbery (1713–67), London publisher and patent manufacturer of medicines.

2. See William Hawes, 'An Account of the Late Dr Goldsmith's Illness', included in this book.

3. Alexander Pope, *Epitaph on John Gay*, I, 2.

4. See Samuel Glover, 'Authentic Anecdotes of the Late Dr Goldsmith', *Universal Magazine*, 53 (May 1774) pp. 252–5.

An Account of the Late Dr Goldsmith's Illness*

WILLIAM HAWES

On Friday the twenty-fifth of March, 1774, the late Dr Goldsmith was taken ill, and at eleven o'clock the same night sent for me to his Chambers. He complained of a violent pain extending all over the forepart of his head; his tongue was moist; he had no cold shiverings or pain in any other part, and his pulse beat about ninety strokes in a minute. He then acquainted me he had taken two ounces of ipecacuanha wine as a vomit, and that it was his intention to take Dr James's Fever-Powders, which he desired me to send him. I replied, that in my opinion this was a medicine very improper at that time, and begged he would not think of it: but I am sorry to say, that every argument used, seemed only to render him more determined in his own opinion; which gave me much concern, as I could not avoid thinking, that the man whom I had all the reason in the world to esteem, was about to take a step which might prove extremely injurious to him. I, therefore, endeavoured to reason medically with him, and observed, that his complaint appeared to be more a nervous affection than a febrile disease. He said [that] he thought so too. I replied, 'Then, Sir, as you have already taken a vomit, which has operated very well, I would advise you to take a gentle opiate, which may be a means of quieting the stomach; as after the operation of an emetic it generally produces for a few hours refreshing sleep; after which, in all probability, the complaint in the head will gradually go off, as repeated experience has confirmed.' To this he answered, 'I like your mode of reasoning well' and for a short time he appeared to be convinced, but soon after insisted upon taking the Powder. I now found myself in a more disagreeable situation, than can easily be conceived by any person whatever, except a brother-practitioner: for with great concern I speak it, the

---

* *An Account of the Late Dr Goldsmith's Illness, So Far As Relates to the Exhibition of Dr James's Powders* (London: W. Brown & H. Gardner, 1774) pp. 1–8.

more we endeavour to convince, the more our good intentions are too frequently treated with disregard; and I solemnly declare, that I felt at that time more anguish of mind than I had done in fifteen years preceding practice. And this for three reasons: First, the consequence of this patient's health and life to his friends and society: Secondly, the desire which every Practitioner has, or ought to have, of doing good when consulted; at least not suffering his patient to do himself an injury: Thirdly, from the real friendship I entertained for the Doctor, on the principles of gratitude for his countenance towards an Undertaking, which I have for a considerable time endeavoured to establish in this kingdom, and which, by the assistance of a worthy and able physician, and the favour of the Public, is now likely to take place. For these reasons, I could not take my leave without again endeavouring to convince him: and tho' some of the Faculty may perhaps smile at me for theorising (to which they have my full consent), I now pursued that plan; and as I had before surmounted his objections, in preceding complaints, by entering a little minutely into the progress of diseases, and the action of medicines on the human body, I hoped it would prove successful in the present instance. I told the Doctor, that his stomach was yet hardly settled from the operation of the emetic, and that his frame in general seemed a good deal agitated; and therefore the Fever-Powder would be more likely to act as a simple stimulant on the *primæ viæ*[1] than as a febrifuge, and thus be a means of reproducing the vomiting in a very violent degree, or induce a purging, and that if it acted upon either stomach or intestines, it might in the end be productive of the most serious consequences.

However, tho' I reasoned with him on the subject, for near half an hour, by his bed-side, and earnestly entreated him not to take Dr James's Powders, yet I could not prevail upon him to say that he would not. – At last I addressed him, to the best of my remembrance, in the following manner, 'Please, Sir, to observe, that if you do take the Fever-Powder, it is entirely without my approbation; and at the same time remember, how very anxious I have been to persuade you to desist from it: and now I will take my leave, if you will be kind enough to grant me one request.' He very warmly asked me what that was? I told him, that as he had always consulted Dr Fordyce in preceding illnesses, and had expressed the greatest opinion of his abilities as a physician, I hoped he would permit me to send for him. It was full a quarter of an hour before I could obtain his consent to this, as the taking Dr James's Powders appeared to be the only object which employed his attention; and even then he endeavoured to throw an obstacle in my way, by saying, that Dr Fordyce was gone to spend the evening in Gerrard-Street, 'where', adds he, 'I should also have been, if I had not been indisposed'. I told him, that the distance was a matter of no consequence, and that if he would permit it, my man should immediately be sent for him. He replied, 'Well, you may send for him, if you will.' I frankly declare, that this last sentence was the most agreeable to me, of any that he had uttered during my stay with him. I then came home, and immediately wrote a note to Dr Fordyce, and dispatched my servant, with orders first to call in Essex-Street, and enquire whether he was returned; and if not at home, to proceed to Gerrard-Street. Fortunately, the messenger found him at home, who sent me word that he would wait on Dr Goldsmith directly.

As I did not attend at the same time with Dr Fordyce, I am ignorant of the conversation that passed during his visit; but it was evident that he did not approve of the Fever-Powder, as he prescribed other medicines. And, indeed, early the next morning the Doctor called at my house, and informed me, that he had represented to Dr Goldsmith the preceding night, the impropriety there would be in his taking Dr James's Powders; but that instead of paying any attention to his remonstrances on this subject, he had unhappily persisted in his own resolution, and taken two or three doses of the Powder, tho' it had operated both as a purgative and an emetic.

When I called to see him on Saturday morning (the twenty-sixth of March) Dr Goldsmith's servant told me, he believed his master was dozing, as he lay very quiet. I then said, I would call in the evening; which I accordingly did, and his man, with great appearance of concern, when I asked him how his master was, replied he was very bad, for he had been vomiting all day, and had had a great many loose stools; notwithstanding which, the servant observed, the Doctor would make him give him James's Fever-Powders, so that he still continued the use of the medicine, and of consequence it increased in its pernicious operation, by which means the evacuations were continued for at least eighteen hours. I afterwards went into Dr Goldsmith's chamber, and found him extremely reduced, and his pulse was now become very quick and small. When I enquired of him how he did, he sighed deeply, and in a very low voice said he 'wished he had taken my friendly advice last night' (meaning Friday night, the twenty-fifth of March): and this was all he said during this visit; for whatever other questions I thought proper to ask him, he appeared so much exhausted as not to be able to make any reply to them; and I clearly perceived he was so very weak and low, from the large and copious evacuation, that he seemed to have neither strength nor spirits to speak.

As Dr Fordyce had visited him a little before my attendance on him at this time, I thought it unnecessary to trouble him to make a reply to many enquiries: accordingly I took my leave; at the same time being firmly convinced in my own mind, that every bad consequence was to be expected from the violent operation of this medicine.

I was very soon too well confirmed in my opinion of Dr Fordyce's calling upon me at my house the same evening, and acquainting me with much regret, that Dr Goldsmith by taking Dr James's Powders had done himself so much injury, that he thought it right to propose calling in another Physician, as he would not follow his advice; in hopes that by so doing, the patient would be convinced of the danger of his situation, and consequently be more inclined to conform to the mode of treatment prescribed. Dr Fordyce said he knew that Dr Goldsmith had a great opinion of Dr Turton; and desired I would go very early in the morning, and if I found him no better, to persuade him to call in that gentleman. Accordingly at eight o'clock, the next morning (being Sunday) I went, and found him much worse. He had passed a very bad night, having vomited several times, and had many loose stools; he lay absolutely sunk with weakness; and I was so very clear respecting the exceeding bad situation he was in, that instead of fatiguing him with any questions, I immediately exerted my utmost endeavours to persuade him to send for Dr Turton; to which he (being now, tho' too late, convinced of his unfortunate mode of proceeding) very readily consented, and desired me to order his servant to go directly. I accordingly did, and the Doctors Fordyce and Turton met at the time appointed, to assist at a consultation, which was continued twice a day till his death. . . . [2]

NOTES

William Hawes, an apothecary who attended Goldsmith in his last illness. Because there had been a good deal of discussion of the circumstances surrounding Goldsmith's death, Hawes prepared a pamphlet describing in detail his handling of the case and maintaining that, although Dr James's Fever Powders had on occasion done much good, they should not be taken without the advice of a physician.

1. The primary passages.

2. Francis Newbery, proprietor of the company which prepared the powders, promptly printed in the newspapers a denial of Hawes's claims, including with it statements from Goldsmith's servants and his nurse, intimating that the powders given to Goldsmith were not genuine Dr James's Fever Powders.

A Tribute to Goldsmith as a Poet*

JOHN TAIT

The moon shone bright – I stray'd along,
    Where Thames so sweetly flows,
And oft I rais'd the rustic song,
    Impell'd by fancied woes.

I sung of love, and all its charms,
    of love with scorn repaid,
I sung of jealousy's alarms,
    And blam'd th' inconstant maid.

'Farewell, I cried, ye giddy train,
    'So fickle and untrue,
'And heav'n protect that hapless swain,
    'Who builds his hopes on you.

'These hopes, alas! will quickly fly,
    'Nor leave a shade behind,
'And cold disdain shall arm that eye,
    'Which lately beam'd so kind.

'Tho' now the Spring, so blythe and gay,
    'Adorns the fields with flow'rs,
'Tho' now the Linnet pours her lay
    'Amid yon sylvan bow'rs:

* *The Druid's Monument* (London: T. Davies, 1774) pp. 5–14.

'Yet to that slighted youth, the Spring
  'Smiles cheerfully in vain,
'And tho' the Linnets sweetly sing,
  'They cannot ease his pain.' –

Thus flow'd my strain, as fancy bade,
  I thought no mortal nigh –
I turn'd me to the sylvan shade,
  A stranger caught my eye.

Grief mark'd his face, his locks were grey,
  An ancient harp he bore,
And plain and rude was his array,
  As that which Druids wore.

'Mortal, he said, thy cares are vain,
  'Such cares thou must forgo;
'It ill becomes thee to complain,
  'Or grieve at fancied woe.

'If grief you love, come follow me,
  'And where yon elms appear,
'A mournful monument you'll see
  'That justly claims a tear.

'That monument the DRUIDS rais'd,
  'It bears a Poet's name,
'Whom Britain's children long have prais'd,
  'A fav'rite son of fame.

'Oft have we seen him on these plains,
  '(He lov'd the calm retreat)
'Oft have we heard his polish'd strains,
  'And every note was sweet.

'Say, *Nature* say, for thou canst tell,
  'Are not the words thy own,
'When to the *hermit's*[1] peaceful cell –
  'The poet leads us on.

'Do not thy thoughts appear,
  'Does not thy voice adorn,
'When these sweet sounds salute the ear,
  '*Turn, gentle hermit, turn.*

'O! say what beauties grace the song,
  'What heavenly Ardor warms,
'When ANGELINA, lost so long,
  'Is lock'd in EDWIN's arms.

'This strain the *Druids* oft repeat
  'In some sequester'd grove,
'Where with the *Fairy* train they meet,
  'To hear the tales of love.

'For still the Druids haunt this isle,
  'And fairies oft are seen,
'When sleep rewards the ploughman's toil,
  'And shepherds leave the green.

'Oft hand in hand, in mirthful mood,
  'At night we tread the lawn,
'And hide us in this lonely wood,
  'When day begins to dawn.

'And here with some bewitching strain,
  'We cheat the ling'ring hours,
'Till the pale moon returns again,
  'And makes all nature ours.

'And oft in hearing GOLDSMITH's lays,
  'These lays that touch the soul,
'We've pass'd the longest Summer days,
  'And wonder'd how they stole.

'But ah! these strains we'll hear no more,
  'For to yon darksome dell,
'This morn the weeping shepherds bore,
  'The bard we lov'd so well:

'With decent grace we saw them bend,
  'And lay in yonder grave,
'The friend of man, the muse's friend,
  'Whom virtue could not save.

'And can we stay when he is gone?
  'Can we enjoy these plains?
'Ah! no, their sweetest charms are flown,
  'They've lost their poet's strains. –

'*Auburn* farewell[2] – no more we'll stray
  "Mid thy *deserted* bow'rs,
'T'applaud thy poet's plaintive lay,
  'And pluck thy withering flow'rs.

'No more the Druids shall appear,
  'But like thy hapless train,
'Drop, as they pass, a silent tear,
  'And seek some happier plain.

'Yet on that plain, where'er it is,
  'We'll oft together join,
'And fondly tell the scenes of bliss
  'The joys that once were thine.

'Ev'n there we'll crown thy bard with bays,
  'And give him just applause,
'When we recall his pleasing lays,
  'And think what *Auburn* was.

'Perhaps where *Alpine* hills[3] ascend,
  'We'll sit us down at last,
'And see fair ITALY extend,
  'And think of pleasures past;

'Then turning, trace the various scenes
  'Which GOLDSMITH's pencil drew,
'And own, with tears, that all his strains
  'Are just, are strictly true.

'Yet ere we left our native land,
  'We rais'd this sacred stone,
'Where SCULPTURE, with an artful hand,
  'The poet's worth hath shown.

'Then turn and read – nor rail at love,
  'Nor drop that useless tear,
'Nor let *unreal* sorrow move,
  'But pay a tribute *here*.'

I turned, I read, I heav'd a sigh,
  My conduct who can blame,
For every bard that passes by
  Will always do the same.

The INSCRIPTION[4]

'Adieu, sweet bard, to each fine feeling true,
'Thy virtues many, and thy foibles few,
'Those form'd to charm, ev'n vicious minds, and these
'With harmless mirth the social soul to please,
'Another's woe thy heart could always melt,
'None gave more free, for none more deeply felt.
Sweet bard adieu, thy own harmonious lays
'Have sculptur'd out thy monument of praise.
'Yes – these survive to time's remotest day,
'While drops the bust, and boastful tombs decay. –
'Reader, if number'd in the muse's train,
'Go tune the lyre, and imitate his strain;
'But, if no poet thou, reverse the plan,
'Depart in peace, and imitate the man.'

NOTES

John Tait, a minor writer who flourished during 1774–6.
1. This alludes to Goldsmith's well-known *Ballad of the Hermit*. The poem is 'Edwin and Angelina.'
2. *The Deserted Village.*
3. *The Traveller.*
4. The inscription is by William Woty (1731–91).

An Ingenious Writer*

EDMUND BURKE

Sir,

I have received a poem on the death of Dr Goldsmith[1] which the author has done me the honour to inscribe to me. I am very much flattered by a compliment on so distinguished a subject and from so

* In *The Correspondence of Edmund Burke*, vol. 2, ed. Dame Lucy S. Sutherland, (Cambridge: University Press, 1960) p. 546. Editor's title.

very ingenious a writer. I shall take it as an additional favour (if I do not intrude too much into his secret) if the gentleman will let me know to whom I owe the obligation of this great politeness and the satisfaction I have had in the perusal of the fine poem in which he has been pleased to give me a particular interest.

I am, Sir,

Your most obedient and humble servant,

EDM. BURKE.

NOTES

Edmund Burke (1729–97), Irish statesman and philosopher. He wrote this letter to Thomas Davies, Goldsmith's publisher, on 28 June 1776. In *Retaliation*, (line 32), Goldsmith said that Burke 'to party gave up what was meant for mankind'. However, Burke never replied to the accusation and continued to think of Goldsmith as a great writer.

1. Possibly John Tait's *The Druid's Monument* or *A Monody on the Death of Dr Oliver Goldsmith* (London: Thomas Davies, 1774), which was dedicated to Burke.

Goldsmith*

W. M. THACKERAY

. . . the career, the sufferings, the genius, the gentle nature of Goldsmith, and the esteem in which we hold him. Who, of the millions whom he has amused, doesn't love him? To be the most beloved of English writers, what a title that is for a man! A wild youth, wayward, but full of tenderness and affection, quits the country village, where his boyhood has been passed in happy musing, in idle shelter, in fond longing to see the great world out of doors, and achieve name and fortune; and after years of dire struggle, and neglect and poverty, his heart turning back as fondly to his native place as it had longed eagerly for change when sheltered there, he writes a book and a poem, full of the recollections and feelings of home: he paints

* *The English Humourists of the Eighteenth Century* (London: Smith, Elder & Co., 1853) pp. 248–71.

the friends and scenes of his youth, and peoples Auburn and Wakefield with remembrances of Lissoy. Wander he must, but he carries away a home-relic with him, and dies with it on his breast. His nature is truant; in repose it longs for change: as on the journey it looks back for friends and quiet. He passes to-day in building an air-castle for tomorrow, or in writing yesterday's elegy; and he would fly away this hour, but that a cage and necessity keep him. What is the charm of his verse, of his style, and humour? His sweet regrets, his delicate compassion, his soft smile, his tremulous sympathy, the weakness which he owns? Your love for him is half pity. You come hot and tired from the day's battle and this sweet minstrel sings to you. Who could harm the kind vagrant harper? Whom did he ever hurt? He carries no weapons, save the harp on which he plays to you; and with which he delights great and humble, young and old, the captains in the tents, or the soldiers round the fire, or the women and children in the villages, at whose porches he stops and sings his simple songs of love and beauty. With that sweet story of the *Vicar of Wakefield* he has found entry into every castle and every hamlet in Europe. Not one of us, however busy or hard, but once or twice in our lives has passed an evening with him, and undergoing the charm of his delightful music.

Goldsmith's father was no doubt the good Doctor Primrose, whom we all of us know. Swift was yet alive, when the little Oliver was born at Pallas, or Pallasmore, in the county of Longford, in Ireland. In 1730, two years after the child's birth, Charles Goldsmith removed his family to Lissoy, in the county Westmeath, that sweet 'Auburn' which every person who hears me has seen in fancy. Here the kind parson[1] brought up his eight children; and loving all the world, as his son says, fancied all the world loved him. He had a crowd of poor dependants besides those hungry children. He kept an open table; round which sat flatterers and poor friends, who laughed at the honest rector's many jokes, and ate the produce of his seventy acres of farm. Those who have seen an Irish house in the present day can fancy that one of Lissoy. The old beggar still has his allotted corner by the kitchen turf; the maimed old soldier still gets his potatoes and buttermilk; the poor cottier still asks his honour's charity, and prays God bless his reverence for the sixpence; the ragged pensioner still takes his place by right and sufferance. There's still a crowd in the kitchen, and a crowd round the parlour table, profusion, confusion, kindness, poverty. If an Irishman comes to London to make his fortune, he has a half-dozen of Irish dependants who take a percentage of his earnings. The good Charles Goldsmith left but little provision for his hungry race when death summoned him; and one of his daughters being engaged to a Squire of rather superior dignity, Charles Goldsmith impoverished the rest of his family to provide the girl with a dowry.

The smallpox, which scourged all Europe at that time, and ravaged the roses off the cheeks of half the world, fell foul of poor little Oliver's face, when the child was eight years old, and left him scarred and disfigured for his life. An old woman in his father's village taught him his letters, and pronounced him a dunce: Paddy Byrne, the hedge-schoolmaster, took him in hand: and from Paddy Byrne, he was transmitted to a clergyman at Elphin. When a child was sent to school in those days, the classic phrase was that he was placed under Mr So-and-so's *ferule*. Poor little ancestors! It is hard to think how ruthlessly you were birched; and how much of needless whipping and tears our small forefathers had to undergo! A relative – kind uncle Contarine – took the main charge of little Noll; who went through his schooldays righteously doing as little work as he could; robbing orchards, playing at ball, and making his pocket-money fly about whenever fortune sent it to him. Everybody knows the story of that famous 'Mistake of a Night', when the young schoolboy, provided with a guinea and a nag, rode up to the 'best house' in Ardagh, called for the landlord's company over a bottle of wine at supper, and for a hot cake for breakfast in the morning; and found, when he asked for the bill, that the best house was Squire Featherstone's, and not the inn for which he mistook it. Who does not know every story about Goldsmith? That is a delightful and fantastic picture of the child dancing and capering about in the kitchen at home, when the old fiddler gibed at him for his ugliness, and called him Æsop; and little Noll made his repartee of 'Heralds proclaim aloud this saying – See Æsop dancing and his monkey playing.' One can fancy a queer pitiful look of humour and appeal upon that little scarred face – the funny little dancing figure, the funny little brogue. In his life, and his writings, which are the honest expression of it, he is constantly bewailing that homely face and person; anon he surveys them in the glass ruefully; and presently assumes the most comical dignity. He likes to deck out his little person in splendour and fine colours. He presented himself to be examined for ordination in a pair of scarlet breeches, and said honestly that he did not like to go into the Church, because he was fond of coloured clothes. When he tried to practise as a doctor, he got by hook or by crook a black velvet suit, and looked as big and grand as he could, and kept his hat over a patch on the old coat: in better days he bloomed out in plum-colour, in blue silk, and in new velvet. For some of those splendours the heirs and assignees of Mr Filby, the tailor, have never been paid to this day: perhaps the kind tailor and his creditor have met and settled their little account in Hades.[2]

They showed until lately a window at Trinity College, Dublin, on which the name of O. Goldsmith was engraved with a diamond. Whose diamond was it? Not the young sizar's, who made but a poor figure in that place of learning. He was idle, penniless, and fond of pleasure: he learned his way early to the pawnbroker's shop. He wrote ballads, they say, for the street-singers, who paid him a crown for a poem, and his pleasure was to steal out at night and hear his verses sung. He was chastised by his tutor for giving a dance in his rooms, and took the box on the ears so much to heart, that he packed up his all, pawned his books and little property, and disappeared from college and family. He said he intended to go to America, but when his money was spent, the young prodigal came home ruefully, and the good folks there killed their calf – it was but a lean one – and welcomed him back.

After college he hung about his mother's house, and lived for some years the life of a buckeen – passed a month with this relation and that, a year with one patron, a great deal of time at the public-house. Tired of this life, it was resolved that he should go to London, and study at the Temple; but he got no farther on the road to London and the woolsack than Dublin, where he gambled away the fifty pounds given to him for his outfit, and whence he returned to the indefatigable forgiveness of home. Then he determined to be a doctor, and uncle Contarine helped him to a couple of years at Edinburgh. Then from Edinburgh he felt that he ought to hear the famous professors of Leyden and Paris, and wrote most amusing pompous letters to his uncle about the great Farheim, Du Petit, and Duhamel du Monceau, whose lectures he proposed to follow. If uncle Contarine believed those letters – if Oliver's mother believed that story which the youth related of his going to Cork, with the purpose of embarking for America, of his having paid his passage-money, and having sent his kit on board; of the anonymous captain sailing away with Oliver's valuable luggage, in a nameless ship, never to return; if uncle Contarine and the mother at Ballymahon believed his stories, they must have been a very simple pair; as it was a very simple rogue indeed who cheated them. When the lad, after failing in his clerical examination, after failing in his plan for studying the law, took leave of these projects and of his parents, and set out for Edinburgh, he saw mother, and uncle, and lazy Ballymahon, and green native turf, and sparkling river for the last time. He was never to look on old Ireland more, and only in fancy revisit her.

> But me not destined such delights to share,
> My prime of life in wandering spent and care,
> Impelled, with steps unceasing, to pursue
> Some fleeting good that mocks me with the view;
> That like the circle bounding earth and skies!
> Allures from far, yet, as I follow, flies:
> My fortune leads to traverse realms alone,
> And find no spot of all the world my own.

I spoke in a former lecture[3] of that high courage which enabled Fielding, in spite of disease, remorse, and poverty, always to retain a cheerful spirit and to keep his manly benevolence and love of truth intact, as if these treasures had been confided to him for the public benefit, and he was accountable to posterity for their honourable employ, and a constancy equally happy and admirable I think was shown by Goldsmith, whose sweet and friendly nature bloomed kindly always in the midst of a life's storm, and rain, and bitter weather. The poor fellow was never so friendless but he could befriend some one; never so pinched and wretched but he could give of his crust, and speak his word of compassion. If he had but his flute left, he could give that, and make the children happy in the dreary London court. He could give the coals in that queer coal-scuttle we read of to his poor neighbour: he could give away his blankets in college to the poor widow, and warm himself as he best might in the feathers: he could pawn his coat to save his landlord from gaol: when he was a school-usher he spent his earnings in treats for the boys, and the good-natured school-master's wife said justly that she ought to keep Mr Goldsmith's money as well as the young gentlemen's. When he met his pupils in later life, nothing would satisfy the Doctor but he must treat them still. 'Have you seen the print of me after Sir Joshua Reynolds?' he asked of one of his old pupils. 'Not seen it? not bought it? Sure, Jack, if your picture had been published, I'd not have been without it half-an-hour.' His purse and his heart were everybody's, and his friends' as much as his own. When he was at the height of his reputation, and the Earl of Northumberland, going as Lord Lieutenant to Ireland, asked if he could be of any service to Doctor Goldsmith, Goldsmith recommended his brother,[4] and not himself, to the great man. 'My patrons,' he gallantly said, 'are the booksellers, and I want no others.' Hard patrons they were, and hard work he did; but he did not complain much: if in his early writings some bitter words escaped him, some allusions to neglect and poverty, he withdrew these expressions when his works were republished, and better days seemed to open for him; and he did not care to complain that printer or publisher had overlooked his merit, or left him poor. The Court face was turned from honest Oliver, the Court patronised Beattie,[5] the fashion did not shine on him – fashion adored Sterne.[6] Fashion pronounced Kelly to be the great writer of comedy of his day. A little – not ill-humour, but plaintiveness – a little betrayal of wounded pride which he showed, render him not the less amiable. The author of the *Vicar of Wakefield* had a right to protest when Newbery kept back the manuscript for two years; had a right to be a little peevish with Sterne; a little angry when Colman's actors declined their parts in his delightful comedy, when the manager refused to have a scene painted for it, and pronounced its damnation before hearing. He had not the great public with him; but he had the noble Johnson, and the admirable Reynolds, and the great Gibbon, and the great Burke, and the great Fox – friends and admirers illustrious indeed, as famous as those who, fifty years before, sat round Pope's table.

Nobody knows, and I dare say Goldsmith's buoyant temper kept no account of, all the pains which he endured during the early period of his literary career. Should any man of letters in our day have to bear up against such, Heaven grant he may come out of the period of misfortune with such a pure kind heart as that which Goldsmith obstinately bore in his breast. The insults to which he had to submit are shocking to read off – slander, contumely, vulgar satire, brutal malignity perverting his commonest motives and actions; he had his share of these, and one's anger is roused at reading of them, as it is at seeing a woman insulted or a child assaulted, at the notion that a creature so very gentle and weak, and full of love, should have had to suffer so. And he had worse than insult to undergo – to own to fault and deprecate the anger of ruffians. There is a letter of his extant to one Griffiths, a bookseller, in which poor Goldsmith is forced to confess that certain books sent by Griffiths are in the hands of a friend from whom Goldsmith had been forced to borrow money. 'He was wild, sir,' Johnson said, speaking of Gold-

smith to Boswell with his great, wise benevolence and noble merci-
fulness of heart – 'Dr Goldsmith was wild, sir; but he is so no more.'
Ah! if we pity the good and weak man who suffers undeservedly, let
us deal very gently with him from whom misery extorts not only
tears, but shame; let us think humbly and charitably of the human
nature that suffers so sadly and falls so low. Whose turn may it be tomorrow! What weak heart, confident before trial, may not succumb
under temptation invincible? Cover the good man who has been
vanquished – cover his face and pass on.

For the last half-dozen years of his life, Goldsmith was far removed from the pressure of any ignoble necessity: and in the receipt,
indeed, of a pretty large income from the booksellers his patrons.
Had he lived but a few years more, his public fame would have been
as great as his private reputation, and he might have enjoyed alive a
part of that esteem which his country has ever since paid to the vivid
and versatile genius who has touched on almost every subject of
literature, and touched nothing that he did not adorn. Except in rare
instances, a man is known in our profession, and esteemed as a
skilful workman, years before the lucky hit which trebles his usual
gains, and stamps him a popular author. In the strength of his age,
and the dawn of his reputation, having for backers and friends the
most illustrious literary men of his time, fame and prosperity might
have been in store for Goldsmith, had fate so willed it, and, at forty-
six, had not sudden disease carried him off. I say prosperity rather
than competence, for it is probable that no sum could have put order
into his affairs or sufficed for his irreclaimable habits of dissipation.
It must be remembered that he owed £2000 when he died. 'Was ever
poet,' Johnson asked, 'so trusted before?' As has been the case with
many another good fellow of his nation, his life was tracked and his
substance wasted by crowds of hungry beggars and lazy dependants. If they came at a lucky time (and be sure they knew his affairs
better than he did himself, and watched his pay-day), he gave them
of his money: if they begged on empty-purse days, he gave them his
promissory bills: or he treated them to a tavern where he had credit;
or he obliged them with an order upon honest Mr Filby for coats, for
which he paid as long as he could earn, and until the shears of Filby
were to cut for him no more. Staggering under a load of debts and
labour, tracked by bailiffs and reproachful creditors, running from a
hundred poor dependants, whose appealing looks were perhaps the
hardest of all pains for him to bear, devising fevered plans for the
morrow, new histories, new comedies, all sorts of new literary

schemes, flying from all these into seclusion, and out of seclusion
into pleasure – at last, at five-and-forty, death seized him and closed
his career. I have been many a time in the chambers in the Temple
which were his, and passed up the staircase, which Johnson and
Burke and Reynolds trod to see their friend, their poet, their kind
Goldsmith – the stair on which the poor women sat weeping bitterly
when they heard that the greatest and most generous of all men was
dead within the black oak door. Ah! it was a different lot from that
for which the poor fellow sighed, when he wrote with heart yearn-
ing for home those most charming of all fond verses, in which he
fancies he revisits Auburn:

> Here, as I take my solitary rounds,
> Amidst thy tangling walks and ruined grounds,
> And, many a year elapsed, return to view
> Where once the cottage stood, the hawthorn grew,
> Remembrance wakes, with all her busy train,
> Swells at my breast, and turns the past to pain.
>
> In all my wanderings round this world of care,
> In all my griefs – and God has given my share –
> I still had hopes, my latest hours to crown,
> Amidst these humble bowers to lay me down;
> To husband out life's taper at the close,
> And keep the flame from wasting by repose;
> I still had hopes – for pride attends us still –
> Amidst the swains to show my book-learned skill,
> Around my fire an evening group to draw,
> And tell of all I felt and all I saw;
> And, as a hare, whom hounds and horns pursue,
> Pants to the place from whence at first he flew –
> I still had hopes, my long vexations past,
> Here to return, and die at home at last.
>
> O blest retirement, friend to life's decline!
> Retreats from care that never must be mine –
> How blest is he who crowns, in shades like these,
> A youth of labour with an age of ease;
> Who quits a world where strong temptations try,
> And, since 'tis hard to combat, learns to fly!
> For him no wretches born to work and weep
> Explore the mine or tempt the dangerous deep;

No surly porter stands in guilty state
To spurn imploring famine from the gate:
But on he moves to meet his latter end,
Angels around befriending virtue's friend;
Sinks to the grave with unperceived decay,
Whilst resignation gently slopes the way;
And all his prospects brightening to the last,
His heaven commences ere the world be past.

In these verses, I need not say with what melody, with what touching truth, with what exquisite beauty of comparison – as indeed in hundreds more pages of the writings of this honest soul – the whole character of the man is told – his humble confession of faults and weakness; his pleasant little vanity, and desire that his village should admire him; his simple scheme of good in which everybody was to be happy – no beggar was to be refused his dinner – nobody in fact was to work much, and he to be the harmless chief of the Utopia, and the monarch of the Irish Yvetor. He would have told again, and without fear of their failing, those famous jokes which had hung fire in London; he would have talked of his great friends of the Club – of my Lord Clare and my Lord Bishop, my Lord Nugent – sure he knew them intimately, and was hand and glove with some of the best men in town – and he would have spoken of Johnson and of Burke, and of Sir Joshua who had painted him – and he would have told wonderful sly stories of Ranelagh and the Pantheon, and the masquerades at Madame Cornelis'; and he would have toasted, with a sigh, the Jessamy Bride – the lovely Mary Horneck.

The figure of that charming young lady forms one of the prettiest recollections of Goldsmith's life. She and her beautiful sister, who married Bunbury, the graceful and humorous amateur artist of those days, when Gilray had but just begun to try his powers, were among the kindest and dearest of Goldsmith's many friends, cheered and pitied him, travelled abroad with him, made him welcome at their home, and gave him many a pleasant holiday. He bought his finest clothes to figure at their country-house at Barton – he wrote them droll verses. They loved him, laughed at him, played him tricks, and made him happy. He asked for a loan from Garrick, and Garrick kindly supplied him, to enable him to go to Barton: but there were to be no more holidays and only one brief struggle more for poor Goldsmith. A lock of his hair was taken from the coffin and given to the Jessamy Bride. She lived quite into our time. Hazlitt saw her an old lady, but beautiful still, in Northcote's painting-room, who told the eager critic how proud she always was that Goldsmith had admired her. The younger Colman has left a touching reminiscence of him (vol. i. 63, 64).[7]

Think of him reckless, thriftless, vain, if you like – but merciful, gentle, generous, full of love and pity. He passes out of our life, and goes to render his account beyond it. Think of the poor pensioners weeping at his grave; think of the noble spirits that admired and deplored him; think of the righteous pen that wrote his epitaph – and of the wonderful and unanimous response of affection with which the world has paid back the love he gave it. His humour delighting us still: his song fresh and beautiful as when first he charmed with it: his words in all our mouths: his very weakness beloved and familiar – his benevolent spirit seems to smile upon us; to do gentle kindnesses; to succour with sweet charity: to soothe, caress, and forgive: to plead with the fortunate for the unhappy and the poor.

His name is the last in the list of those men of humour who have formed the themes of the discourses which you have heard so kindly.

Long before I had ever hoped for such an audience, or dreamed of the possibility of the good fortune which has brought me so many friends, I was at issue with some of my literary brethren upon a point – which they held from tradition I think rather than experience – that our profession was neglected in this country; and that men of letters were ill-received and held in slight esteem. It would hardly be grateful of me now to alter my old opinion that we do meet with goodwill and kindness, with generous helping hands in the time of our necessity, with cordial and friendly recognition. What claim had any one of these of whom I have been speaking, but genius? What return of gratitude, fame, affection, did it not bring to all?

What punishment befell those who were unfortunate among them, but that which follows reckless habits and careless lives? For these faults a wit must suffer like the dullest prodigal that ever ran in debt. He must pay the tailor if he wears the coat; his children must go in rags if he spends his money at the tavern; he can't come to London and be made Lord Chancellor if he stops on the road and gambles away his last shilling at Dublin. And he must pay the social penalty of these follies too, and expect that the world will shun the man of bad habits, that women will avoid the man of loose life, that prudent folks will close their doors as a precaution, and before a demand should be made on their pockets by the needy prodigal. With what difficulty had any one of these men to contend, save that eternal and mechanical one of want of means and lack of capital, and of which thousands of young lawyers, young doctors, young soldiers and sailors, of inventors, manufacturers, shopkeepers, have to complain? Hearts as brave and resolute as ever beat in the breast of any wit or poet, sicken and break daily in the vain endeavour and unavailing struggle against life's difficulty. Don't we see daily ruined inventors, grey-haired midshipmen, baulked heroes, blighted curates, barristers pining a hungry life out in chambers, the attorneys never mounting to their garrets, whilst scores of them are rapping at the door of the successful quack below? If these suffer, who is the author, that he should be exempt? Let us bear our ills with the same constancy with which others endure them, accept our manly part in life, hold our own, and ask no more. I can conceive of no kings or laws causing or curing Goldsmith's improvidence, or Fielding's fatal love of pleasure, or Dick Steele's mania for running races with the constable. You never can outrun that sure-footed officer – not by any swiftness or by dodges devised by any genius, however great; and he carries off the Tatler to the spunging-house, or taps the Citizen of the World on the shoulder as he would any other mortal.

Does society look down on a man because he is an author? I suppose if people want a buffoon they tolerate him only in so far as he is amusing; it can hardly be expected that they should respect him as an equal. Is there to be a guard of honour provided for the author of the last new novel or poem? how long is he to reign, and keep other potentates out of possession? He retires, grumbles, and prints a lamentation that literature is despised. If Captain A. is left out of Lady B.'s parties, he does not state that the army is despised: if Lord C. no longer asks Counsellor D. to dinner, Counsellor D. does not announce that the bar is insulted. He is not fair to society if he enters it with this suspicion hankering about him; if he is doubtful about his reception, how hold up his head honestly, and look frankly in the face that world about which he is full of suspicion? Is he place-hunting, and thinking in his mind that he ought to be made an Ambassador like Prior, or a Secretary of State like Addison? his pretence of equality falls to the ground at once: he is scheming for a patron, not shaking the hand of a friend, when he meets the world. Treat such a man as he deserves; laugh at his buffoonery, and give him a dinner and a *bon jour*; laugh at his self-sufficiency and absurd assumptions of superiority, and his equally ludicrous airs of

martydom: laugh at his flattery and his scheming, and buy it, if it's worth the having. Let the wag have his dinner and the hireling his pay, if you want him, and make a profound bow to the *grand homme incompris*, and the boisterous martyr, and show him the door. The great world, the great aggregate experience, has its good sense, as it has its good humour. It detects a pretender, as it trusts a loyal heart. It is kind in the main: how should it be otherwise than kind, when it is so wise and clear-headed? To any literary man who says, 'It despises my profession,' I say, with all my might – no, no, no. It may pass over your individual case – how many a brave fellow has failed in the race and perished unknown in the struggle! – but it treats you as you merit in the main. If you serve it, it is not unthankful; if you please it, it is pleased; if you cringe to it, it detects you, and scorns you if you are mean; it returns your cheerfulness with its good humour; it deals not ungenerously with you weakness; it recognises most kindly your merits; it gives you a fair place and fair play. To any one of those men of whom we have spoken was it in the main ungrateful? A king might refuse Goldsmith a pension, as a publisher might keep his masterpiece and the delight of all the world in his desk for two years; but it was mistake, and not ill-will. Noble and illustrious names of Swift, and Pope, and Addison! dear and honoured memories of Goldsmith and Fielding! kind friends, teachers, benefactors! who shall say that our country, which continues to bring you such an unceasing tribute of applause, admiration, love, sympathy, does not do honour to the literary calling in the honour which it bestows upon *you*?

NOTES

W. M. Thackeray (1811–63), English novelist.
1. At church, with meek and unaffected grace,
    His looks adorn'd the venerable place;
    Truth from his lips prevail'd with double sway,
    And fools who came to scoff remain'd to pray.
    The service past, around the pious man,
    With steady zeal each honest rustic ran;
    E'en children follow'd with endearing wile,
    And pluck'd his gown to share the good man's smile.
    His ready smile a parent's warmth exprest,
    Their welfare pleased him, and their cares distrest;
    To them his heart, his love, his griefs were given,
    But all his serious thoughts had rest in heaven.

As some tall cliff that lifts its awful form,
Swells from the vale, and midway leaves the storm,
Though round its breast the rolling clouds are spread,
Eternal sunshine settles on its head.

The Deserted Village.

2. 'When Goldsmith died, half the unpaid bill to Mr William Filby (amounting in all to £79) was for clothes supplied to this nephew Hodson' – Forster's *Goldsmith*, p. 520. As this nephew ended his days 'a prosperous Irish gentleman,' it is not unreasonable to wish that he had cleared off Mr Filby's bill (Thackeray's note).
3. Thackeray's volume on the *English Humourists* was originally published as *A Series Delivered in England, Scotland and the United States of America.*
4. Henry.
5. James Beattie. See his recollections in this book.
6. Goldsmith attacked Sterne obviously enough, censuring his indecency, and slighting his wit, and ridiculing his manner, in the 53rd letter in the 'Citizen of the World'. 'As in common conversation,' says he, 'the best way to make the audience laugh is by first laughing yourself; so in writing, the properest manner is to show an attempt at humour, which will pass upon most for humour in reality. To affect this, readers must be treated with the most perfect familiarity; in one page the author is to make them a low bow, and in the next to pull them by the nose; he must talk in riddles, and then send them to bed in order to dream for the solution,' &c. (Thackeray's note)
7. See Colman's recollections of Goldsmith in this book.

The Personality of Goldsmith*

RICHARD BRINSLEY SHERIDAN KNOWLES

. . . But at least his works procured for him a great reputation. Goldsmith's name was spread far beyond the circle of his intimates, or even of his acquaintances; but these, after all, form a man's world; and it is surprising how small, with these, was the consideration ensured to him by his great renown. There was something in his manner that had the effect of checking at once any disposition to respect which even strangers might have entertained before seeing him. He was awkward, had no dignity of bearing, no power of

* *Dublin University Magazine*, 88 (September 1876) pp. 364–7.

concealing his thoughts or feelings, either by facial expression or by silence. Added to these superficial defects, there were his poverty and his extreme good-nature. He had not much power to favour, and too much generous sensibility to wound. As he inspired no fear, and did no harm to any one, he was regarded with a certain tolerant liking – as being a butt for practical jokes, and an amusing piece of absurdity – but certainly not with deference. In such a one it was found hard to acknowledge the presence of genius. His seat in the Literary Club he owed to Johnson's domineering support. When the poem of *The Traveller* fell like a thunder-clap among the members of the Club, they consoled themselves by mutual assurances that the best parts had been dictated by Johnson; and when Johnson repudiated the credit thrust upon him, and marked the eight unimportant lines which were the sum of his contribution, and when repeated successes had put its author's genius beyond dispute, what he had done was all but ignored, and his friends founded their treatment of him, not upon his worth, but upon his weaknesses.

And what were these? His faults of manner have been already alluded to. His generosity was proverbial: it amounted to an inability to say 'no' to anyone who came to him with a tale of suffering, and to a longing to relieve, which he would gratify regardless of consequences to himself. Therefore, while he was himself always in pecuniary straits, he was always surrounded by a crowd poorer than himself, to whose wants he administered. Had he been rich, his generosity would never have been condemned.

But his poverty was only partly due to his generosity. It was owing in a far greater degree to a sturdy independence which would neither suffer him to truckle nor abate one jot of principle at the call of self-interest. As a student in Edinburgh, he was sometimes the guest of the Duke of Hamilton; but discovering that he was valued chiefly on account of his oddity and the amusement he occasioned, he ceased to avail himself of the hospitality which was open to him, and relinquished the chances to which it might have led. When his first poem had made him famous, and the Earl of Northumberland, sending for him, asked whether he could advance his interests in any way in Ireland, whither he was going as Lord Lieutenant, Goldsmith's petition was for his brother the clergyman, and not for himself. And later on, during a time of great political excitement, when the Ministry, reeling under the attacks of Junius, were looking about to recruit their strength in the press, one Parson Scott, their emissary, waited on Goldsmith, and his account of what passed, as it is completely unsympathetic, will not be considered partial. 'I found him,' said Parson Scott, 'in a miserable suite of chambers in the Temple. I told him my authority, I told how I was empowered to pay most liberally for his exertions; and, would you believe it? he was so absurd as to say, "I can earn as much as will supply my wants without writing for any party; the assistance you offer is therefore unnecessary to me" – and so I left him in his garret!'

Thus could Goldsmith turn a deaf ear to the prompting of selfishness, while he could never resist the story of another's distress. Yet his contemporaries for the most part refused to credit him with lofty motives. Such behaviour on the part of Johnson would have been in accordance with his ordinary bearing – invariably dignified, ever conscious of his superiority to which he compelled all to bow by the overwhelming force of his character, and the resistless readiness of his tongue. In him such conduct would have been applauded. But in Goldsmith it was folly and a proof of his overweening conceit. 'He is an inspired idiot,' said Walpole, and in this expression he epitomised the prevalent feeling with regard to poor Goldsmith. He was one who seemed born to be personally undervalued, and this was the harder, as it cannot be pretended that he was insensible to the incense of fame. There is a pretty story told of his meeting one day in the Strand with a young man who had formerly been his pupil at Dr Milner's school at Peckham.

'Come, my boy,' he said, 'come, Sam, I am delighted to see you. I must treat you to something. What shall it be? Will you have some apples? Sam,' added Goldsmith suddenly, 'have you seen my picture by Sir Joshua Reynolds? Have you seen it, Sam? Have you got an engraving?' The former pupil answered that he had not, but that he was going to get one. 'Sam,' returned Goldsmith, with some emotion, 'if *your* picture had been published, I should not have waited an hour without having it.'

On another occasion he complained at the Literary Club, with the candour that was natural to him, of the slighting treatment he had received from a certain peer, who meeting him at a country house, 'took no more notice of me,' said Goldsmith, 'than if I had been an ordinary person'. Expressions like these show that he was not insensible to the deference which was certainly due to his reputation; and he, no doubt, often wondered why it was denied to him. Something he attributed to his ugliness and his awkward figure; and to counteract these, he would attire himself in the gayest and costliest garments that his tailor could supply. In part he accounted for it by the meanness of his circumstances and surroundings; and to remedy this, he bought the lease of a suite of chambers in the Temple, and furnished them sumptuously, to entertain his friends. But his efforts to win esteem were of worse than no avail; for upon these very grounds his character has been handed down to posterity as a marvel of improvidence and vanity.

Goldsmith himself benefited but little by his works. If he enjoyed anything of happiness in life, he owed it to the buoyancy of spirit which may be found apart from genius; and to have seen this in full play, we should not have followed him to the Literary Club, or to those spheres of society to which his reputation introduced him – where he was generally undervalued and where his personality suffered by contrast with his fame, – but to the free-and-easy clubs, of a type akin to that of the 'Three Jolly Pigeons' of earlier days; where the entertainment consisted of recitations, songs, jokes, and dramatic imitations; or we should have taken part in what he termed his 'shoemakers' holidays,' when a party of his 'Three Jolly Pigeon' associates would breakfast with him at his chambers, and afterwards stroll off to some resort within a few miles of London – Blackheath, Wandsworth, Chelsea, Highgate, or Islington – where they would dine simply at some rustic tavern: or again, we should have made one in those gatherings of young people which he delighted to hold at his chambers when the middle-aged man would become the willing butt of his guests, and would play at hunt the slipper and blind-man's buff, with all the zest of youth, to the inconvenience of Mr Blackstone on the floor beneath, who would pause in his learned labours to wonder at the unseemly din overhead.

Before the close of Goldsmith's life, however, even his spirit was to be broken. During his latter years the clouds gradually gathered, and enveloped him in hopelessness, and he endured secretly worse than all the hardships of his early years, in the dread of their return. Partly by extravagance, partly because of the crowd of needy adventurers whom he assisted, but most of all by reason of the inadequate sums which he received for his works, he had become heavily involved in debt. The load had been growing for a long time back, and it no longer sat lightly on his shoulders. But all his efforts to shake it off were useless. It was in vain that he engaged himself in advance for new histories, new novels, and plays; it was to no purpose that the town was convulsed with laughter by *She Stoops to Conquer*, or melted with the sad beauty of *The Deserted Village*. Hope cannot allure him with prospects of greater success than he had gained, and even its repetition would be powerless to assuage his necessities; and so the 'knack of hoping' which had sustained him in the struggles of his youth takes flight, and in addition, his apprehensive mind suffers the anguish of a supposed desertion of his powers. 'I am afraid,' said an acquaintance to whom he had one day narrated the plot of his comedy, *She Stoops to Conquer*, in the hope of a little encouragement – for manager and actors were all sure that the play would be damned – 'I am afraid that the audience, under their present sentimental impressions, will think it too broad and farcical for comedy.' Goldsmith remained silent, looking very serious, and presently taking the other by the hand, he 'piteously' said, 'I am much obliged to you, my dear friend, for the candour of your opinion; but it is all I can do; for, alas! I find that my genius, if ever I had any, has of late totally deserted me.'

The extent of his anxiety during the last few months of his life can only be surmised. He unburdened himself to no one, not even to his trusty friend Johnson, not even to Reynolds. He tried to obtain a pension; but he had before, as we have seen, declined to serve the Ministry, and he was now met with a refusal. Some of his friends remarked that he was changed, and looking old and haggard, and that his mirth had quite abandoned him. A slight fever caused him to take to his bed, but the doctor feeling his pulse, found it much higher than could be accounted for by the fever. 'Is your mind at ease?' he inquired; and Goldsmith answered, 'No, it is not.'

These words are the last recorded of him; and they throw a deep mournfulness over the close of a life in which misfortune prevailed. He died in his forty-sixth year.

The undiminished popularity of what Goldsmith wrote has caused his name to survive. But the interest that attaches to him personally in the mind of posterity is hardly enviable. We are apt to dwell on his oddities, his mistakes, and the practical jokes of which he was the subject. We shake our heads over his debts, and we unconsciously echo the phrase with which the friends of his hero, 'The Man in Black,' commented on his miscarriages, as we say, 'it is a pity he was so weak, he who had not the least harm in him, and was so very good-natured.'

But Goldsmith deserves a more dignified treatment at the hands of his readers, were it only from selfish motives. There is about his writings a peculiar charm of freshness that survives many a reading; and they gain a new significance when – remembering that no writer has more intimately bound up his own nature and his own history with his works – we read them by the light of his life. They can stand on their own merits, it is true; but they acquire a more vivid interest when we alight, here and there, upon the embalmment of what were once real events and living emotions.

Thus indirectly we render a kind of poetical justice to Goldsmith by thoroughly identifying him with his works. For, after all, they are only the outcome of himself. The elevation of tone and sentiment, the purity of thought, the independence of judgement, and the perception of truth which prompted what he wrote, are conspicuous to a remarkable degree in the actions of his life. When we have considered his career with candour and sympathy, we shall be tempted to wish that his worst failings were more commonly the worst, and we shall be inclined to admit that his impartial friend Johnson was simply just when he wrote, 'Let not his faults be remembered; he was a very great man.'

Memoir*

WILLIAM SPALDING

The fame of Goldsmith, while it is one of the highest in English literature, has likewise been one of the steadiest, and is certain to be one of the most lasting. Of all our standard authors, there are very few who please so many readers; and, perhaps, none who is as widely popular is at the same time so heartily appreciated by persons of refined and critical taste.

The Vicar of Wakefield has been read, and liked, oftener than any other novel in any European language. The Citizen of the World, if less various and less dramatic than the essays of Addison and his friends, is inspired by warmer feeling than they, and guided by a deeper sense of human interests. She Stoops to Conquer, overflowing with native gaiety, and seasoned by the truest humour, is one of the most pleasant comedies in existence. From The Traveller, our poetry has received much, from The Deserted Village it has received still more, of imagery flowing out of a fine and original fancy, of pathos which frequently dissolves into tenderness and sometimes swells into pas-

* In The Complete Works of Oliver Goldsmith (London: James Blackwood 1872) pp. 7–20.

sion, and of expression so apt and so suggestive, that phrases and lines recur to us more readily than from any other works, except those of Shakespeare and Pope. The ever-living interest of Goldsmith's imaginative pictures lies mainly in the glow of kindness, wishful rather than hopeful, by which they are brightened. The landscape stretches out in clear sunshine, from which a gentle breeze is always chasing the scattered clouds. The same amiable spirit characterises his observation of real life: the thoughts look always toward social or individual good; the satire, when keenest, is never harsh. Over everything he does, too, his spontaneous grace of manner diffuses a charm which art could never reach.

In his less prominent writings, also, there present themselves many hints towards thoughts which those greater works elaborated, and many expansions of thoughts at which those works had only hinted, and many other thoughts, and images, and sentiments, which he did not elsewhere use. Such things give an attraction and a value to his miscellaneous *Essays*. They occur abundantly in his Letters, few, but exceedingly interesting, and most instructive as illustrations of his disposition; and they may be dug out of those compilations, and those perishable contributions to reviews and magazines, on which (and even on toils meaner still) the man of genius was condemned to waste so many of his precious days. For the works which have made Goldsmith immortal were but the fruit of hours snatched, at intervals, from the hard labour forced on him for bread, during seventeen weary years of professional authorship. The fact makes us inquisitive as to the events of his life, and prepares us for looking on his history and character with respectful sympathy and indulgence.

Of all those many men of letters, whom we cannot but love in spite of weaknesses and errors, there is none whose character is more vexingly anomalous than Goldsmith's. He was spontaneously frank beyond the bounds of prudence, yet he often shut up his most profound emotions within an impenetrable veil of reserve, or yet oftener disguised them in a way which made loose observers do him grievous injustice. He was naturally and habitually unassuming; yet he broke out, now and then, into fits of defiant pretension. He was thoroughly unselfish, devotedly affectionate and grateful; and yet destitute of the strength of will to do what gratitude and affection dictated. He was inspired by the feelings of a gentleman, and prone towards rushing impetuously to the relief of all distress; and yet he was unable (even when he had the means, which did not come to him for long,) to protect himself from degrading money-embarrass-ments, and equally unable to think, with a view to action, either of his own future fate, or of the mischief which his wasteful careless-ness was inflicting on others. Such are among the contradictions which we gather from the best-known passages of his history, and which are detected as attaching especially to his latest years. To some of them, the key is yielded by the facts of his life, taken with the evidence we have of his native tendencies. A long and sad appren-ticeship to poverty and depreciation; sudden elevation into a cele-brity which might have turned a more steady head; the attainment, for the last few years of his life, of a social position, which was essentially a false one: these were circumstances frightfully danger-ous for a man of genius, impulse, and imagination – for a man who sensitively shrank from the contemplation of external evils, and who had the power of throwing himself back on dreams when he found it hard to act. The worst of Goldsmith's aberrations, and all the little follies which were scorned so much by his inferiors, are traceable to a disappointed desire of approbation – a desire which, felt with painful intensity, was, throughout his life, in one way or another, doomed to continual and irritating frustration. The brightest side in his character, as in his works, consisted in his extraordinary and unquenchable sweetness of heart and temper: he often desponded, and sometimes despaired; but he never hated or waxed bitter.

A character like this holds out to its analysts temptations towards exaggeration on either side. The biographers of Johnson, while bent on sacrificing every one to their own idol, were not only incompetent to understand Goldsmith, but informed very ill as to his history, even for the time he was among them. These men accordingly painted him in colours supplied by avowed contempt and secret dislike. There have now been wiped off all the stains which were thus rubbed on the portrait, whether by the malignity of Hawkins,[1] or by the envious silliness of Boswell.[2] We are no longer in danger of judging Goldsmith harshly. But, in accordance with the usual law of reactions, the pendulum has perhaps oscillated too far in the oppo-site arc. Mr Prior, in his *Life*,[3] of 1837, has collected an invaluable mass of new facts and documents, which suffice to correct mistakes innumerable. In 1848, and more fully in 1854, Mr Forster's *Goldsmith*[4] has digested all the attainable knowledge into a masterly biography of the poet, and has touched his character with a hand which, skil-fully bringing his virtues into just prominence, errs only, if at all, by passing somewhat too softly over his faults.

For the story of a life so diversified as Goldsmith's, some distribution is needed. In a hasty sketch like the present, it may be enough to arrange the events under three periods. The first of these, extending from his birth to the end of his twenty-seventh year (1728–55), comprises his childhood and youth, and his wanderings before he settled in London. The second (1756–61), closing with his thirty-third year, stretches over those six years of obscurity and wretchedness which were his training in the trade of authorship. The third period, of twelve years (1762–74), exhibits him from his introduction into the society of Johnson and his friends, through his brief literary triumphs, to his untimely death at the age of forty-five.

I.   In the year 1718, Charles Goldsmith, a young Irish clergyman, descended of a clerical family, married Ann Jones. Though his father had some property, he was a younger son. His wife, whose father was master of the diocesan school at Elphin, brought a very small portion; and he himself had not obtained a living. In a word, while his heart seems to have been as warm as his son's, his prudence, in this and other matters, is shewn to have been no greater. For twelve years after his marriage, his means of support were both very narrow and very precarious. He farmed a little land; he officiated occasionally in the parish of Kilkenny West, in the county of Westmeath, the rector of which was his wife's uncle; and he seems to have been regularly the curate of the parish of Forney, lying next to the other, but in the county of Longford. There, also, he occupied a house belonging to the uncle, and situated in a hamlet called Pallas, or Pallasmore. Mr and Mrs Goldsmith had eight children, five of whom were sons. Oliver, the fifth child, and second son, was born in the house at Pallas, on the 10th of November, 1728. Two years later, his father succeeded to the rectory of Kilkenny West. The living is understood to have been then worth less than two hundred a year; and he obtained, also, a lease at a low rent, renewable for ever, of some seventy acres of the Lissoy estate, said to have been, afterwards, worth to him about forty pounds a year. He resided in his parish, in the village of Lissoy, ejections from which were commemorated in the history of of his son's 'Auburn.'

Oliver, in his childhood, was admittedly a slow scholar, but held to be indolent rather than dull. Shy and sensitive, with outbursts of spirit and whim, petulant and unstable, but generous and affectionate, the boy was far from being unlike the man; and there is unpleasant proof of his having thus early become a victim to the same course of sneering and depreciation, under which he was made to smart to the end of his days. Some of the attacks on him, recorded as having been met by keen retorts, were aimed at a disfigurement of his face, which was caused by smallpox. In such facts as these, Mr Forster thoughtfully seeks for the clue, by which may be traced some of the besetting weaknesses of his character in manhood. He was, at first, destined for some 'common trade;' and this might have been no better than that found for one of his younger brothers, who became a cabinet-maker. Hopes of him, however, sprang up; and the mother's love and faith were strong. Accordingly, he was sent from lower teachers to spend four years at the classical school of Edgworthstown. In his last journey between that place and home, he is said to have actually committed the blunder of his own comedy, mistaking a squire's house for an inn. Obstacles rose between him and college. The oldest son, Henry (the beloved brother of *The Traveller*), was there already; and now Mr Goldsmith, acting on a mistaken view of honour, beggared himself and his children, by giving a large portion to a daughter[5] who had secretly married a wealthy pupil of Henry's.[6] For Oliver, there was no road to the university unless through a sizarship. His pride revolted against the humiliations then accompanying that position; and he was with difficulty encouraged to submit, by the kindest of his relations, the only one of them, indeed, except Henry, to whom, in mature life, he looked with confidence. This was Mr Contarine, the husband of his paternal aunt, who had been the college friend of Bishop Berkeley, and was now a beneficed clergyman, of moderate means.

On the 11th of June, 1745, Goldsmith, then half-way on in his seventeenth year, was enrolled as a sizar of Trinity College, Dublin. In the beginning of 1747, his father died; and the poverty which had weighed down his son from the beginning grew hopelessly heavy. Gifts from his uncle, Contarine, were received, but were insufficient; an exhibition of thirty shillings was obtained, but held for one year only; books were pawned, and money was borrowed from fellow-students, and street-ballads were composed, and sold for five shillings a-piece. Self-respect was thus impaired sadly; but, behind this, there lurked another evil, in itself sufficient, for a temperament like Oliver's, to destroy all chance of academical success. Wilder, his tutor, in his dealings with all his pupils, had, as his rules of conduct, caprice and violence, partialities and dislikes; and the poor Lissoy sizar, unsatisfactory, and probably lazy, in his study of mathematics and logic, and receiving no credit either for his respectable classical knowledge, or for his clever knack of versification, was an object of incessant contempt and vituperation. On occasion of a supper, which he had foolishly given (probably to celebrate the gaining of the exhibition), the tutor fairly knocked him down. He left Dublin with a shilling in his pocket, but was soon starved into submission, and returned to college through the mediation of Henry. On the 27th of February, 1749, being a little more than twenty years old, he received the degree of Bachelor of Arts.

What was now to be done with him, was a question of grave perplexity. He spent two years at home, in almost complete useless-ness and general lounging, and, certainly, with the effect of exhaust-ing the patience both of mother and of brother. He became a tutor, but retired on charging one of the family with cheating at cards. He presented himself, with great reluctance, to examination for orders; but he was rejected – why, is not known: by tradition, it was for appearing in red breeches. He started for America, but returned from the Irish coast after a series of mishaps, which he had the courage to describe in a comic letter to his mother. Again he set off, to eat his way to the bar; but, inveigled into play in Dublin by a country acquaintance, he lost every farthing of the fifty pounds with which his kind uncle had supplied him.

In autumn, 1752, when he had almost completed his twenty-fourth year, he was again fitted out by the same friendly hand, and left Ireland, never to return. He entered, in Edinburgh, on a course of medical study, which was continued in the same University till the spring of 1754, when it closed without the appearance, in his corre-spondence with his uncle, of any very strong reason for a change of place. The period was too short to qualify for a degree; and no assurance can be gathered that the profession was rightly or in-dustriously studied. But the young Irishman was known as a warm-hearted fellow, an admirable companion, and an excellent story-teller and comic singer; and he satirised Scotland in letters to his family as humorous and diverting as anything he ever wrote. The strange, wilful scapegrace and dreamer was already bent on distinguishing himself; but he was bent, quite as resolutely, on not doing so in the one only course, which promised him the certain means of being useful in his generation, and of making good to his friends the anxieties and cost they had suffered for him. That he should fall into pecuniary entanglements, was a matter of course with one who, while he had very little to spend, never learned how to fit his own expenditure to his income, and could never find it in his heart to resist the cry of another person's distress. The Dublin sizar had given away his blanket to a shivering beggar-woman; the Edinburgh medical student became security for a comrade as poor as himself. Accordingly, though he now received from his uncle the last which can positively be traced of the small supplies which had been his chief dependence, his departure from Scotland had something of the nature of an escape. He was bound for the Continent; but odd mishaps befell him on the way. However, in April or May, 1754, he had resumed, at Leyden, his attendance on medical lectures; and this course was continued for a year under heavy difficulties, but closed, like the former one, without a degree. Of his proceedings during the next year, hardly more can peremptorily be affirmed than this, that he was travelling through Europe on foot. His means of support are asserted to have been those of his 'Vicar's son', who played the flute to French peasants, and earned lodging or more by disputing in Italian universities. But something is hinted, also, of a tutorship held for a while; and the title of 'Doctor,' which he afterwards assumed, is vaguely alleged to have been justified by a bachelorship in medicine, conferred either at Louvain or at Padua.

II.   The second era in Goldsmith's life, commencing with his return to England, opens with a change of purposes, which, in our ignorance of the connecting facts, startles us like the transformations of a dissolving view. It seems as if the 'philosophical vagabond' had learned that he had sown his wild oats broadly enough, and that it was time to grow wheat for penny-loaves. In plain terms, he sought no longer either for knowledge or for amusement, but set himself seriously about earning his daily bread.

He had been taught the lesson of independence. He received no further aid from home: he asked for none; and, if he had, it is unlikely he would have received it. His mother, always poor, was now becoming blind; Uncle Contarine had sunk into dotage; and Henry was labouring, as curate and schoolmaster, in that life-long poverty, in respect of which, he, rather than the father, was the model of the clergyman of Auburn. To his nearest relatives, he now addresses, instead of complaints or petitions, over-drawn pictures of his prosperity; in belief of which, when his affairs were at their very lowest ebb, a younger brother walked over from Ireland into Oliver's garret to have his fortune made. In those representations, to say nothing of past disappointments, may be found some excuses for the silent neglect with which his other Irish kinsfolk and friends received the only requests he made to them, which were for obtaining subscribers or purchasers for his works. By one or two fellow-students, who accidentally crossed his path, he was treated more generously. But, for a long time after he came to London, Goldsmith stood almost utterly unfriended and alone.

Black, indeed, was the prospect which lay before him. He had entered his twenty-eighth year, without having made one real step, either in his nominal profession or in any other available pursuit. It is particularly to be observed, that towards literature, as a means of livelihood, he looked even less than towards medicine; and, in truth, if he knew the state of the trade, as we know it from the records of Johnson's life, voluntary dependence on it would have been as foolish as anything he ever did. He thought of no such thing; he thought of nothing but keeping himself alive, no matter how. He understood the true bent of his own powers quite as ill as he understood the business-side of the world. His judgement and imagination, doubtless, were by this time mature: in Switzerland, he had composed passages of the *Traveller*; and his letters, even earlier, are as good as the best of his published works. Still, it is far from being unlikely, that the indolent man of genius would never have gone farther than the composition of fragments; had not the consciousness of his own strength, and a longing after the fame which that strength might win, been pressed on him by slow degrees, as he drudged sadly on in that routine of hack authorship on which starvation had driven him.

In February 1756, Goldsmith was again in England; and, within a few weeks, he had found his way to London. There, except for short intervals, the remainder of his life was spent.

The first three years of this period are buried in an obscurity, through which there emerge glimpses of much and constant misery. We discover, with great uncertainty of dates and order, several attempts at pursuits other than literary. Perhaps he was for a short while a strolling player: certainly he was a chemist's shopman in Monument Yard: he was a country-usher, probably in Kent: and he was more than once employed similarly in the school of a Dr Milner at Peckham. He is conjectured to have at one time corrected the press in the printing-house of Richardson the novelist: and, assisted by a loan from a college-friend, he endeavoured in vain to establish a humble medical practice on the Bankside in Southwark. Speedily after this, his professional aspirations were rudely extinguished.

A surgical appointment to Coromandel, in the Company's service, obtained through Dr Milner, came to nothing, for reasons which do not directly appear. Hereupon, though he must have read *Roderick Random*, he was driven to think of being a surgeon's mate in the navy. But, alas! the record of examinations at the College of Surgeons bears, on the date of 21st December, 1758, these words: 'Oliver Goldsmith, found not qualified.'

When he sought these medical appointments, he had had experience of authorship, and was desirous to escape from it. The leading periodicals were then two. Of the *Critical Review*, Smollett was the editor: the *Monthly Review* was edited by the proprietor and publisher Griffiths, assisted actively by his wife. Introduced to Griffiths by Dr Milner, Goldsmith was, in February 1757, engaged to write criticisms for his *Review*, receiving a small salary, and boarding in the bookseller's house. Griffiths's memoranda have enabled the collectors of Goldsmith's works to identify a good many essays as contributed under this agreement: and several of these are well worth study for their own merits, not less than as illustrative of the writer's mental history. Though the engagement was for a year, his regular working for the *Review* lasted only seven months. The employer said the scribe was idle and proud: the scribe said the employer and the lady were uncivil to him, starved him, and (worst of all) mutilated and interpolated his writings. A total breach did not ensue. Goldsmith continued to supply Griffiths with translations from the French. But the secession from the periodical opened up to him the *Critical Review*, to which he began to contribute in the end of 1758. About the same time there broke out a humiliating quarrel, which shews painfully how little way Goldsmith had made in the world, at the close of his third year in London. Requiring a suit of clothes for his appearance at the College of Surgeons, he obtained it on Griffiths's security. Four days after his rejection, the poor man with whom he lodged was arrested for a small debt: and the lodger was tempted, by the tears of the family, to pawn the clothes for money to pay the demand. In another week his own necessities drove him to pledging with an acquaintance four books, which Griffiths, again employing him as a critic, had lent him to be reviewed. Immediately the bookseller angrily demanded the books and clothes, or payment of their value: and there has been preserved a letter of Goldsmith's, affecting, but not exactly candid, which was sent in the course of the correspondence.

The sky began to clear up. The three years beginning with 1759 raised Goldsmith into a position, in which, though unfortunately it was not solid enough for his wavering footsteps, a man particularly prudent might have stood firm. The booksellers had learned to value him as an excellent workman: nor was it likely to be a disqualification in their eyes, that his hopeless incapacity in money-matters was sure to put him constantly at their mercy. Some of the leading professional authors welcomed cordially a man who could no longer be confounded with the herd. Smollett, who was still fighting bravely against the difficulties he was never able to overcome, made his acquaintance in the end of 1759, and secured him as a regular coadjutor. In the summer of 1761, Johnson, whose troubles were nearly over, (the pension was given him in the year after) supped in the first decent lodging which poor Goldsmith was able to occupy.

Those three years gave birth, with all those that followed, to many pieces of task-work not worth naming here, and probably to some that have not been identified. But he now wrote with hope and courage. He drudged and copied when there was not room for anything better: he cheerfully threw away wit and thinking on ephemeral criticisms of worthless books: and he speculated and imagined originally whenever originality could find a vent. In April, 1759, appeared his *Enquiry into the present state of Polite Learning in Europe*; an essay fulfilling very imperfectly the promise of its title, but spirited and interesting, abundant in miscellaneous knowledge, shrewd observation, and striking hints towards general principles. In the same year he set on foot a periodical called *The Bee*, which, though it did not survive its eighth number, contained some of his liveliest essays. In one of them the text is the maxim commonly fathered on Talleyrand; that the use of language to man is that of concealing his thoughts: but he characteristically turns aside from the serious philosophy which the irony veils, to work up from it diverting rules for the guidance of gentlemen who are out at elbows. The year 1760 would, by itself, have sufficed to make Goldsmith an English classic. While writing valuable papers for Smollett's new adventure, *The British Magazine*, he eclipsed, in another periodical, the novel of *Sir Launcelot Greaves*, which was the leading feature in his friend's miscellany. To *The Public Ledger*, a daily newspaper projected by the same bookseller Newbery, he undertook to furnish two articles every week, at the price of a guinea apiece. He fulfilled the agreement by writing, chiefly in the course of that year, the exquisite series of sketches, which, in 1762, was collected and reprinted as *The Citizen of the World*. Beau Tibbs, and the elegant Mrs Tibbs, and the philanthropic humourist, 'The Man in Black,' can never be forgotten: as little can the liveliness of descriptive fancy, and the acuteness of observation, with which the misplaced Chinaman wanders through the scenes of European society; or the kindly thoughtfulness with which he discovers and rebukes the weaknesses which lay beneath. Mr Forster, indeed, claims, not unjustly, for Goldsmith's works generally, and most emphatically for this series of essays, the merit of a deeper and more serious wisdom than any which is usually attributed to him. 'One marked peculiarity its best admirers have failed to observe upon; its detection and exposure, not simply of the follies and foibles which lie upon the surface, but of those more pregnant evils which rankle at the heart of society. The occasions were frequent on which the Chinese Citizen so lifted his voice, that only in a later generation could he find his audience; and they were not few, in which he has failed to find one even yet.'

III.   We are now able to look at the last twelve years of Goldsmith's life, through a medium cleared from the distortions thrown over them by Boswell and his rivals in the art of gossiping. The unamiable features which had been attributed to his character fall away the moment they are closely handled. There might be, now and then, a short access of jealousy, natural and excusable in one who probably felt himself to stand, in some points, higher than any with whom he was compared: but much oftener the protests which are triumphantly set down for us as explosions of envy, are nothing else than expressions of scorn for the toadyism with which Johnson's London friends, and his Scottish visitors yet more humblingly than they, licked incessantly the feet of the really great man who was weak enough to allow them. As to the alleged silliness, again, of Goldsmith's conversation, it must be allowed that his talk was not always the wisest; and that, like many men of still higher mark, he was far from speaking in a manner worthy of his writings. But not infrequently there may be discovered, in what he said, a thinking which was too deep for the hearers: while the most glaring of the rash sayings came, naturally and without imputation on his real ability, from one whose thoughts were more fluent than systematic, whose imagination and feelings were characteristically and naturally quick, and who, when he did speak much, spoke either to indulge for his own pleasure a boyish elasticity of spirits, or else (and this but too often) to divert his thoughts from secret misery, the causes of which his associates neither knew nor cared for, and which he stubbornly and proudly buried in his own breast.

His obligations to Johnson were great: but Johnson himself, with honourable indignation, denied that they were what his sycophant called them. For the development of his genius, Goldsmith did not owe him anything whatever: and the rise of his fame was only somewhat quicker because of Johnson's aid. Goldsmith did owe to him much kind and good advice, and might have owed him both this and active help, but for the reserve in which, even to him, he wrapped up from an early stage of their friendship all that was bad and dangerous in the state of his affairs: Goldsmith owed to him, further, the comfort and the mighty benefit of friendly and familiar intercourse with himself and other men of distinguished intelligence and elevated character: Goldsmith owed also to him the precious hope and encouragement which a man, who has still his way to make, receives from the countenance of the man who is the acknowledged chief in the art he practises. But the gains were not taken without payment of costs. Especially there subsisted, in the relations between those two celebrated men, one peculiarity which, though it strikes one very forcibly, has been much left in the background by the biographers. Johnson, who had never been familiar with professional authors at large, was now, when he had actually ceased to be a professional author himself, shaking off, quite unequivocally, association with the fraternity. He continued to assist and counsel many of them; but it was in the character of a gentleman and patron. To friendly and habitual intercourse he did not admit one of them except Goldsmith alone. Scrutinise the lists of the 'Literary Club,' which represent Johnson's usual society: you will find that every name but Goldsmith's is that of a man well-to-do in the world, or otherwise entitled to hold up his head in contempt of Grub Street. Reynolds and Garrick and Colman were professional men indeed, but thriving or wealthy, in reality or in appearance; Burke had soared from literature to the dignity of the House of Commons: the rest were clergymen or others who merely dabbled in literature as an amusement or accomplishment, with a few men of rank or fortune, who, without having any literary ambition, liked letters, or respected Samuel Johnson. In a word, while these were the men with whom Goldsmith was continually mixing, he stood alone in the circle, among them but not of them. Evidently they looked down upon him for his station and presumed poverty, not less than for his *étourderie*[7] and his somewhat coarse breeding: the air of superiority is evident, even with better and more sensible men than the frothy Boswell, the good-naturedly supercilious Beauclerk, or the languidly polite Bennet Langton. Goldsmith, on the other hand, clearly felt the falseness of his position, without having the strength of mind either to reconcile himself to it or to retire from the field. Johnson's thoroughgoing and frank reception of Goldsmith into the small society which he gathered about him, was doubtless the strongest evidence of sincerity, both in his love for the man and in his admiration for his singular gifts. But, if he had, by keeping himself more at a distance, saved his friend from the Turk's-Head and the half-intimacies it led to, Goldsmith would probably have fallen into fewer of those explosions of assumption for which he was laughed at; and he might even, perhaps, have failed to contract some of those expensive habits which kept him constantly on the rack, and ended by breaking his heart.

In 1762, Goldsmith was far from being idle; though he was ill, and for a while at watering-places. His principal publication, in 1763, was his small and pleasant *History of England, in Letters from a Nobleman to his Son*. It became popular at once, and was ascribed to this, that, and the other man of rank, oftenest to Lord Lyttelton. His debts, though still of no great amount, began to torment him anew: and next year a crisis took place. Johnson, obeying an urgent summons to his lodgings, found him arrested by his landlady: and a consultation was held about the means of relief. The despairing debtor drew from his desk a novel which he had written in snatches of leisure. Johnson glanced through the manuscript, carried it off and sold *The Vicar of Wakefield* for sixty pounds: 'a sufficient price, too,' he said, 'when it was sold'; for the author was not yet famous. Yet, when he thus exhibited a work, whose hearty and natural pictures of life and character will make it live as long as the language it is written in, Goldsmith did not venture to exhibit, to his friendly but severe critic, another work, having pretensions still higher, which also lay by him completed. He had at length executed, with the ripened consciousness of power and skill, the poetical design which had possessed his mind since he trod the mountains of Switzerland, and which he now addressed to that unforgotten brother whose life of patient poverty was to end even sooner than his own. *The Traveller, or a Prospect of Society*, at last shown to Johnson, was declared by him to be a poem 'to which it would not be easy to find anything equal since the death of Pope'. The work was published in December, 1764. Instantly it ceased to be true that Goldsmith was not famous. The price paid for the copyright is uncertain; but there is reason for believing that it did not exceed twenty guineas.

Next year the same sum was paid, on the strength of his growing celebrity, for an edition of his *Essays*, collected from periodicals. In the same year he made a faint endeavour after medical practice, acting on an advice of Reynolds, kindly meant, but not over-judicious. The publication of the *Vicar*, the delay of which has not been well accounted for, took place in February, 1766: and it went through three editions before the end of August. But in June, after the second edition, the bookseller to whom it belonged refused to honour the author's bill for fifteen pounds: in December the same person paid him five guineas, when he had earned them by 'writing a short English Grammar;' and about New-Year's-Day thereafter, the bookseller's notebook received this entry: 'To lent Doctor Goldsmith one pound one.' The man who not only possessed genius, but had now acquired fame, was still the compiler and translator and literary journeyman: and the money was still sliding, like quicksilver, out of the hands of one who never could be taught what money is worth.

In 1767, his first comedy was submitted to Garrick, whom, by the way, Goldsmith had imprudently affronted in the *Enquiry*. The negotiation failed; principally, it would seem, because the manager was disposed to be forgiving and patronising, while the author would not submit to be either patronised or forgiven. Two other facts of this year claim notice. A mere compilation by a man of celebrity being a pretty safe speculation, Goldsmith was offered, and accepted, a contract, at the price of two hundred and fifty guineas, for a History of Rome, in two volumes, to be completed in two years if it were possible. Somewhat later, though having a general agreement with the policy of Lord North's government, he refused to write in its defence for liberal payment. The next year began with the performance of his comedy, *The Good-natur'd Man*, at Colman's theatre, Covent Garden. Its success was no more than fair; nor is the partial failure to be wondered at. He had designed to deviate from the sentimental school of comedy, then fashionable though waning, and to return, as far as morals would permit, to the comedy of manners: but the work hangs hesitatingly between the two spheres. The characters, also, are drawn strongly rather than interestingly: and the plot is heavy and heavily carried out. A new poem was now designed, the composition of which must have been a delightful relief from the toils which had still to be prosecuted. Early in 1769, just before the appearance of his agreeable but superficial *Roman History*, he entered on a new and very formidable bargain. This was for the writing of the *History of the Earth and Animated Nature*; for which he had certainly no specific qualifications, beyond the power of translating from Buffon, and that of telling felicitously the results of a few isolated observations he had made of the habits of common animals. The work was to be in eight volumes; and for each of these he was to receive a hundred guineas. It is sad to discover that his embarrassments were already so heavy, as to make those eight hundred guineas really useless to him. Before the year was closed, and when probably nothing, and certainly very little of the work was written, he prevailed on the publisher to advance five hundred guineas of the price. The payment is noticeable as having presumably been prompted by kindness, because performed with loss to the bookseller, who had to make up the sum by selling a large proportion of his interest in the copyright. This was not all: it seemed as if the careless and improvident man of impulse were bent on overwhelming himself under difficulties. Hardly had the money been received for the one unwritten work, than he contracted with another bookseller for a second, – a History of England, in four volumes, – for which, on its completion, he was to receive five hundred pounds.

Yet again has it to be marked, how, in the midst of this imprudence, with its accompaniments of anxiety, and fear, and self-reproach, the poetic fancy could revel in unrealities, and the poet forget, in the luxury of imaginative creation, the sufferings and danger both of himself and of his creditors. In circumstances no less unpromising than these was it, that Goldsmith poetised the recollections of his youth, immortalised those whom he had loved best, and framed one of the sweetest and most touching of poetical landscapes. *The Deserted Village*, a poem, was published on the 26th of May, 1770: a second, a third, and a fourth edition appeared in June, and a fifth in August. The leaning then prevalent towards the didactic in poetry made Johnson and other critics of the day prefer the earlier poem; but the public did not share that opinion then, nor is any one likely to do so now. Nature and pathos are a more poetical groundwork than speculation, even were it much more profound than Goldsmith's; and the loving interest we are enticed into feeling, for Auburn and its inhabitants, makes us forget the false theory of society which the poet here tried to inculcate, though he had denied and refuted it in his prose writings. What price was paid for the poem is not known: but the publisher was the same who had contracted for the *Animated Nature*. In the same summer, Goldsmith sought distraction of a different kind, by paying a visit to Paris in company with ladies of some rank.[8] The following year gave birth, through another aristocratic companionship, to his playful poem, *The Haunch of Venison*; and then also the *History of England* was published. Before the end of the year he had nearly finished his second comedy, working at it, as recently on the descriptive poem, chiefly in the country, in lodgings on the Edgeware Road.

While he was thus imagining, alternately, scenes of pathos and of broad fun, the real gloom was gathering round him more and more thickly. In June, 1772, the bookseller who had been so indulgent before was induced to advance the whole remainder of the price for the *Animated Nature*. Certainly a large part of the compilation was still unwritten; and it may be enough to say of the work, that it did not appear till three months after the author's death. A novel which he had engaged to write was rejected when offered to the publishers, being alleged to be merely a paraphrase of his first comedy: small aid can have been gleaned from small compilations, or from several of his last Essays, contributed to a new magazine: and obstacles, which threatened to be insurmountable, kept back his new play from the stage.

At length, in March, 1773, *She Stoops to Conquer* was played for the first time. It is amusing now, and might soon have given a half-malicious amusement to the dramatist, to look back on the distrust and fear with which all who were concerned either about him or about the theatre regarded this attempt to substitute humour, and life, and incident, for whining sentimentalism. The success of the play was brilliant: and popularity has never since deserted it. It is supposed to have gained for him four or five hundred pounds. In June of the same year, the bookseller who had twice paid him large sums in advance, acted similarly for a third time, though the *Natural History* still hung on hand: the author received from him two hundred and fifty pounds, for a *History of Greece*, which was published soon after his death.

He had not long to live. Nor can it be doubted that his strength and health were undermined by the gnawing uneasiness, which his desperate circumstances were now incessantly inflicting on him. New literary schemes, were formed in vain. He was not only penniless, but in debt; and that to an amount for which, when the large receipts he had recently had are considered, it is very difficult to

account by the supposition of mere neglect, or of any probable lavishness in personal expenditure. This difficulty, and some of the false steps which he certainly made in early manhood, supply the only ostensible ground for the charge of gambling in his latest years, so often brought against him. In the worst of the sufferings which he now endured, he found no comforter, and asked for none. To none of his condescending associates in the Literary Club was one word breathed, to hint at his poverty or his anguish: and they, good easy men, put no questions. Not even to Johnson, formerly so active in emergency, did he ever unbosom himself after the one occasion long past; nor to the friendly Reynolds, or the generous Burke, who would have saved him if it had been in mortal man to do so. But he did not disappear from among those well-bred gentlemen, without bequeathing to them pregnant proof, that the forbearance on which they had trespassed so long had not been caused by impotence to resist attack. In an encounter of jests, at one of the merry suppers, a biting epitaph on him by Garrick was heard by the company with shouts of laughter. Goldsmith, saying nothing at the time, began at home to write his poem 'Retaliation,' one of the finest and most characteristic of satires, and one of the truest also, because it does not forget fairness or indulgence in its deep-cutting dissections of character. It was his latest effort, and was found among his papers unfinished after his death.

Of that event the immediate cause was dysuria, aggravated by an injudicious treatment which he had insisted on using in defiance of his medical attendants. To one of them, however, who feared that the evil lay deeper than the body, he confessed mournfully that his mind was ill at ease. The distemper, after enduring for a few days, destroyed him on the morning of the 4th of April, 1774, when his age was forty-five years and about five months. He died in chambers, which he had occupied for a considerable time, in Brick Court in the Temple; and in the Temple churchyard he was buried. The visitor to Westminster Abbey reads, on a niche in Poets' Corner, a Latin epitaph, in remembrance of him, written by Samuel Johnson.

NOTES

William Spalding, critic and Professor of Logic and Rhetoric.

1. See Hawkins's recollections of Goldsmith in this book.
2. See Boswell's recollections of Goldsmith in this book.

3. James Prior, *The Life of Oliver Goldsmith, MB, from a Variety of Original Sources*, 2 vols (London: John Murray, 1837). The first full-length biography.
4. John Forster, *The Life and Times of Oliver Goldsmith* (London: Bradbury et al, 1848).
5. Catherine.
6. Daniel Hodson.
7. Inadvertence.
8. The Hornecks.

Portrait of Goldsmith*

SIR JOSHUA REYNOLDS

If anyone thinks that Dr Goldsmith was a man not worth the investigation, we must refer him to the public advertisements, where he will find the booksellers have lived upon his reputation, as his friends have lived upon his character, ever since his death.

The literary world seemed to deplore his death more than could be expected, when it is considered how small a part of his works were [written] for fame; yet epigrams, epitaphs and monodies to his memory were without end. And what is still a greater proof of his popularity, the booksellers still continue to live upon his name, which they shamefully prostitute by prefixing it to works which he never saw, and which were probably written since his death.

Dr Goldsmith's genius is universally acknowledged. All that we shall endeavour to do is to show what indeed is self-apparent, that such a genius could not be a fool or such a weak man as many people thought him.

Dr Goldsmith was, in the truest as the most common sense of the word, a man of genius. But if we take the popular opinion of genius – that it is a gift, or supernatural power, entirely distinct from wisdom, knowledge, learning, and judgement, and that all these acquisitions contribute to destroy, rather than increase, the operations of genius – the Doctor must be acknowledged to have in this sense greater claim to the name of genius than any other man whatever,

---

* In *Portraits by Sir Joshua Reynolds*, ed. Frederick W. Hilles (London: William Heinemann; New York: McGraw-Hill, 1952) pp. 44–59.

not excepting M. La Fontaine.[1] I do not mean that the Doctor entirely wanted all these qualities, but he appeared to want them in conversation.

Among those, therefore, who knew him but superficially, many suspected he was not the author of his own works, whilst others pronounced him an idiot inspired.[2] The supposition that he did not write his own works had a great appearance of probability to those who knew him but superficially, but whoever knew him intimately and still continued of that opinion, it would reflect no great compliment to his sagacity. His more intimate acquaintances easily perceived his absurdities proceeded from other causes than from a feebleness of intellect, and that his follies were not those of a fool.

A great part of Dr Goldsmith's folly and absurdity proceeded from principle, and partly from a want of early acquaintance with that life to which his reputation afterwards introduced him.

The author was intimately acquainted with Dr Goldsmith. They unbosomed their minds freely to each other, not only in regard to the characters of their friends, but what contributed to make men's company desired or avoided. It was agreed that it was not superior parts, or wisdom, or knowledge that made men beloved – that men do not go into company with a desire of receiving instruction, but to be amused – that people naturally avoid that society where their minds are to be kept on the stretch.

He was of a sociable disposition. He had a very strong desire, which I believe nobody will think very peculiar or culpable, to be liked, to have his company sought after by his friends. To this end, for it was a system, he abandoned his respectable character as a writer or a man of observation to that of a character which nobody was afraid of being humiliated in his presence. This was his general principle, but at times, observing the attention paid to the conversation of others who spoke with more premeditation, and the neglect of himself though greedy and impatient to speak, he then resolved to be more formal and to carry his character about with him. But as he found he could not unite both, he naturally relaxed into his old manner, and which manner, it must be acknowledged, met with all success for the purposes he intended it.

The Doctor came late into the great world. He had lived a great part of his life with mean people. All his old habits were against him. It was too late to learn new ones, or at least for the new to sit easy on him. However, he set furiously about it. For one week he took one for a model and for another week [another]. This disadvantage, joined to an anxious desire and impatience to distinguish himself, brought him often into ridiculous situations. As he thought, and not without reason, that he had distinguished himself by his writings, he imagined therefore he ought at all times and in all places to be equally distinguished from the rest of the company, which, if neglected, he thought it incumbent on him to do that little service for himself. Without therefore waiting for a fit opportunity, he always took care to stand forward and draw the attention of the company upon himself. He talked without knowledge, not so much for the sake of shining as [from] an impatience of neglect by being left out of the conversation. He would therefore, to draw the attention of the company upon [himself], sing, stand upon his head, [or] dance about the room.

His *Traveller* produced an eagerness unparalleled to see the author. He was sought after with greediness. He knew much was expected from him. He had not that kind of prudence to take refuge in silence. He would speak on subjects [of] which he had not thought, and of which he was ignorant; he was impatient of being overlooked; he wished to be the principal figure in every group. Goldsmith having adopted this mode of conduct forgot that he must with the advantages accept of all the disadvantages that belonged to it. But he envied Johnson. It may easily be conceived what absurdity of conduct he must fall into in whom this restless desire predominates.

No man's company was ever more greedily sought after, for in his company the ignorant and illiterate were not only easy and free from any mortifying restraint, but even their vanity was gratified to find so admirable a writer so much upon a level, or inferior to themselves, in the arts of conversation. The ingenious and the learned, who wished to display their knowledge, were sure to find an opportunity of gratifying their desire by the triumph of refuting his paradoxes. And it must be acknowledged that he often fought like a tiger, and like the tiger he fought when turned on his back. He risked every opinion which that moment came into his head.

He was impatient when praises were bestowed on any person, however remote these might be from interfering with his own department. It was enough for him if they filled the mouths of men, to oppose their pretensions.

With this fighting, absurdity, and ridiculous kind of envy, he made always a sort of bustle, and wherever he was there was no yawning. The conversation never stagnated or languished. The same company [that], the moment he had turned his back, were in open cry on his absurdity and folly, were still desirous of meeting him again the next day.

He considered him as a friend indeed who would ask him to tell a story or sing a song, either of which requests he was always very ready to comply with, and very often without being asked, and without any preparation, to the great amazement of the company. His favourite songs were *Johnny Armstrong*, *Barbara Allen*, and *Death and the Lady*. In singing the last he endeavoured to humour the dialogue by looking very fierce and speaking in a very rough voice for Death, which he suddenly changed when he came to the lady's part, putting on what he fancied to be a lady-like sweetness of countenance, with a thin, shrill voice. His skill in singing those ballads was no ways superior to the professors of this art which are heard every day in the streets, but whilst he was thus employed he was a conspicuous figure at least and was relieved from that horror which he entertained of being overlooked by the company.

It must be confessed that whoever excelled in any art or science, however different from his own, was sure to be considered by him as a rival. It was sufficient that he was an object of praise, as if he thought that the world had but a certain quantity of that commodity to give away, and what was bestowed upon others made less come to his share. This odious quality, however, was not so disagreeable in him as it generally is in other people. It was so far from being of that black malignant kind which excites hatred and disgust, that it was, from its being so artless and obvious, only ridiculous.

The following happened once in a large company, which may serve as an instance to characterise the Doctor's manner. Somebody said that one of Mr Garrick's excellencies, amongst many others, was his powers in telling of a story. This being universally agreed to, excited the Doctor's envy.

'I do not see what difficulty there can be in telling a story well. I would undertake to tell a story as well as Mr Garrick, and I will tell you one now, and I will do my best. There lived a cobbler – some people do laugh at this story and some do not; however, the story is this – there lived a cobbler in a stall. This stall was opposite our house, so I knew him very well. This cobbler a bailie came after, for I must tell you he was a very low fellow.'

('But you was acquainted with him, you say. He used to be often at your house.')

'Ay, he used to come over to fetch our shoes when they wanted mending, but not as an acquaintance, I always kept the best company.'

('Go on with your story, Doctor.')

'This cobbler was afraid of being arrested. – Why, the very best company used to come in our house. Squire Thomson used to dine with us, who was one of the first men in the country. I remember his coach and six, which we used to see come galloping down the hill, and then my mother, who was a little woman, was quite hid at the head of the table behind a great sirloin of beef. You could but just see the top of her head.'

('Well, but go on, Doctor Goldsmith, with your story.')

'When the bailie came to, and knocked at, the door of the cobbler's stall in order to have it opened, the cobbler, being aware, answered in the voice of a child (here the Doctor changes his voice), "Put in your finger into the hole and lift up the latch," which as soon as he had done, the cobbler with his knife cut the finger off, and still speaking in the child's voice, "Put in the other finger, Sir, if you please."'

The Doctor's folly, freaks, and nonsense, though there was seldom anything in it which marked it to be the nonsense of a man of genius, yet neither had it any of those marks of feebleness by which weakness and ignorance is immediately discovered. If he was sometimes foolish out of season, he never was what is worse, wise out of season. For instance, Dr Goldsmith never made common observations with the air and as if he had spoke[n] oracles, or even acquiesced in what others advanced, in order to conceal his own ignorance. On the contrary, he delighted in advancing paradoxes, and opposed others with false authorities, by which he often indeed discovered his ignorance, but not weakness.

Goldsmith had no wit in conversation, but to do him justice, he did not much attempt it. When in company with ladies he was always endeavouring after humour, and as continually failed; but his ill success was equally diverting to the company as if he had succeeded. If they laughed, he was happy and did not seem to care whether it was with him or at him. But when he was in company with the philosophers, he was grave, wise, and very inclinable to dispute established opinions. This immediately produced a general cry. Every man had arguments of confutation ready, and he himself was at once placed in the situation he so much loved, of being the object of attention of the whole company. However this disposition to paradoxes might be sometimes troublesome, it often called out the rest of the company into conversation, and as has been often observed, wherever the Doctor was, the conversation was never known to languish.

What Goldsmith intended for humour was purposely repeated as serious. However, to do justice to the world, a man seldom acquires the character of absurd without deserving it. As the *bons mots* of other wits are handed about the town, the Doctor's blunders and absurdities, circulated with equal success, helped to increase his fame and give everybody a desire of seeing the man, and this perhaps not without some mixture of self-congratulation to find a person whom they were obliged to look up to for superior talent sink below their own level when in conversation.

Goldsmith's mind was entirely unfurnished. When he was engaged in a work, he had all his knowledge to find, which when he found, he knew how to use, but forgot it immediately after he had used it.

He was so far from exciting envy in others by any exhibition of his own superior powers in extempore thinking that he would in a shorter time write the poem in his closet than give a satisfactory account in company of the plan or conduct of the work, or give any satisfactory explanation of a passage. This reminds me of a story of two sculptors who were rival candidates for a great work which was to be given to the most able artist. They were desired, by those who were appointed to be the judges of their respective merit, to speak upon their art with regard to their intention. After one of them had finished his speech with all the ostentation of eloquence, when it came to his rival's turn to speak, who had not the same gift of elocution, though a better sculptor, he only said, 'What this man *says* I can *do*.'

Perhaps one of the reasons why the Doctor was so very inexpert in explaining even the principles of his own art was his ignorance of the scholastic or technical terms by which similar things are distinguished. He professed himself an enemy to all those investigations which he said did not at all increase the powers of doing, but only enabled a person to talk about it, of those researches of which you receive the full result and advantage without study or attention equal to those who have spent their life in the pursuit. He considered this as superfluous and needless a science as that which was taught the *bourgeois gentilhomme*, who was persuaded he had made a great proficiency in rhetoric when he knew the operation of the organs of speech, or, as he himself says, what he did when he said *u*.

No man ever wrote so much from his feelings as Dr Goldsmith. I do not mean here the vulgar opinion of being possessed himself with the passion which he wished to excite. I mean only that he governed himself by an internal feeling of the right rather than by any written rules of art. He judged, for instance, by his ear, whether the verse was musical, without caring or perhaps knowing whether it would bear examination by the rules of the *prosodia*.

He felt with great exactness, far above what words can teach, the propriety in composition, how one sentiment breeds another in the mind, preferring this as naturally to grow out of the preceding and rejecting, another, though more brilliant, as breaking the chain of ideas. In short, he felt by a kind of instinct or intuition all those nice discriminations which to grosser minds appear to have no difference. This instinct is real genius if anything can be so called. But little of this judgement, as was before observed, appeared in conversation. It came when he took up the pen and quitted him when he laid it down.[3] Even his friends did not think him capable of marking with so much sagacity and precision the predominant and striking features of their characters as he did in the epitaphs.

These were the excellencies and the defects of the author of *The Traveller* and *The Deserted Village*, two of the most excellent works in the English language.

His name as a poet must depend upon the quality, not the quantity, of his works. *The Traveller, The Deserted Village*, the ballad in *The Vicar of Wakefield*, his two comedies (*The Good-Natur'd Man* and *She Stoops to Conquer*), and if to these we add his epitaphs on his friends, they make all his works in poetry which he owned.

His *Traveller* alone would have entitled him to a place in the Poets' Corner. It is a small, well-polished gem, the work of many years. It was begun when he was abroad and retouched at different periods since, and is more completely furnished than any of his other works. There is a general commanding air of grandeur that pervades the whole, that never sinks into languor. The general and popular character of each nation is strongly marked.

He is very sparing of epithets, which though they give a richness destroy simplicity, which I think is the peculiar characteristic of his poetry.

His works in prose were *The History of England in Letters from a*

Father to his Son, which the booksellers endeavour to pass upon the world as the work of the late Lord Lyttelton, *The State of Polite Literature in Europe, Chinese Tales*, a periodical paper called *The Bee, The Life of Mr Beau Nash of Bath, The Life of Dr Parnell, The Vicar of Wakefield*, a novel, *The Roman History* in [two] volumes, *The English History* in [four] volumes, and *The History of Animated Nature* in [eight] volumes.

Of his style in prose we may venture to say he was never languid, tedious, or insipid. It is always sprightly and animated. He very well knew the art of captivating the attention of the reader, both by his choice of matter and the lively narration with which it is accompanied.

NOTES

Sir Joshua Reynolds (1723–92), English artist and friend of Goldsmith. This sketch was found among Boswell's papers.

1. Jean de La Fontaine (1621–95), French poet and fabulist who had been one of the greatest literary geniuses of all times.

2. A reference to an unconfirmed comment Horace Walpole is said to have made.

3. 'No man,' remarked Johnson, 'was more foolish when he had not a pen in his hand, or more wise when he had.'

The Eccentric Poet*

JAMES NORTHCOTE

Much of the attention which even Goldsmith personally met with was undoubtedly owing to the patronage of his admired friend; yet Sir Joshua used to say, that Goldsmith looked at, or considered, public notoriety, or fame, as one great parcel, to the whole of which he laid claim, and whoever partook of any part of it, whether dancer, singer, sleight-of-hand man, or tumbler, deprived him of his right, and drew off the attention of the world from himself and which he

* In *Memoirs of Sir Joshua Reynolds* (London: Henry Colburn, 1813) pp. 153–5, 179–80, 204–5, 210–14. Editor's title.

was striving to gain. Notwithstanding this, he lamented that when-ever he entered into a mixed company, he struck a kind of awe on them, which deprived him of the enjoyment and freedom of society, and which he then made it his endeavour to dispel by playing wanton and childish pranks in order to bring himself to the wished-for level.

It was very soon after my first arrival in London, where every-thing appeared new and wonderful to me, that I expressed to Sir Joshua my impatient curiosity to see Dr Goldsmith, and he promised I should do so on the first opportunity. Soon afterwards Goldsmith came to dine with him, and immediately on my enter-ing the room, Sir Joshua, with a designed abruptness, said to me, 'This is Dr Goldsmith; pray why did you wish to see him?' I was much confused by the suddenness of the question, and answered, in my hurry, 'Because he is a notable man.' This, in one sense of the word, was so very contrary to the character and conduct of Gold-smith, that Sir Joshua burst into a hearty laugh, and said, that Goldsmith should, in future, always be called the notable man.

What I meant, however, to say was, that he was a man of note, or eminence.

He appeared to me to be very unaffected and good-natured; but he was totally ignorant of the art of painting, and this he often confessed with much gaiety.

It has been often said of Goldsmith, that he was ever desirous of being the object of attention in all companies where he was present; which the following anecdote may serve to prove.

On a summer's excursion to the continent he accompanied a lady and her two beautiful daughters into France and Flanders, and often expressed a little displeasure at perceiving that more attention was paid to them than to himself. On their entering a town, I think Antwerp, the populace surrounded the door of the hotel at which they alighted, and testified a desire to see those beautiful young women; and the ladies, willing to gratify them, came into a balcony at the front of the house, and Goldsmith with them; but perceiving that it was not himself who was the object of admiration, he pres-ently withdrew, with evident signs of mortification, saying, as he went out, 'There are places where I am the object of admiration also.'

One day when Drs Goldsmith and Johnson were at dinner with Sir Joshua, a poem, by a poet already alluded to, was presented to Sir Joshua, by his servant, from the author. Goldsmith immediately laid hold of it, and began to read it, and at every line cut almost through the paper with his finger nail, crying out, 'What d—d non-sense is this;' when Sir Joshua caught it out of his hands, saying, 'No, no, don't do so; you shall not spoil my book, neither:' for the Doctor could not bear to hear of another's fame.

Sir Joshua was always cautious to preserve an unblemished char-acter, and careful not to make any man his enemy. I remember when he was told of some very indiscreet speech or action of Goldsmith, he quickly said, 'What a fool he is thus to commit himself, when he has so much more cause to be careful of his reputation than I have of mine!' well recollecting that even the most trivial circumstance which tells against an eminent person, will be remembered as well as those in his favour; and that the world watch those who are distinguished for their abilities with a jealous eye . . .

When Goldsmith's comedy, *She Stoops to Conquer*, was to be brought out on the stage, on the 15th of March in this year [1773], he was at a loss what name to give it, till the very last moment, and then, in great haste, called it *She Stoops to Conquer, or the Mistakes of a Night*. Sir Joshua, who disliked this name for a play, offered a much better to him, saying, 'You ought to call it the *Belle's Strategem*, and if you do not I will damn it.' However, Goldsmith chose to name it himself, as above; and Mrs Cowley has since given that name to one of her comedies.

Goldsmith was in great anxiety about its success, he was much distressed in his finances at the time, and all his hopes hung on the event; and at the dinner preceding the representation of his play, his mouth became so parched and dry, from the agitation of his mind, that he was unable to swallow a single mouthful. The actors them-selves had great doubts of its success; but, contrary to their expecta-tions, the play was received with great applause; Sir Joshua and a large party of friends going for the purpose of supporting it if neces-sary. The dinner party, which took place at the Shakespeare, is humourously described by Cumberland. Dr Johnson took the head of the table, and there were present the Burkes, Caleb Whiteford, Major Mills, &c., &c.

I remember Dr Goldsmith gave me an order soon after this, with which I went to see this comedy; and the next time I saw him he inquired of me what my opinion was of it. I told him that I would not presume to be a judge of its merits; he then said, 'Did it make you laugh?' I answered, 'Exceedingly.' 'Then,' said the Doctor, 'that is all I require.' . . .

Just before his death, he had nearly completed a design for the execution of an *Universal Dictionary, of the Arts and Sciences*. Of this he had published the *Prospectus*, or, at least, had distributed copies of it amongst his friends and acquaintances. It did not meet with any warm encouragement, however, from the booksellers, although Sir Joshua Reynolds, Johnson, Garrick, and several others of his literary connections had promised him their assistance on various subjects: and the design was, I believe, entirely given up even previous to his demise.

In the Dedication of his *Deserted Village* to Sir Joshua Reynolds, already noticed, Goldsmith alludes to the death of his eldest brother, Henry, the clergyman; and his various biographers record another, Maurice, who was a younger brother, and of whom it is stated, by Bishop Percy, that having been bred to no business, he, upon some occasion, complained to Oliver that he found it difficult to live like a gentleman. To this Oliver wrote him an answer, begging that he would, without delay, quit so unprofitable a trade, and betake himself to some handicraft employment. Maurice wisely, as the Bishop adds, took the hint, and bound himself apprentice to a cabinet-maker, and when out of his indentures set up in business for himself, in which he was engaged during the viceroyalty of the late Duke of Rutland; and his shop being in Dublin, he was noticed by Mr Orde, later Lord Bolton, the Lord Lieutenant's Secretary, who recommended him to the patronage of the Duke, out of regard to the memory of his brother.

In consequence of this, he received the appointment of inspector of licences in that metropolis, and was also employed as mace-bearer, by the Royal Irish Academy, then just established. Both of these places were compatible with his business: and in the former he gave proof of great integrity by detecting a fraud committed on the revenue in his department; and one by which he himself might have profited, if he had not been a man of principle. He has now been dead not more than fifteen years; I enter more particularly into his history, from having seen the following passage in one of Oliver's letters to him: 'You talked of being my only brother – I don't understand you. Where is Charles?' . . .

Soon after Goldsmith's death, some people dining with Sir Joshua were commenting rather freely on some part of his works, which, in their opinion, neither discovered talent nor originality. To this, Dr Johnson listened, in his usual growling manner, for some time; when, at length, his patience being exhausted, he rose, with great dignity, looked them full in the face, and exclaimed, 'If nobody was suffered to abuse poor Goldy, but those who could write as well, he would have few censors.'

Yet, on another occasion, soon after the death of Goldsmith, a lady of his acquaintance was condoling with Dr Johnson on their loss, saying, 'Poor Goldsmith! I am exceedingly sorry for him; he was every man's friend!'

'No, Madam,' answered Johnson, 'he was no man's friend!'

In this seemingly harsh sentence, however, he merely alluded to the careless and imprudent conduct of Goldsmith, as being no friend even to himself, and when that is the case, a man is rendered incapable of being of any essential service to anyone else.

It has been generally circulated, and believed by many, that Goldsmith was a mere fool in conversation; but, in truth, this has been greatly exaggerated by such as were really fools. In allusion to this notion Mr Horace Walpole, who admired his writings, said he was 'an inspired idiot', and Garrick described him as one,

> for shortness call'd Noll,
> Who wrote like an angel, but talk'd like poor Poll.

Sir Joshua Reynolds mentioned to Boswell that he frequently had heard Goldsmith talk warmly of the pleasure of being liked, and observe how hard it would be if literary excellence should preclude a man from that satisfaction, which he perceived it often did, from the envy which attended it; and therefore Sir Joshua was convinced, that he was intentionally more absurd, in order to lessen himself in social intercourse, trusting that his character would be sufficiently supported by his works. If it was his intention to appear absurd in company, he was often very successful. This, in my own opinion, was really the case; and I also think Sir Joshua was so sensible of the advantage of it, that he, yet in a much less degree, followed the same idea, as he never had a wish to impress his company with any awe of the great abilities with which he was endowed, especially when in the society of those high in rank.

I have heard Sir Joshua say, that he has frequently seen the whole company struck with an awful silence at the entrance of Goldsmith, but that Goldsmith has quickly dispelled the charm, by his boyish and social manners, and he then has soon become the playthings and favourite of the company.

His epitaph in Westminster Abbey, written by Dr Johnson, is a true character of the eccentric poet.

Among the various tributes to his memory, was one by *Courtney Melmoth* (Mr Pratt, I believe,) dedicated to Sir Joshua, 'who will naturally receive with kindness whatever is designed as a testimony of justice to a friend that is no more.' In this, the dedicator has well attempted to portray the feelings of Sir Joshua's heart.

Before I dismiss poor Goldsmith from the stage, it may be proper to notice another dedication to Sir Joshua, prefixed to that edition of his works published by Evans, in which he says:

SIR,

I am happy in having your permission to inscribe to you this complete edition of the truly poetical works of your late ingenious friend, Oliver Goldsmith. They will prove a lasting monument of his genius. Every lover of science must deeply lament that this excellent writer, after long struggling with adversity, finished his mortal career just as his reputation was firmly established, and he had acquired the friendship of Sir Joshua Reynolds, Dr Johnson, Mr Edmund Burke, the Dean of Derry, Mr Beauclerk, and Mr Cumberland, names which adorn our age and nation. It is, Sir, being merely an *echo* of the *public* voice, to celebrate your admirable productions.

In which, to latest time, the artist lives.

Had Dr Goldsmith understood the art of painting, of which he modestly declares himself ignorant, his pen would have done justice to the merits of your pencil. He chose a nobler theme, by declaring his ardent affection for the *virtues of your heart*. That you may long continue, Sir, the ornament of your country and the delight of your friends, is the sincere wish of your most obliged humble servant,

T. EVANS

NOTE

James Northcote (1746–1831), painter and author.

Reynolds's Affection for Goldsmith*

CHARLES ROBERT LESLIE and TOM TAYLOR

Whatever Reynolds might think of the political economy of Goldsmith's exquisite Idyll – which the Doctor maintained to be his own honest deduction from observation – he deserved the honour of this dedication by his fellow-feeling for the subject, as well as his thorough appreciation of the poet. In every loving reminiscence of a humble country birthplace; in every touch descriptive of village character, sports, and enjoyments; in every trait of that unrivalled picture of the good pastor 'passing rich with forty pounds a year,' the painter's heart must have gone along with the poet's.

In none of the great men of the Club could Goldsmith have found a stronger, stancher, more enduring attachment to the scenes and associations of his youth than in Reynolds, who loved, he used to say, every stone in Plympton; who valued the mayoralty of his little native borough beyond all the distinctions that his own Sovereign, or that English or foreign universities and academies could bestow, and whose heart warmed to Northcote[1] for his broad Devonshire dialect. His own good father, Samuel Reynolds, might have sat for the original of Goldsmith's pastor:

> Remote from towns he ran his godly race,
> Nor e'er had changed, nor wish'd to change, his place:
> Unpractised he to fawn, or seek for power,
> By doctrines fashion'd to the varying hour;
> Far other aims his heart had learn'd to prize,
> More bent to raise the wretched than to rise;
> His house was known to all the vagrant train,
> He chid their wanderings, but relieved their pain.
> . . .

* In *The Life and Times of Sir Joshua Reynolds*, vol. 1 (London: John Murray, 1865) pp. 362–6. Editor's title.

Careless their merits or their faults to scan,
His pity gave ere charity began.
. . .
Even children follow'd with endearing wile,
And pluck'd his gown, to share the good man's smile.
His ready smile a parent's warmth express'd,
Their welfare pleas'd him, and their cares distress'd;
To them his heart, his love, his smiles were given,
But all his serious thoughts had rest in heaven.

Few points in the life of Reynolds are calculated to give his biographer more pleasure than the constant evidence he finds of the intimacy and mutual affection subsisting between the painter and Goldsmith. Reynolds, at all events, appreciated the beautiful, tender genius which worked below that crust of awkwardness, uncouthness, and childish vanity. He never started the laugh against poor Goldy's innocent pleasure in his fine clothes, or snubbed his sometimes ineffectual joke; never 'smoked,' or 'hummed,' or 'bit' him, as the slang of the time ran. He seems at this time to have dined oftener with Goldsmith than any one else. They were often seen together at Vauxhall and Ranelagh; the thickset little poet in butterfly brilliancy of colours, and the quiet painter in sober black or brown. Sir Joshua would leave the high play and high-life jokes and scandal of the wits and beaux at the Star and Garter to enjoy the shilling rubbers and the homely company at the Devil or the Globe in Goldsmith's society. Whenever the names of Reynolds and Goldsmith are coupled, it is for some act of kindness, some service, some word of appreciation, some deprecation of a sneer or a rebuke, on the part of Reynolds, for some expression or act of affectionate regard on the part of Goldsmith. The Doctor dedicates his poem to Sir Joshua in language speaking a sincerity of affection which dedications speak but seldom. The painter was now at work on the poet's portrait, ennobled by such an expression of dignity and tenderness as few but himself ever contrived to see in that oddly compounded but most touching face. The year after this he painted his *Resignation*: a subject suggested by the *Deserted Village*, and, when engraved, dedicated to the poet by the painter, with a quotation from the poem. Goldsmith was to have been Reynolds's companion this year in the visit to his native Devonshire which was the relaxation of the President's autumn. One has a pleasure in thinking how naturally such a project might have taken shape. While Goldsmith was sitting for the last touches to his portrait for this year's Exhibition,[2] the two might have been talking over the new poem, which had been for some time in print, and was now on the eve of publication, their kind, gentle hearts warming with the fire of early recollections, and glowing in the rosy memories of childhood and schoolboy days. 'You must come and see *my* native village, Doctor,' one can fancy Reynolds saying. 'Come with *me* this September; we will hunt and shoot, and be merry among my old friends. I will show you there, at Plympton:

> The shelter'd cot, the cultivated farm,
> The never-failing brook, the busy mill,
> The decent church that tops the neighbouring hill.

We will climb the castle-knoll together, where often:

> As I pass'd with careless steps and slow,
> The mingling notes came soften'd from below,
> The swain responsive as the milkmaid sung,
> The sober herd that low'd to meet their young,
> The noisy geese that gabbled o'er the pool,
> The playful children just let loose from school.

Unluckily, when the time came for this pleasant excursion, Goldsmith was in France with the Hornecks, and Sir Joshua had to go alone. But it is Reynolds whom Goldsmith chooses as his correspondent; to him he gossips and prattles artlessly and pleasantly, as one who knows he is safe in being natural, easy, and unaffected.

His pleasant gossiping letters of their adventures in France and Flanders will be found both in Prior's and in Forster's *Life* of the poet. They are certainly not such letters as Goldsmith would have addressed to a cold, ungenial man, such as many of his critics and some of his biographers would fain make out Sir Joshua to have been. Among all Goldy's longings to be back with his friends at 'the Club,' there is nothing more strongly expressed than his eagerness to enjoy once more Sir Joshua's kindly and social humour. The news of his mother's death reached Goldsmith in Paris on his way home.

NOTES

1. James Northcote. See his recollections of Goldsmith in this book.

2. Goldsmith was proud of the popularity which made his face a matter of public interest at this time, and shows this feeling, with his usual affectionate naïveté, in a letter to his brother Maurice (4 February 1770): 'I have sent my cousin Mary a miniature picture of myself, and I believe it is the most acceptable present I can offer. I have ordered it to be left for her at George Faukner's, folded in a letter. The face, you will know, is ugly enough, but it is finely painted. I will shortly, also, send my friends over the Shannon some mezzontinto prints of myself, and some more of my friends here, such as Burke, Johnson, Reynolds, and Colman.' This refers to Marchi's print from Sir Joshua's picture of the Doctor, then in progress.

Oliver Goldsmith*

JOHN WATKINS

In the memoirs of this extraordinary man, prefixed to his poetical works, he is said to have been born in 1729, at Elphin, in the county of Roscommon; but on the tablet erected to his memory in Westminster Abbey, by his most intimate friends, the date of his birth is 1731, and the place is stated to be Fernes, in the county of Longford. This difference is very remarkable, and it may be justly pronounced as an instance, on one side or the other, of a very culpable negligence in not making due enquiry concerning what doubtless might have been accurately determined.

The father of Goldsmith was a clergyman who gave him a good education, and sent him to the University of Dublin, where he was admitted a sizar, in 1744, which seems to give the preference to the first mentioned year, for the time of his birth. At Dublin he had for a fellow-student, Mr Edmund Burke.

Of Goldsmith's proficiency in academical learning we have no other account than that which he gave of himself to Mr Malone, 'that though he made no great figure in mathematics, which was a study much in repute there, he could turn an Ode of Horace better than any of them'.

---

* *Characteristic Anecdotes of Men of Learning and Genius* (London: James Cundee, 1808) pp. 513–28.

After attending a few lectures on anatomy, he went to Edinburgh, with the view of adopting physic as his profession. But though he continued there three years, his application to the peculiar studies of the place, was little, and his prudence less. By becoming surety for a fellow-student, he was involved in difficulties, and to avoid the consequences he made a precipitate retreat from Edinburgh. But his steps were traced, and he was taken at Sunderland. The kindness of Dr Sleigh, and another college friend, relieved him from this embarrassment, and, being once more at liberty, in a spirit of thoughtless extravagance, he took ship, and landed at Rotterdam: from thence he travelled through Flanders, and at Louvaine took the degree of bachelor of physic. After perambulating a great part of Europe, he landed at Dover, with a few pence in his pocket, and making his way to London, applied to several apothecaries for employment as a journeyman. His appearance and brogue were against him, and being reduced to the lowest state of distress, a chemist near Fish Street Hill, out of compassion, took him into his laboratory.

Soon after this, he learnt that his friend Sleigh was in London, and having discovered his abode, he waited upon him. 'It was Sunday,' said Goldsmith, 'when I paid him a visit; and it is to be supposed, in my best clothes. Sleigh scarcely knew me; such is the tax the unfortunate pay to poverty. However, when he did recollect me, I found his heart as warm as ever; and he shared his purse and his friendship with me during his continuance in London.'

By this means Goldsmith obtained the situation of usher in the school of Dr Milner, at Peckham. He did not long continue in that situation, which he never afterwards could bear to hear mentioned, without throwing himself into a passion, but removed to London, took lodgings in Green Arbour Court, and became a writer for the booksellers. It is said, indeed, that on the death of Dr Milner, in 1760, Goldsmith undertook the superintendance of the school for the widow, who allowed him twenty pounds a year, out of which he gave so liberally to objects in distress, that his salary was spent before it became due. This induced Mrs Milner to say to him, 'You had better, Mr Goldsmith, let me keep your money for you, as I do for some of the young gentlemen,' to which he replied, with great good humour, 'In truth, Madam, there is equal need.'

His continuance at Peckham must have been of short duration, for we find him engaged with Griffiths as a writer in the *Monthly Review*, also with Smollett in the *Critical Review*, besides other publications. The friendship of Smollett procured him the acquaintance of several other men of literary eminence, particularly Johnson. By his advice Goldsmith published the poem *The Traveller*, of which Johnson had a high opinion: and when a person in his company was saying, 'that it was a pretty poem,' he caught fire, and exclaimed, 'So, you only call it a pretty poem, do you? Let me tell you, Sir, it is the finest poem since Mr Pope's time.'

A little before this Johnson disposed of the novel of the *Vicar of Wakefield*, for Goldsmith, to Newbery, the bookseller, in a very remarkable manner.[1]

The bookseller, however, did not bring out the novel till Goldsmith's reputation was established by his poem of the *Traveller*. It was received with the applause to which it was entitled, and, in truth, it is impossible to praise this instructive and entertaining moral tale beyond its merits.

Goldsmith now took chambers in the Temple, and joined with a countryman of his, in a small house on the Edgware road, to which he gave the name of *Shoemaker's Paradise*, it having been built in a whimsical style by a person of that occupation.

At this latter place he composed a *History of England, in a series of Letters from a Nobleman to his Son*, in two volumes, duodecimo. This useful and pleasing little work, was very well received and passed for a long time as the performance of Lord Lyttelton. In 1768, Goldsmith brought out at Covent Garden, a comedy called, *The Good Natur'd Man*, which however, was not very successful, owing partly to the defects of the plot, and the perverted taste of the public, which was then extravagantly fond of sentimental pieces.

The poetical fame of Goldsmith attained its summit in 1770, by the publication, of that delightful piece, *The Deserted Village*.

The bookseller at once offered the author one hundred guineas for this poem, which he thought too much, and refused to take, saying it was five shillings a couplet, which was more than any modern poetry was worth.

But whatever may be the value of modern poetry in general, the public soon gave a convincing proof of the excellence of the *Deserted Village*. Several large impressions were sold; and the bookseller paid Goldsmith his full sum.

In 1772,[2] appeared his comedy, *She Stoops to Conquer*, which, for broad humour, stands among the first of that class of dramatic compositions.

Colman, the manager, however, had but indifferent hopes of its success, and even the performers gave the author but little encouragement. On the night of performance, Goldsmith, instead of attending the house early, walked the park in great agitation. There he was found by a friend who urged the necessity of his going to the theatre to see how the piece went on. Immediately on his entrance behind the scenes, the audience hissed that part where Mrs Hardcastle supposes herself fifty miles off. Goldsmith, in great alarm, exclaimed to Colman, 'What's that? What's that?' – 'Pshaw, doctor,' says the manager, 'don't be alarmed at a few *squibs*, when we have been sitting these two hours upon a *barrel of gunpowder.*'

The play, notwithstanding this, went off with great applause, and the author cleared by it eight hundred pounds.

But though it succeeded so well on the stage, it was attacked with great severity, in some of the public prints, particularly in one published by Evans the bookseller, and conducted by the noted Dr Kenrick. It happened at this time that Goldsmith, who was always vain of a very ordinary person, dressed beauishly to make himself agreeable to a lady of fortune, with whose brother he was intimate. The critic in censuring his play, did not overlook this circumstance, and in language which nothing could excuse, compared the author to the monkey in the fable who went to see the world. Goldsmith was highly exasperated at this attack, and with his usual want of consideration, hastened to Paternoster Row, where poor Evans happened to be in his shop, whom the doctor, in great wrath, immediately assailed with a volley of execrations, at the same time elevating his cane, which striking against the lamp, broke it all to pieces, the oil pouring down upon Goldsmith's clothes. Evans saved his pate by ducking behind the counter, but the irritated poet gave him two or three smart strokes upon the shoulders, and was still exercising this discipline, when Kenrick, the original cause of the mischief, came in; to him the doctor made his complaint, and Kenrick, to prevent farther mischief, persuaded him to go home with him in a hackney coach. An account of this affair getting into the newspapers, Goldsmith published an ingenious defence of his conduct in the *Daily Advertiser*; but Evans had recourse to the law, and the matter was determined in his favour by arbitration.

The extravagance of Goldsmith kept pace with his gains, and it affords matter of astonishment, that a man fond of company, the tavern, and the gaming-table, should have had so much industry, and fertility of composition. He had copious resources in his mind, and it was his reliance upon these which made him so indifferent to the patronage of the great, and regardless of the money he acquired by his literary labour.

Goldsmith used to say, that he once waited upon the Earl, afterwards Duke of Northumberland, by appointment, but that on being shewn into the antichamber, he met a gentleman very elegantly dressed, and mistaking him for his lordship, he paid him all the compliments which he had previously prepared, when, to his great astonishment, he found that this fine gentleman was the servant and not the master. At that instant, said Goldsmith, the duke came into the apartment, and I was so confounded on the occasion, that I wanted words to express the sense I entertained of the duke's politeness, and went away exceedingly chagrined at the blunder I had committed.

The story, however, is differently told by Sir John Hawkins, who, as having been present at Northumberland House at that time, is more entitled to belief.[3]

Goldsmith was a member of the literary club, established by Johnson and Reynolds, at the Turk's Head, in Gerard Street; and as Hawkins was also one of that association, he had abundant opportunities to be acquainted with his singularities.

Sir John says of him, 'that he had some wit, but no humour, and never told a story but he spoiled it.' . . .

Goldsmith, like many other poets, was a very bad reciter of verse, yet he had the vanity to think that his voice was harmonious, and his judgement correct. 'Several years ago,' says Mr Malone, 'I was in company with him and Dr Johnson; and after dinner, the conversation happening to turn on this subject, Goldsmith maintained that a poet was more likely to pronounce verse with accuracy and spirit than other men. He was immediately called upon to support his argument by an example; a request with which he readily complied; and he repeated the first stanza of the ballad, beginning with the words 'At Upton on the Hill', with such false emphasis, by marking the word *on* very strongly, that all the company agreed he had by no means established his position.'[4]

One great point in the doctor's pride, was to be liberal to his poor countrymen who applied to him in distress. The expression *pride* is not improper, because he did it with some degree of ostentation. One that was very artful never failed to apply to him as soon as he had published any new work, and while it was likely that the doctor would be in cash. Goldsmith, tired of his application, told him, that he should write himself; and ordered him to draw up a description of China, interspersed with political reflections, which a bookseller had applied to the doctor for, at a price he despised, but had not rejected. The idle carelessness of his temper may be collected from this, that he never gave himself the trouble to read the manuscript, but sent to the press, an account which made the Emperor of China a Mohammedan, and placed India between China and Japan. Two sheets were cancelled at the expense of Goldsmith, who kicked his newly created author downstairs.

Among his numerous pensioners, and he generally enlarged his list as he enlarged his finances, was the late unfortunate Jack Pilkington of scribbling memory, who had served the doctor so many tricks, that he despaired of getting any more money from him without coming out with a master-stroke once for all. He accordingly called on the doctor one morning, and running about the room in a fit of joy, told him his fortune was made. 'How so, Jack?' says the doctor, 'Why,' says Jack, 'the Duchess of Marlborough, you must know has long had a strange wish for a pair of white mice; now as I knew they were sometimes to be had in the East Indies, I commissioned a friend of mine who was going thither, to get them for me, and he is just arrived with two of the most beautiful little animals in the world.' After Jack had finished this account in raptures, he lengthened his visage by telling the doctor all was ruined, for without two guineas to buy a cage for the mice, he could not present them. The doctor unfortunately, as he said himself, had but half a guinea, which he offered to him; but Jack was not to be beat out of his scheme; he perceived the doctor's watch hanging up in his room, and hinted that if he could spare it for a week, he could raise a few guineas on it, which he would repay with gratitude. The doctor would not be the hindrance of a man's fortune for such a trifle: he accordingly gave him the watch, which the other immediately took to the pawnbroker, and Goldsmith heard no more of his friend Jack, till a message came to inform him, that he was on his death-bed, and requesting a guinea, which he readily sent to him.

Goldsmith, himself, had often suffered from a strangury, and this disorder at last increased upon him to such a degree as to produce considerable irritation of mind, and a nervous fever. Contrary to the counsel of his apothecary and physician, he took too large a dose of James's powder, which hastened his end [on] April 4th, 1774. His remains were interred in the Temple burial ground, and a monument was erected to his memory by the literary club, of which he was a member.

Johnson's opinion of Goldsmith was finely expressed in a conversation with Boswell. 'Goldsmith,' said the latter, 'has acquired more fame than all the officers last war, who were not generals.' – *Johnson:*

'Why, Sir, you will find ten thousand fit to do what they did, before you find one who does what Goldsmith has done. You must consider that a thing is valued according to its rarity. A pebble that paves the street is in itself more useful than the diamond upon a lady's finger.'

NOTES

1. See Johnson's version of this anecdote in this book.
2. *She Stoops to Conquer* was produced on 15 March 1773, not 1772.
3. See Sir John Hawkins's recollections of Goldsmith in this book.
4. *Life of Dryden*, p. 518. (Watkins's note).

Memoir of Goldsmith*

DAVID MASSON

And now, having, with one exception, completed our inventory of Goldsmith's writings, whether of the compilation kind or of the finer and more permanent kind, during the last years of his life, we are free for a look at the dear fellow himself, and his habits and circumstances socially, during all this exercise of his pen.

His headquarters were his chambers in No 2, Brick Court, Middle Temple. Not only had he furnished them expensively; but the breakfasts, dinners, and suppers which he frequently gave in them, whether to his friends of the Johnson and Reynolds set, or to the needier Hiffernans, Glovers, Kellys, and other literary Irishmen, of whom he had always a retinue attached to him, were extravagantly lavish. This, with his perpetual giving away of guineas to poor blackguards, or better fellows, who wanted them, and his general carelessness of money, kept him always poorer than, with his receipts, he need have been. His receipts during the last six years of his life may be calculated at between 3,000*l*. and 4,000*l*. in all, which was worth in those days about double what such a sum would be worth now; and yet he was always in debt. Something may have gone to his relations in

---

* In *The Miscellaneous Works of Oliver Goldsmith* (London: Macmillan, 1869) pp. xlvi–lx.

Ireland – to his much-loved brother Henry, before his death in May 1768; to his mother, who survived till 1770, and was blind in her old age; and then to his younger brother Maurice, to whom at any rate we find him resigning a small legacy that had been left him by Uncle Contarine. Some expense to Goldsmith was also caused by the arrival in London of his nephew Hodson, and his residence there for some time without means of his own. Goldsmith's famous accounts with his tailor, Filby, which ran high – one year as high as 70*l*., – were swelled by orders of clothes for this inconvenient young gentleman. But, on the whole, his general recklessness in his Brick Court Chambers, where he never kept a drawer locked, and let his man Dennis manage everything – this and his open-handedness to all about him in the London streets, account sufficiently for his expenditure. Often, however, he was out of London, taking his open-handedness with him to the fields, or along country roads, and into roadside inns or country houses. He was particularly fond of starting with one or two Irish friends, after breakfast in Brick Court, on a ramble to Islington, Kilburn, Hampstead, or some other suburb, returning late or not till next day. He and his friend Bott[1] rented together for some time in 1768, and again in 1769, a convenient cottage eight miles from London on the Edgeware Road; and in this 'Shoemaker's Paradise,' as Goldsmith called it in honour of the trade of its builder, he worked away for weeks together, in those years, at his *Roman History* and other things, running up to London when he liked. The neighbourhood was a favourite one with him, for he returned to it during portions of 1771 and 1772, for greater leisure to write his *Animated Nature* – not this time to the 'Shoemaker's Paradise,' or with Bott, but to a farmhouse, in Hyde Lane, near the six-mile stone on the same Edgeware Road. Here, occupying a single room, and boarding with the farmer's family, who became exceedingly fond of him, he wrote not only a good portion of his *Animated Nature*, but also, it is said, *She Stoops to Conquer*. Of course, in addition to these occasional retirements to the quiet of the Edgeware Road, there were longer journeys at intervals into various parts of England. He is traced into Hampshire, Sussex, Suffolk, Derbyshire, Leicestershire, Lincolnshire, and Yorkshire; and in 1771 he was, for a good while together, with his friend Lord Clare at Bath. Some of these country excursions appear to have been undertaken in the interests of his *Animated Nature*; at all events, in the course of the excursions, he now and then jotted down an observation for use in that compilation. More purely for pleasure was a visit of six weeks to France in the autumn of 1770 – his only visit to the Continent since his long and strange vagabond ramble in it fifteen years before. On this occasion he went as one of a family-party, with Mrs Horneck, a widow lady, whose acquaintance he had recently made through Sir Joshua Reynolds, and her two daughters, beautiful girls of twenty and eighteen respectively. The elder, for whom Goldsmith had invented the playful name of 'Little Comedy', was engaged to be married to a Mr Bunbury;[2] the younger, Mary Horneck, or 'The Jessamy Bride', as Goldsmith called her, was unengaged, and — ! Well, who knows? Of no feminine creature, at all events, save this 'Jessamy Bride', do we hear, in all Goldsmith's life, so near to him, and in such circumstances, that the world can fancy he was in love with her and can wish that they had wedded. 'The Jessamy Bride!' what a suggestion of the jasmine-flower, of gracefulness and white muslin, in the very sound of her name! Poor, plain, mean-looking Goldy! – two-and-forty years of age, too! – did he only look and sigh, and know it to be hopeless? Everything was against him even in this journey. For example, there was that wretched Hickey, the attorney, who joined the party in Paris, and would make a butt of Goldy even in the presence of the ladies, and came back with the story how, maintaining a certain distance from one of the fountains at Versailles to be within reach of a leap, he made a jump to prove his assertion and his muscular power to the Jessamy, and tumbled into the water. Who could marry a man like that? One comfort is that she did not marry Mr Hickey. When she was engaged, which was not till a year after Goldsmith's death, it was to a Colonel Gwyn, whose wife she became about three years after that. She was alive as late as 1840, having survived Goldsmith sixty-six years. She talked of him fondly to the last.

The reader may remember a certain Kenrick, who succeeded Goldsmith as Griffiths's hack on the *Monthly Review* in 1757, and who had ever since been, for some reason, his deadly enemy. In March 1773, when Goldsmith had reached the very height of his living reputation, and *She Stoops to Conquer* was winning the plaudits of the town, this envious brute, who was editing the *London Packet* newspaper, inserted in its columns an anonymous letter of abuse against Goldsmith and all that he had done. Not content with condemning all Goldsmith's writings and especially his last comedy, as worthless, flimsy, and what not, he ventured on such elegancies as this:

Your poetic vanity is as unpardonable as your personal: would
man believe it, and will woman bear it, to be told that for hours
the *great* Goldsmith will stand surveying his grotesque orang-
outang figure in a pier-glass? Was but the lovely H—k as much
enamoured, you would not sigh, my gentle swain, in vain!

When Goldsmith read this, his blood was properly up; and, accompanied by Captain Horneck of the Guards, the brother of the lady
whose name had been dragged in, he was off to the bookseller
Evans's in Paternoster Row, where the newspaper was published.
What passed was described to Mr Prior, when he was writing his *Life
of Goldsmith*, by Mr Harris, the publisher of St Paul's Churchyard,
who had been in Evans's employment at the time in question, and
was a witness to the scene.

> 'I have called,' said Goldsmith to Evans, 'in consequence of a
> scurrilous attack in your paper upon me (my name is Goldsmith),
> and an unwarrantable liberty taken with the name of a young
> lady. As for myself I care little, but her name must not be sported
> with.'

Evans, professing that he knew nothing of the matter, stooped down
as if to look for the offensive article in a file of the newspaper, when
Goldsmith, unable to resist the sight of the big Welsh back so tempt-
ingly exposed, came down upon it with a whack of his cane. Instantly it was big Welshman against little Irishman; a lamp which
hung overhead was broken in the scuffle, and they were both
drenched with the oil; one of the shopmen ran for a constable, and
the sneak Kenrick himself, coming out from his editor's room, helped
Captain Horneck to separate the combatants, and send Goldsmith
home in a coach. For a week the town was merry over the affray,
chiefly at Goldy's expense; who had, moreover, to pay 50*l.* to a
Welsh charity, to avoid an action by Evans. One's wish now is that
time could be rolled back to the moment of the scuffle, so that the
lamp-oil that was spilt might have been poured down Kenrick's
throat.

There is an abundance of stories of Goldsmith in his last years, his
ways in society, and his table-talk. They are all to the same effect –
what a sensitive, guileless, tender-hearted, and really high-minded,
creature he was, so that everybody that knew him liked him; and yet
how absurd, blundering, alternately consequential and bashful, so

that everybody took liberties with him, and it was only when people remembered what a writer he was, or now and then when his wits did clear in the course of talk, and he flashed out a brilliancy as keen as any in his books, that he was looked at with adequate respect. 'Dr Goldsmith,' said some one, 'is this sort of man: when he comes into a room, if you have not seen him before, you look at him with reverence because of his writings; but, before he leaves the room, you may be riding on his back.' Again, when the poet Rogers asked Conversation Cooke, as he was called, who had known Goldsmith well and been much with him, what he really was in talk, this was the answer he received, 'Sir, he was a fool. The right word never came to him. If you gave him back a bad shilling, he'd say, "Why, it is as good a shilling as ever was *born.*" You know he ought to have said *coined. Coined,* Sir, never entered his head. He was a fool, Sir.' Or take Boswell's report of one of his conversations with Johnson. 'Of our friend Goldsmith he said, "Sir, he is so much afraid of being unnoticed that he often talks merely lest you should forget that he is in the company."

BOSWELL.   Yes, he stands forward.

JOHNSON.   True, Sir; but, if a man is to stand forward, he should wish to do it not in an awkward posture, not in rags, not so that he shall only be exposed to ridicule.

BOSWELL.   For my part, I like very well to hear honest Goldsmith talk away carelessly.

JOHNSON.   Why, yes, Sir; but he should not like to hear himself.'

To the same purpose is another conversation of Goldsmith's friends about him, recorded by Boswell. 'Goldsmith being mentioned:

JOHNSON.   It is amazing how little Goldsmith knows. He seldom comes where he is not more ignorant than any one else.

SIR JOSHUA REYNOLDS.   Yet there is no man whose company is more liked.

JOHNSON.   To be sure, Sir. When people find a man of the most distinguished abilities as a writer their inferior while he is with them, it must be highly gratifying to them. What Goldsmith comically says of himself is very true – he always gets the better when he argues alone; meaning that he is master of a subject in his study, but, when he comes into company, grows confused, and unable to talk.

Among the best stories of Goldsmith are certainly those preserved by Boswell. The young Scotchman, it is to be understood,
whom Johnson had seen off at Harwich on his way to Utrecht, had
returned from abroad in February 1766, with his head full of a new
enthusiasm for Corsica and Paoli. He at once renewed his intimacy
with Dr Johnson, whom he found now residing in Johnson's Court,
Fleet Street; and, as during his absence Goldsmith had published his
Traveller and other things, he no longer wondered at finding Johnson
and Goldsmith so much together. The three again supped at the
Mitre, and met once or twice at Johnson's, before Boswell's return to
Edinburgh to begin the practice of law. But in 1768 Boswell was
again in London for a considerable time; again in 1769; again in 1772,
having in the meantime married; and again in 1773, when he had the
honour of being elected a member of the Gerrard Street Club, already reinforced since its commencement by some other new members, among whom were Percy, Chambers, Colman, and Garrick. In
Boswell's pages, accordingly, and chiefly in the form of his own
recollections of those visits to London, we have a pretty continuous
history, from 1768 to 1774, of that Johnsonian world which so fasci-
nated him. It was the time, in general politics, of the continued fame
of Wilkes and Liberty – the time of Chatham's obscuration, of the
Grafton and other unpopular ministries, of the Letters of Junius, and
of those discontents in the American colonies which led to the War
of American Independence. Nor, amid these public events, were
matters stationary in private with the members of the Johnsonian
group. Burke's political career as a Rockingham Whig had begun in
1766, and his voice was now powerful in the House of Commons.
Johnson had added his edition of Shakespeare to his many previous
publications, had had his famous interview with young George III in
the royal library, had begun his intimacy with the Thrales, and had
entered on his sixties. The Royal Academy having been founded in
1768, Reynolds had become its first President and received his knight-
hood. What Goldsmith had been doing has been already told – save
that we have yet to advert to an honour that came to him, in association with Johnson, in consequence of this last-mentioned fact of the
foundation of the Royal Academy. 'Dr Johnson,' says the *Public
Advertiser* of December 22, 1769, 'is appointed Professor of Ancient
Literature, and Dr Goldsmith Professor of History, to the Royal
Academy. These titles are merely honorary, no salary being annexed
to them.' It was Reynolds who had arranged these distinctions for
his friends in connexion with the new institution. About the same

time he painted his well-known portrait of Goldsmith, engravings from which were to be seen in 1770 in the windows of all the print-shops. Its only fault is that it represents Goldsmith without a wig, whereas he invariably wore one. Reynolds, doubtless, foresaw that posterity would like to know the real shape of the head.

And now, with these preliminaries, let Boswell tell some of his stories of Goldsmith's ridiculous ways:

Goldy's Envy of Johnson on account of his Interview with the King:

During all the time in which Dr Johnson was employed in relating to the circle at Sir Joshua Reynolds's the particulars of what passed between the King and him, Dr Goldsmith remained unmoved upon a sofa at some distance, affecting not to join in the least in the eager curiosity of the company. He assigned as a reason for his gloom and seeming inattention that he apprehended Johnson had relinquished his purpose of furnishing him with a Prologue to his play, with the hopes of which he had been flattered; but it was strongly suspected that he was fretting with chagrin and envy at the singular honour Dr Johnson had lately enjoyed. At length, the frankness and simplicity of his natural character prevailed. He sprung from the sofa, advanced to Johnson, and, in a kind of flutter, from imagining himself in the situation which he had just been hearing described, exclaimed, 'Well, you acquitted yourself in this conversation better than I should have done; for I should have bowed and stammered through the whole of it.'

Goldy's Bloom-Coloured Coat:

He [Dr Johnson] honoured me with his company at dinner on the 16th of October (1769) at my lodgings in Old Bond Street, with Sir Joshua Reynolds, Mr Garrick, Dr Goldsmith, Mr Murphy, Mr Bickerstaff, and Mr Thomas Davies. . . . One of the company not being come at the appointed hour, I proposed, as usual on such occasions, to order dinner to be served; adding, 'Ought six people to be kept waiting for one?' 'Why, yes,' answered Johnson, with a delicate humanity, 'if the one will suffer more by your sitting down than the six will do by waiting,' Goldsmith, to divert the tedious minutes, strutted about, bragging of his dress, and I believe was seriously vain of it, for his mind was wonderfully prone to such impressions. 'Come, come,' said Garrick, 'talk no more of that. You are perhaps the worst – eh, eh!' Goldsmith was eagerly attempting to interrupt him, when Garrick went on, laughing ironically, 'Nay, you will always *look* like a gentleman; but I am talking of being well or ill *drest*.' 'Well, let me tell you,' said Goldsmith, 'when my tailor brought home my bloom-coloured coat, he said, "Sir, I have a favour to beg of you. When anybody asks you who made your clothes, be pleased to mention John Filby, at the Harrow, in Water Lane."' JOHNSON: 'Why, Sir, that was because he knew the strange colour would attract crowds to gaze at it, and thus they might hear of him, and see how well he could make a coat even of so absurd a colour.'

Goldy's Facts in Natural History:

On Thursday, April 29 [1773], I dined with him [Johnson] at General Oglethorpe's, where were Sir Joshua Reynolds, Mr. Langton, Dr. Goldsmith, and Mr. Thrale. . . .

GOLDSMITH.   There is a general abhorrence in animals at the signs of massacre. If you put a tub full of blood into a gable, the horses are like to go mad.

JOHNSON.   I doubt that.

GOLDSMITH.   Nay, it is a fact well authenticated.

THRALE.   You had better prove it before you put it into your book on Natural History. You may do it in my stable if you will.

JOHNSON.   Nay, Sir, I would not have him prove it. If he is content to take his information from others, he may get through his book with little trouble, and without much endangering his reputation. But, if he makes experiments for so comprehensive a book as his, there would be no end to them; his erroneous assertions would then fall upon himself.

Goldy trying to shine, and resenting familiarity:

Goldsmith's incessant desire of being conspicuous in company was the occasion of his sometimes appearing to such disadvantage as one should hardly have supposed possible in a man of his genius . . . [Once] when [he was] talking in a company with fluent vivacity, and, as he flattered himself, to the admiration of all who were present, a German who sat next him, and perceived Johnson rolling himself, as if about to speak, suddenly stopped him, saying, 'Stay, stay – Toctor Shonson is going to say something.' This was, no doubt, very provoking, especially to one so irritable as Goldsmith, who frequently mentioned it with strong expressions of indignation. It may also be observed that Goldsmith was sometimes content to be treated with an easy familiarity, but upon occasions would be consequential and important. An instance of this occurred in a small particular. Johnson had a way of contracting the names of his friends: as Beauclerk, Beau; Boswell, Bozzy; Langton, Lanky; Murphy, Mur; Sheridan, Sherry. I remember, one day when Tom Davies was telling that Dr Johnson said, 'We are all in labour for a name to *Goldy's* play,' Goldsmith seemed much displeased that such a liberty should be taken with his name: 'I have often desired him not to call me *Goldy*.'

The foregoing are from Boswell's *Life of Johnson*, where there is more of the same sort; but other stories, as good, have come down by other channels of tradition. One or two of these may be added to the string:

Gibbon making game of Goldy

While Goldsmith was busy with his 'Grecian History,' Gibbon is said to have called upon him at his chambers in Brick Court. 'You are the very person I wanted to see,' said Goldsmith, 'for I can't remember the name of that Indian king who gave Alexander the Great so much trouble.' 'Montezuma,' said Gibbon mischievously; till, perceiving that Goldsmith took the information in good faith, and was making a note of it, he thought the jest might go too far, and added, 'No, I mistake: it was not Montezuma; it was Porus.'

Burke making game of Goldy

Burke and his friend Mr (afterwards Colonel) O'Moore, were walking together to Sir Joshua Reynolds's to dine, when they saw Goldsmith, who was also going there, standing near a crowd that had gathered to stare and shout at some foreign women who were looking out from the windows of a house in Leicester Square. 'Observe Goldsmith,' said Burke to his companion, 'and mark what passes between him and me at Sir Joshua's.' They arrived at Sir Joshua's before Goldsmith; and, when he appeared, Burke received him with a grave face, as if seriously offended. When Goldsmith had pressed some time for an explanation, Burke, with seeming reluctance, said it was really too much to expect that one could continue to be intimate with him after the indiscreet way in which he had been behaving in the square. With great earnestness Goldsmith professed his ignorance of having done anything wrong,and asked what it was. 'Why,' said Burke, 'did you not exclaim, as you were looking up at those women, what stupid beasts the people must be for staring with such admiration at those painted Jezebels while a man of your talents passed by unnoticed!' 'Surely I did not say that,' said the astonished Goldsmith. 'Nay, if you had not said so,' replied Burke, 'how should I have known it?' 'That's true,' said Goldsmith humbly; 'I am very sorry – it was very foolish. I do recollect that something of the kind passed through my mind, but I did not think I had uttered it.'

Goldy and the Pig-Butcher

At the humble Wednesday's Club at the Globe in Fleet Street, according to Mr Forster, no less than at the Gerrard Street Club and the parties at Sir Joshua's, Goldsmith was the subject of practical jokes. Mr Forster tells some of these and adds this story: A frequent attendant at the Club was 'a certain Mr B., described as a good sort of man and an eminent pig-butcher, who piqued himself very much on his good fellowship with the author of the *Traveller*, and whose constant manner of drinking to him was, "Come, Noll, here's my service to you, old boy!" Repeating this one night after the comedy (*the Good-natur'd Man*) was played, and when there was a very full club, Glover went over to Goldsmith, and said in a whisper that he ought not to allow such liberties. "Let him alone," answered Goldsmith, "and you'll see how civilly I'll let him down." He waited a little; and, on the next pause in the conversation, called out aloud, with a marked expression of politeness and courtesy, "Mr. B., I have the honour of drinking your good health." "Thankee, thankee, Noll," returned Mr. B., pulling the pipe out of his mouth, and answering with great briskness."'

Enough in this vein! Quite as numerous are the anecdotes of Goldsmith's extreme tenderness of nerve, his generosity, his quick sympathy with all kinds of distress. Once, at a whist-table, we are told, hearing a woman sing in the streets, and struck by something peculiarly mournful in the tones of her voice, he could not rest till he had run out, given her some silver, and sent her away. In his own poverty he was ready with help and kind words not only for the Purdons, Hiffernans and other poor Grub Street hacks, personally known to him, but also for any unknown young fellow he might casually encounter walking about the Temple Gardens and looking aimless and woebegone. Remembering this, one cannot help wondering sometimes what might have happened or been prevented, if the boy Chatterton, during his fatal three months in London (May–August 1770) had chanced upon Goldsmith in his weary ramblings. One cannot but imagine, at all events, a certain sad significance in the fact that the hour of the last agony of that marvellous young life, the hunger-and-arsenic agony in the dreadful garret in Brooke Street, Holborn, coincided with the time of Goldsmith's absence from London on his Paris journey. As it was, he was one of the first, on his return, to hear of Chatterton's fate, and to talk of him and the Rowley Poems. But what more is needed to attest the essential goodness of Goldsmith's heart, his singular unselfishness and placability than the story which Boswell tells of his momentary quarrel with Johnson?

I dined with him (Johnson) this day (May 7, 1773), at the house of my friends, Messrs Edward and Charles Dilly, booksellers, in the Poultry: there were present – their elder brother, Mr Dilly of Bedfordshire; Dr Goldsmith; Mr Langton; the Rev. Dr Mayo, a Dissenting minister; the Rev. Mr Toplady; and my friend, the Rev. Mr Temple. There was much talk; they came at last on the subject of toleration; and Johnson, whom the presence of a Dissenting minister made unusually loud and pugnacious, was hammering away on this subject, without much success against Dr Mayo's calm stolidity in the common opinion. During this argument, Goldsmith sat in restless agitation, from a wish to get in and *shine*.

Finding himself excluded, he had taken his hat to go away, but remained for some time with it in his hand, like a gamester, who, at the close of a long night, lingers for a little while, to see if he can have a favourable opening to finish with success. Once when he was beginning to speak, he found himself overpowered by the loud voice of Johnson, who was at the opposite end of the table and did not perceive Goldsmith's attempt. Thus disappointed of his wish to obtain the attention of the company, Goldsmith in a passion threw down his hat, looking angrily at Johnson, and exclaimed in a bitter tone, 'Take it.' When Toplady was going to speak, Johnson uttered some sound, which led Goldsmith to think that he was beginning again, and taking the words from Toplady. Upon which he seized this opportunity of venting his own envy and spleen, under the pretext of supporting another person: 'Sir,' said he to Johnson, 'this gentleman has heard you patiently for an hour; pray allow us now to hear *him*.' JOHNSON (sternly) 'Sir, I was not interrupting the gentleman; I was only giving him a signal of my attention. Sir, you are impertinent.' Goldsmith made no reply, but continued in the company for some time. After he had gone, the rest talked a while longer; but at last, it being the club night, the company broke up. He (Johnson), and Mr Langton, and I, went together to the club, where we found Mr Burke, Mr Garrick, and some other members, and amongst them our friend Goldsmith, who sat silently brooding over Johnson's reprimand to him after dinner. Johnson perceived this, and said aside to some of us, 'I'll make Goldsmith forgive me;' and then called to him in a loud voice, 'Dr Goldsmith, something passed to-day where you and I dined; I ask your pardon.' Goldsmith answered placidly, "It must be much from you, Sir, that I take ill." And so at once the difference was over, and they were on as easy terms as ever, and Goldsmith rattled away as usual.'

Goldsmith, as Boswell had to admit, did not always drivel in conversation. Forked lightnings now and then came out of the fog, and he said excellent and memorable things. We have already quoted his definition of Boswell's main faculty, and Boswell has himself honestly recorded two or three sallies of Goldsmith at his expense:

One evening, in a circle of wits, he found fault with me for talking of Johnson as entitled to the honour of unquestionable superiority. 'Sir,' said he, 'you are for making a monarchy of what should be a republic.'

Again, in 1773, when Boswell had booked Johnson for his three months' tour that autumn in Scotland and the Hebrides, and it was more than flesh and blood could stand to hear him exulting in the prospect and talking of the matchlessness of his great man. 'Is he like Burke, who winds into a subject like a serpent?' said Goldsmith angrily. Even Johnson himself was occasionally outwitted by Goldy, and took it good-humouredly.

JOHNSON. I remember once being with Goldsmith in Westminster Abbey. While we surveyed the Poets' Corner, I said to him:

> *'Forsitan et nostrum nomen miscebitur istia.'*

When we got to Temple Bar, he stopped me, pointed to the heads upon it, and slyly whispered me,

> *'Forsitan et nostrum nomen miscebitur istia.'*

Again, when Goldsmith, in talk with Johnson and Reynolds, spoke of the difficulty of fable-writing, and gave as an instance 'the fable of the little fishes who saw birds fly over their heads, and envying them, petitioned Jupiter to be changed into birds'. While he was dilating on this and pointed out very earnestly that the skill consisted in 'making them talk like little fishes,' Johnson's laughter roused him. 'Why, Dr Johnson,' he proceeded smartly, 'this is not so easy as you seem to think; for, if *you* were to make little fishes talk, they would talk like *whales.*' Again, these two often-quoted sayings about Johnson are Goldsmith's: 'There is no arguing with Johnson; for, when his pistol misses fire, he knocks you down with the butt-end of it;' and, 'Johnson, to be sure, has a roughness of manner, but no man has a better heart: he has nothing of the bear but his skin.' Finally, take the story of the *tête-à-tête* supper of Johnson and Goldy off rumps and kidneys at Jack's Coffee House in Dean Street:

> 'Sir,' said Johnson, 'these rumps are pretty little things, but then a man must eat a great many of them before he is satisfied.' 'Ay, but how many of these would reach to the moon?' said Goldsmith.

'To the moon!' echoes Johnson; 'that, sir, I fear, exceeds your calculation.' 'Not at all,' said Goldy firmly; 'I think I could tell.' 'Pray then let us hear?' 'Why,' said Goldy slowly – and Mr Forster must be right in supposing that here he edged off as far as possible from Johnson – 'one, if it were long enough.' 'Sir, I have deserved it,' gasped Johnson at last.

Poor Goldsmith's successes in this way, however, bore no proportion to his failures. 'I have been but once at the club since you left England,' wrote Beauclerk to Lord Charlemont, another member of the club, on the 5th of July, 1773; 'and we were entertained as usual by Dr Goldsmith's absurdities.' This had become the common way of talking of him. More especially since Garrick, with his love of mimicry and mischief, had become a member of the club, it had become the fashion there to laugh at Goldy and all he said and did. But the fashion extended beyond the club; and, whenever Goldy's friends met together, and Garrick chanced to be among them, Goldy's 'absurdities' were sure to be the theme. One such place was St James's Coffee House in St James's Street, where for some time a company of persons, partly belonging to the club and partly not, had been in the habit of dining together periodically. Here, one day in February 1774, when Goldy was absent, it was proposed to write jocular epitaphs upon him. Several such were written, and among them this by Garrick:

> Here lies Poet Goldsmith, for shortness called Noll,
> Who wrote like an angel, but talked like poor Poll.

But it was not very safe to challenge Goldsmith at this kind of sport, as Garrick and others found to their cost when, in the course of the next month, fragments of Goldsmith's little poem called *Retaliation* began to be whispered about. Who does not know this exquisite masterpiece of satire, or rather of humorous character-painting? For there is not a touch of malice or mere caricature in it, but only the keenest and kindliest observation, and the quintessence of happy expression? How all the friends that had been laughing at him are paid off, one by one, with what is at once most gracious compliment and most delicate banter, so that they must have both liked it and not liked it, and must have known that the tables were turned upon the whole pack of them, by this one retort of Goldy, for all time to come! Especially what three portraits in miniature are those of Burke,

Garrick, and Reynolds! Burke lived five-and-twenty years longer, and was to be and do during those five-and-twenty years a great deal more than he had yet been or done; but it is Goldsmith's character of him that we always quote when we want epigram or epitome. In vain Garrick tried, by subsequent verses, not in the best taste, to out-epitaph Goldy after he was dead; his clever 'Poor Poll' couplet does last, but Goldy's thirty-two lines on Garrick in his *Retaliation* last also, and are a settlement for ever of the account between them. And what portrait of any one has come to us from the pencil of Reynolds more graphic than the unfinished pen-and-ink sketch of Reynolds himself with which *Retaliation* ends?

> To coxcombs averse, yet most civilly steering,
> When they judged without skill, he was still hard of hearing;
> When they talked of their Raphaels, Correggios, and stuff,
> He shifted his trumpet, and only took snuff.
> By flattery unspoilt . . .

So, with this loving tribute to Sir Joshua, the poem breaks off. He had more to say in honour of the great painter who had been so truly his friend. Did he contemplate the addition of a portrait of Johnson? Most probably not. 'It must be much from you, Sir, that I take ill,' the gentle creature had said to the terrible Samuel on receiving his apology for a gross insult; and, notwithstanding his tetchy observation about Johnson to Boswell, 'Is he like Burke, who winds into a subject like a serpent?' it is clear that there was no human being for whom Goldsmith felt so profound and absolute a regard.

They were not to be troubled, any of them, with poor Goldy much longer. His *Animated Nature* and his *Grecian History*, though not published, were off his hands; and except that *Retaliation* may have been lying on his desk to have a few lines added to it now and then when he was in the humour, we hear of nothing particular that was occupying him in the months of February and March 1774. He had come to the end of some years of labour in compiling; and now, if ever, was the time for carrying into effect the resolution, to which he had been persuading himself, of retiring permanently into some quiet part of the country and coming to London only for two months every year. But, in fact, either to go or stay would have been difficult for him. All his resources were gone; his feet, as he walked in the streets, were in a meshwork of debt, to the extent of about 2,000*l.*; and all that he could look forward to, with any promise of relief in it, was the chance of a new stretch of some ten thousand acres of additional ditch-work and compilation, for some bookseller who would not mind prepaying for the labour in part. He did talk of something of the kind to the publisher Nourse, into whose hands the property of the *Animated Nature* had passed, and who had it now at press. What would Mr Nourse say to taking shares with Griffin in a large sequel to the *Animated Nature*, in the form of a work on the *'vegetable* and *fossil* kingdoms?' Mr Nourse does not appear to have had time to consider this proposal when, as far as Goldsmith was concerned, it became unnecessary for him to think more about it. Goldy had gone in March, for a week or two, to his retreat at Hyde on the Edgeware Road, when an attack of a local complaint to which he had for sometime been subject brought him back to his chambers in the Temple. The immediate illness passed off, but a kind of nervous fever followed; and at eleven o'clock at night on the 25th of March, Mr Hawes,[3] an apothecary and a friend of Goldsmith's, was sent for. He found Goldsmith very ill, and bent on doctoring himself with 'James's fever-powders,' a patent medicine the property in which had belonged to Newbery the publisher, and in which Goldsmith had great faith. In spite of all that Mr Hawes could say, he would take one of these powders; after which he became worse and worse. Dr Fordyce, who had been just elected a member of the Gerrard Street Club, and Dr Turton, another physician of celebrity, were called in to assist Mr Hawes, but without avail. 'Your pulse,' said Dr Turton to his patient, 'is in greater disorder than it should be from the state of your fever: is your mind at ease?' 'It is *not*,' said Goldsmith. And so, with varying symptoms, he lay on in his chambers in Brick Court till Monday, the 4th of April, 1774, on which day it was known through town that Goldsmith was dead. He died at half-past four that morning in strong convulsions. When Burke was told the news, he burst into tears. When Reynolds was told it, he left his painting-room, where he then was, and did no more work that day. How Johnson was affected at the moment we can only guess; but three months afterwards he wrote as follows to Bennet Langton, in Lincolnshire:

> Chambers, you find, is gone far, and poor Goldsmith is gone much farther. He died of a fever, exasperated, as I believe, by the fear of distress. He raised money and squandered it by every artifice of acquisition and folly of expense. But let not his frailties be remembered; he was a very great man.

When Goldsmith died he was forty-five years and five months old. His body was buried, on the 9th of April, in the burying-ground of the Temple Church. The monument to him in Westminster Abbey, with the Latin inscription by Johnson, was erected in 1776.

About Goldsmith personally we can add but few particulars to those already given. As is implied by the very name 'Goldy,' so persistently attached to him in spite of his remonstrances, he was a little man – not above five feet five inches high, it is said, though stout and thick about the chest and limbs. To have seen him walking down Fleet Street, with the gigantic Johnson by his side, must have been a sight indeed. His pale and pitted face taken along with his figure, people thought him one of the plainest little bodies that ever entered a room; they even called his appearance 'mean'. Looking at his portrait now, and knowing what he was, we do not find this, but only a certain oddness, caused by the outbulging forehead, the lax mouth and chin, and in general the pouting, sulky, 'You don't sufficiently respect me' expression. Though sociable and convivial, and lavishly expensive in his style of entertaining others, he seems himself to have had simple enough tastes in eating and drinking; he never had a habit of excess in wine, and he was fond of a bowl of milk to the last. One of his peculiarities – he himself notes it as a peculiarity in one who professed to write on Natural History – was a strong antipathy to mice, eels, and most little animals of the crawling kind, such as worms and caterpillars. Of all the rest of that strange mixture, or jumble, of qualities that went to make Goldy, a sufficient account has already been given; and, if one were bent on summing it all up in some one general idea or impression, to be easily remembered, it must be that impression or idea in which his contemporaries concurred unanimously through every period of his life, and which has been transmitted to us in so many forms, *viz.* that he was one of the best-hearted creatures ever born, but a positive idiot except when he had the pen in his hand.

Except when he had the pen in his hand! Ay! there has been his power with the world! And what shall one say now of Goldsmith's writings? Take four brief remarks:

(1) Not to be forgotten is that division of them, already dwelt on, into two distinct orders – *compilations* and *original pieces*. As the division was a vital one to Goldsmith himself – for his literary life

consisted, as we have said, of a succession of glitterings of spontaneous genius amid dull habitual drudgery at hackwork – so it is of consequence in our retrospect of him. Probably much that Goldsmith did in the way of anonymous compilation lies buried irrecoverably in the old periodicals for which he wrote, and which are now little better than lumber on the shelves of our great libraries. But his compilations of English, Roman, and Grecian History, and his *Animated Nature*, once so popular, are still known, and are to be distinguished from that class of his writings of which the present volume is a collection. Even in the present volume there are some small things that must be regarded as mere compilations, and may serve as minor specimens of Goldsmith in that line – the wretched shred called a *Life of Bolingbroke*, for example, and the better, but still poor, *Life of Parnell*, if not indeed also the *Memoir of Voltaire*, and the *Life of Beau Nash*. Deduct these, and in the *Inquiry into the State of Polite Learning*, the *Essays*, the *Bee*, the *Citizen of the World*, the *Vicar of Wakefield*, and the *Poems and Plays*, you have, in various forms, the pure and real Goldsmith.

(2) In all that he wrote, his compilations included, there was the charm of his easy, perspicuous style. This was one of Goldsmith's natural gifts; with his humour, his tenderness, and his graceful delicacy of thought, he had it from the first. No writer in the language has ever surpassed him, or even equalled him, in that witching simplicity, that gentle ease of movement, sometimes careless and slip-shod, but always in perfect good taste, and often delighting with the subtlest turns and felicities, which critics have admired for a hundred years in the diction of Goldsmith. It is this merit that still gives to his compilations what interest they have, though it was but in a moderate degree that he could exhibit it there. '*Nullum fere scribendi genus non tetigit; nullum quod tetigit non ornavit*' ('There was no kind of writing almost that he did not touch; none that he touched that he did not adorn,') said Johnson of him in his epitaph in Westminster Abbey; and the remark includes his compilations, In *matter*, his *History of England*, for example, has become quite worthless; and if you want a good laugh over Goldy's notion of what sort of thing a battle might be, open the book at his descriptions of the battles of Cressy and Agincourt. What 'letting fly' at the enemy! and how it is the Black Prince in the one case, and Henry V. in the other, that settles everything with his own hand, and tumbles them over in droves! But read on, and you will see how the style could reconcile people to the meagreness of the matter, and keep the compilation so

long popular. And so with his *Animated Nature*. Johnson prophesied that he would make the work as pleasant as a Persian tale; and the prophecy was fulfilled. The 'style' of Goldsmith – which includes, of course, the habitual rule of sequence in his ideas, his sense of fitness and harmony, the liveliness of his fancy from moment to moment, and his general mental tact – this is a study in itself.

(3) In his original writings, where the charm of his style is most felt, there is, with all their variety of form, a certain sameness of general effect. The field of incidents, characters, sentiments, and imagined situations, within which the author moves, is a limited one, though there is great deftness of recombination within that horizon. We do not mean merely that Goldsmith, as an eighteenth-century writer, did not go beyond the intellectual and poetic range to which his century had restricted itself. This is true; and though we discern in Goldsmith's writings a fine vein of peculiarity, or even uniqueness, for the generation to which they belonged, there is yet abundant proof that his critical tenets did not essentially transcend those of his generation. Even more for him than for some of his contemporaries, Pope was the limit of classic English literature, and the older grandeurs of Shakespeare and Milton were rugged, barbaric mountain-masses, well at a distance. But, over and above this limitation of Goldsmith's range by essential sympathy with the tastes of his time, there was a something in his own method and choice of subjects causing a farther and inner circumscription of his bounds. All Goldsmith's phantasies, whether in verse or prose – his *Vicar of Wakefield*, his *Traveller*, his *Deserted Village*, his *Good-Natur'd Man* and *She Stoops to Conquer*, and even the humorous sketches that occur in his *Essays* and *Citizen of the World* – are phantasies of what may be called *reminiscence*. Less than even Smollett, did Goldsmith *invent*, if by invention we mean a projection of the imagination into vacant space, and a filling of portion after portion of that space, as by sheer bold dreaming, with scenery, events, and beings, never known before. He drew on the recollections of his own life, on the history of his own family, on the characters of his relatives, on whimsical incidents that had happened to him in his Irish youth or during his continental wanderings, on his experience as a literary drudge in London. It is easy to pick out passages in his *Vicar*, his *Citizen*, and elsewhere, which are, with hardly a disguise, autobiographical. Dr Primrose is his own father, and the good clergyman of the *Deserted Village* is his brother Henry; the simple Moses, the Gentleman in Black, young Honeywood in the *Good-Natur'd Man*, and even

Tony Lumpkin in *She Stoops to Conquer*, are so many reproductions of phases of himself; the incident on which this last play turns, the mistake of a gentleman's house for an inn, was a remembered blunder of his own in early life; and more than once his device for ending all happily is a benevolent uncle in the background. That of these simple elements he made so many charming combinations, really differing from each other, and all, though suggested by fact, yet hung so sweetly in an ideal air, proved what an artist he was, and was better than much that is commonly called invention. In short, if there is a sameness of effect in Goldsmith's writing, it is because they consist of poetry and truth, humour and pathos, from his own life, and the supply from such a life as his was not inexhaustible.

(4) Though so much of Goldsmith's best writing was generalised and idealised reminiscence, he discharged all special Irish colour out of the reminiscence. There are, of course, Irish references and allusions, and we know what a warm heart he had to the last for the island of his birth. But in most of his writings, even when it may have been Irish recollections that suggested the theme, he is careful to drop its origin, and transplant the tale into England. The ideal air in which his phantasies are hung is an English air. *The Vicar of Wakefield* is an English prose-idyll; *She Stoops to Conquer* is a comedy of English humour, and Tony Lumpkin is an English country lout; and, notwithstanding all the accuracy with which Lissoy and its neighbourhood have been identified with the Auburn of the *Deserted Village*, we are in England and not in Ireland while we read that poem. Goldsmith's heart and genius were Irish; his wandering about in the world had given him a touch of cosmopolitan ease in his judgement of things and opinions, and especially, what was rare among Englishmen then, a great liking for the French; but in the form and matter of his writings he was purposely English.

NOTES

1. Edward Bott, lawyer.
2. Catherine Horneck married W. H. Bunbury, brother of Sir Charles Bunbury.
3. William Hawes. See his account of Goldsmith's illness in this book.

Goldsmith and his First Biography*

ALICE C. C. GAUSSEN

It will be remembered that Dr Goldsmith had entrusted Percy with many of his papers, and had begged him to undertake to write his biography; but the Bishop either found no time to discharge the trust committed to him by his friend, or he was deterred through fear of associating himself with anything that might appear inconsistent with his episcopal position. In his day a bishop was expected, above all things, to be pompous. Sir William Pepys wrote of a newly chosen Bishop of Durham that he was 'as proper a person as could have been appointed, as his coldness and distance of manner will be less imputed to him as a fault in that very elevated station to which he is raised'.

When Goldsmith died, in 1774, Percy handed over the memoranda that he had received from the poet himself, with other materials collected by his relations, to Dr Johnson, in order that he should write a biography, to be published as a separate work, for the benefit of Goldsmith's family.

Prior excuses Johnson for not having included Goldsmith in his *Lives of the Poets* on the score of a dispute with Carnan, the bookseller, about the copyright of *She Stoops to Conquer*. It was probably also owing to the impracticability of Carnan, who was a man 'at variance with all his brethren,' that the project of this other work fell to the ground. But what appears less excusable is Dr Johnson's indifference in the matter, for 'he utterly forgot the whole subject, and lost many of the papers that Dr Percy had transferred to him.'

For nearly thirty years nothing was done. During his residence in Dublin, Bishop Percy discovered the destitute condition of Goldsmith's family and begged the assistance of his literary friends in

* In *Percy: Prelate and Poet* (London: Smith, Elder & Co., 1908) pp. 210–16. Editor's title.

London. He suggested that each member of the Club should subscribe a guinea, but this small mark of appreciation of one of its most
distinguished members was refused. After several years of starvation, the honest cabinet-maker, Maurice Goldsmith, was given a
small place in the Licence Office in Dublin, and was made mace-
bearer to the newly formed Irish Academy, and in 1793 Esther Goldsmith begged for the post of housekeeper to the same institution, a
position in which she would be permitted to sweep out the academic
dust. Under a sudden impulse of compassion for the family, Bishop
Percy had, in 1785, issued proposals for an edition of Goldsmith's
writings to be published for their benefit. The men of letters in
Goldsmith's native land welcomed this attempt, and one of their
number, William Jessop, wrote from Lismore on September 26, 1785:

> I am happy to find that your Lordship has again employed your
> pen for the public. Otherwise I should conclude that your genius
> had been chilled by the damps of our Bœotian climate. I have no
> doubt that you have erected for Goldsmith a more valuable monu-
> ment than sculpture even in Westminster Abbey could bestow.
> He was my college class-fellow; but with regret I own that I knew
> him little, and was very seldom in his company. I had not suffi-
> cient penetration to discover in Admetus's herdsman the con-
> cealed Apollo. You never saw him until an intercourse with life
> must have, in some degree, planed down his ruggedness. But it is
> a fact that in his college days his aspect and manners were uncom-
> monly against him. Nor was he at all distinguished in the aca-
> demic line. His tutor, Dr Wilder, often said that he had parts, but
> nobody believed him. To us he seemed nothing but a lounger.
> I still indeed fancy it was distress that scourged him into the
> temple of fame. It is remarkable that our other genius of the same
> period, Edmund Burke, was among us equally unnoticed. A col-
> lege was too narrow a stage for such a tumbler to show his feats
> of activity. But that a lad so mild, bashful, and retired, should
> change at once into a capital orator, demagogue, and statesman,
> was a metamorphosis almost as incredible as the wildest that
> Ovid has imagined. It was fortunate however both for him and
> Goldsmith that they crossed the Channel. England is the sunny
> side of the hill, where the seedlings of genius shoot quickly into
> fruitage; this kingdom is its northern aspect, where bleakness,
> and a total want of sunshine, condemn them to stunting and
> sterility.

After years passed in collecting material, nothing was done until an enthusiastic Irish clergyman, Dr Thomas Campbell, offered to edit the *Life of Goldsmith*, under Bishop Percy's direction. He is described by Mrs Thrale [Hester Lynch (Thrale) Piozzi] as a 'flashy, handsome, hot-headed, loud and lively Irishman'; his good humour was of that irrepressible kind that could boast of being able to live with a man of 'ever so odd a temper'. He professed himself equally ready to black Dr Johnson's shoes or shed his blood for him. In the matter of flattery he outran Mrs Thrale to such an extent that she could only borrow one of his own phrases and exclaim 'Upon my honour, sir, I'm but a twitter to him.' When Campbell came from the North of Ireland on purpose to see Johnson, with the same enthusiasm that Corelli had come to England to see Purcell, only to find that he had died, the Doctor exclaimed 'I should not wish to be dead in order to disappoint so foolish a person.' Dr Campbell was fond of dabbling in literature during his leisure hours in his comfortable Irish Rectory of Clones in Monaghan. He promised to conduct the work in a way that would not 'make the Bishop blush,' adding that it would always be in Percy's power to expunge, till it was 'brought into some shape that would not disgust him.' Though the Bishop declared he had 'particular reasons for not wishing to appear as Goldsmith's ostensible biographer', Campbell naturally desired to introduce his name, for he had not only supplied the material, but had also added many notes which he had taken down from Goldsmith's own mouth. Even in the account of his first visit to Goldsmith the Bishop wished his identity to be concealed. 'Could there be any harm,' urged Campbell, 'in letting the world know who the visitant was? If the dignity of the guest were concealed, the facts would lose their authenticity.'

Campbell was engaged in this work from the spring of 1790 to the autumn of 1791. The manuscript was sent to the Bishop, who made copious notes in its margin, which his chaplain, Dr Boyd, embodied in the text, rewriting portions at Percy's suggestion, and putting the whole into shape. In January 1796 everything remained still unsettled as to the publication of the work, for the 'trade' were already reaping a rich harvest from Goldsmith's works, and were unwilling that on this one edition a reasonable percentage should go to the benefit of the author's family. The dispute raged for over a year and a half, in spite of the assurance of Percy's literary friends that the booksellers would hardly think it prudent to 'provoke a pen so pointed and popular as his'. Percy insisted that the family should have a sum of money and a few copies for sale. Cadell and Davies, on behalf of the booksellers, refused to make any money payment, and only offered 250 unbound copies, all of which were to be sold in Ireland, the Bishop himself being charged with the carriage and the cost of binding. If the right of selling them in England was granted, the family were to content themselves with 200 copies stitched in 'blue paper'. Great anger and excitement prevailed on both sides during the prolonged dispute that followed. The Bishop at length reluctantly consented to take, in exchange for the Memoir which he had placed in Cadell and Davies's hands, 250 unbound copies of the *Miscellaneous Works*, to which it was prefixed – 125 to be sold in Dublin, and 125 in London, on behalf of the Goldsmith family.

But fresh trouble arose, for the trade could not settle among themselves what the edition was to contain; the Bishop's patience was exhausted, and he refused further help. A new editor was chosen in the person of Mr Rose (the friend of Cowper); Malone joined Percy in protesting against any tampering with the Memoir, but this protest was disregarded, and the Bishop's name was finally withdrawn from the scheme. So the matter stood in 1800.

In the meanwhile Goldsmith's last surviving brother had died in London in great poverty, with little or no relief. The only daughter of his eldest brother Henry also died in Dublin before her small share of the profits could be apportioned to her, while her mother was matron of the Meath Infirmary. Maurice Goldsmith's widow and sisters were in abject poverty. 'A few sold and unsold shabby books' in sheets 'represented their gains, while the booksellers, having sold all the impressions of the collected works reserved for themselves, had since issued two handsome editions, unencumbered with any obligations to the family of the author,' whose welfare the English public showed little zeal to promote.

This edition of Goldsmith's *Miscellaneous Works* was finally issued in 4 vols 8vo. in 1801.

Dr Percy's assistance was also sought by Boswell for his famous biographical work. On March 20, 1785, after the death of Dr Johnson, he wrote to the Bishop:

It is a great consolation to me now that I was so assiduous in collecting the wisdom and wit of that wonderful man. It is long since I resolved to write his life and conversation. He communicated to me a thousand particulars, from his earliest years upwards to the dignified intellectual state in which we have beheld him with awe and admiration. If your Lordship will favour me with anything concerning him, I shall be much obliged to you.

In answer to this letter the Bishop sent Boswell a Greek epitaph of Dr Johnson's on his poor friend Oliver Goldsmith, with a few details of Johnson's early life. He added:

I have neglected to commit to writing the many *bon mots* I have heard, but I recollect one. He was told of a man who had been obliged to apply to his neighbour, with whom he was not on very cordial terms, for a small piece of ground, which he thought necessary to complete his fine gardens. 'See,' said the sage, 'how inordinate desires enslave a man, and how they humiliate and enthral the proudest mind; here is a man submits to beg a favour from one he does not love, because he has made a garden-walk essential to his happiness!'

The Bishop, as usual, desired his name might not be mentioned. Boswell answered:

As to suppressing y^r Lordship's name when relating the very few anecdotes of Johnson with which you have favoured me, I will do anything to oblige you but that very thing. I owe it to the authenticity of my work, to its respectability, and to the credit of my illustrious friend, to introduce as many names of eminent persons as I can. It is a very small portion which is sanctioned by that of your Lordship, and there is nothing even bordering on impropriety. Believe me, my Lord, you are not the only Bishop in the number of great men with which my pages are graced. I am quite resolute as to this matter.

Memorandum*

OLIVER GOLDSMITH

Dr Oliver Goldsmith is Descended from a Spanish Family of the name of Romeiro or Romero, wch. came over to England[1] *in the time of Philip and Mary.*[2] From a marriage with a Miss Goldsmith the Descendents took the latter name.

His, the Doctor's, Father, the Revd Charles Goldsmith, was a native of the *County of Durham,*[3] but educated at Dublin College: he got a small Living in England, & afterwds. a good Benefice in Ireland: being rector of Kilkenny West. He died while his son Oliver was at College (about 25 years ago, 1773). *General Wolfe was allied to the Goldsmith Family.*

His mother was Ann, Daughter of the Revd Mr Jones, Rector of Elphin. Her maternal Uncle & Grandfather & other of her Family has been successively Rectors of Kilkenny West aforesd. *She was allied to Oliver Cromwell, in compliment to whom our Author was named Oliver.*

They had 7 children, sc.

1. Catharine, wife of Daniel Hudson Esq. of St Johns in the County of Roscommon.

2. Henry, who was curate of Kilkenny West, & left a son & Daughter at his Death, which happened 4 or 5 years ago. To this Brother the *Traveller* was inscribed.

3. Jane, wife of Mr Johnson a farmer in Ireland.

4. Oliver, born at a Place called Pallas in the County of Longford in the Parish of Forney (a house belonging to his Wife's Uncle the Revd Mr Green Rector of Kilkenny West with whom his Father & Mother then resided.) He was born 29th Novr 1731 (or 1730, h[4]

6. Charles, who went to Jamaica as a Cabinet Maker

5. Maurice, who lives now in Dublin a cabinet-maker.

7. John, who died young, circ. Aet. 12.

---

* In Katharine C. Balderston, *The History and Sources of Percy's Memoir of Goldsmith* (Cambridge: University Press 1926) pp. 13–16.

Th. Doctor's Mother died at Athlone, about 2 years & half ago.

The Doctor was educated chiefly under the Direction of his great Uncle Green, who placed him first at the Grammar School of Elphin[5] whence he removed him to Revd Mr Campbel's at Athlone, thence to Rev Mr Patrick Hughes's at Edgworthstown where he profitted more than any where, as the Master conversed with him on a footing very difft. from that of a young Scholar which the Doctor mentions with great gratitude & Respect. This Revd Gentleman is still alive.

At 13[6] years of age he was entered at Dublin University under the Tuition of Theaker Wilder, who used him very harshly *and was a debauched licentious Man.*[7]

After taking the Degree of A.B. he proceeded upon the Line of Physic and took the Degree of M.B. when he was about 20, he however ceased to reside after his degree of A.B.[8]

While he was an undergraduate his Father died & left his family in distressed Circumstances, upon wch. the Revd Mr Contarine,[9] who had mard his Father's sister, took him under his care & finished his Education.

After his Degree of M.B.[10] (about 1751) he removed to Edinburgh[11] where he persued his Medical Studies under Monro for about 2 years and half, and then removed to Leiden where he staid about a year studying Chimistry under Gaubius & Anatomy under Albinus.

He then went (about 1753) *to Padua in Italy,*[12] where he staid 6 months & saw *Venice, Florence, Virona, & all the North Part of Italy.* His Uncle dying while he was at Padua,[13] he was obliged to return back thro France &c. on Foot, lodging at Convents chiefly of the Irish Nation. After spending in this perigrination once a year he came to settle in London this was about the breaking out of the War in 1756:— Here he first tried to practice Physic, living in the Bank Side, *& then removed to the Temple,*[14] where he had plenty of Patients, but got no Fees.

The Revd Dr Milner, a dissenting Minister of note, who kept a Classical School, at Peckham in Surrey, having a long fit of illness of which he soon after died, becoming acquainted with him thro' his son, who was also a young Physician, invited him to take the Care of School During his illness, upon promise of securing him the Place of Chief Surgeon aboard an Indiaman: which promise he effectually fulfilled thro the Interest of Mr Jones then a Director, the Doctor had accordingly made preparations for going abroad (in the spring of 1757)[15] when happening to dine with Mr Griffith the Bookseller, who was acquainted in Dr Milner's Family, he was drawn into an agreemt.

to write in his *Review*, in consideration of his board, Lodging, & *100 Pd. per annum*.[16] In this Thraldom[17] he lived 7 or 8 Months[18] Griffith and his wife continually objecting to everything he wrote & insisting on his implicitly submitting to their corrections [ ] & since Dr Goldsmith lived with Griffith & his wife during this intercourse the Dr and he[19] thought it incumbt. to drudge for his Pay constantly from 9 o'clock till 2. The above agreemt. (which was in writing) was to hold for a twelve-month, but by mutual consent was dissolved at the end of 7 or 8 months; when the Dr removed into Green Arbour Court in the Old Bailey where he wrote his *Review of the Present State of Polite Literature in Europe printed for Dodsley* & published in 1759.[20] Here I first became acquainted with Dr Goldsmith from supping along with him at the lodgings of our common Friend Dr Grainger.

He afterwards removed to Lodgings at Mrs Carnan's in Wine License Court, Fleet Street: where he wrote his *Vicar of Wakefield*.

He then had Lodgings at Canonbury House Islington.

He afterwards Lodged up the Library Staircase in the Temple with Mr Jeffs, the Butler of the Temple.

He then removed to Chambers of his own at No. 2 Brick Court in the Temple.

His *Traveller* was published about 1764.

His *Deserted Village* in 1770.

NOTES

On 28 April 1773 Goldsmith dictated his own biographical notes to Bishop Thomas Percy, whom he had designated as his biographer. Although Percy used this document as a basis for his *Memoir of Goldsmith*, he sometimes deviated from it. Words in italics (other than titles of poems, books) indicate Percy's underlining. All notes are Balderston's.

1. 'To England' is crossed out.
2. On the opposite page, marked 'Corrections from Dr Goldsmith's Brother Maurice', is the following: 'The Doctor's great grandfather Juan Romero came over to Ireland as private tutor to a Spanish Nobleman in the last Century, who was then on his travels.'
3. The correction reads, 'A native of the County of Roscommon in the Diocese of Elphin at a place called Ballyoughter.'
4. '1731 (or 1730, h' is crossed out and '1728' added in the margin. This correction must have been Maurice's, since in the Memoir Percy offers 'a member of the Goldsmith's family' as authority for giving 1728 as the birth year.
5. Here is added on the correction sheet, 'under the Revd Michl Griffin.'
6. 'Or 15 or 16' is added above.

7. On the correction sheet opposite this statement is written, 'He was rusticated from college for being concerned in a riot to set at large a Prisoner confined for Debt, who had been arrested within the Precincts of the College.' The statement is made evidently on the authority of Thomas Wilson's letter to Malone, a copy of which is in the Meade collection.

8. Percy has written here in the margin, 'He most probably took no degree.' The entire paragraph is bracketed, as if to express doubt.

9. Opposite is written, 'Contryon or) Contarini.'

10. Above 'his Degree of M.B. is written, 'he left Dublin College', evidently as a substitute statement.

11. Here is added on the opposite sheet, 'at the expense of his Uncle Contarine who was like a Father to him'.

12. On the correction sheet opposite is written, 'To Switzerland.'

13. 'At Padua' is crossed out, and 'thus abroad' substituted.

14. The underlining of this shows that Percy doubted it, although he retained it in the Memoir. Proof of its veracity is found in an excised passage in Goldsmith's letter to his brother Henry, written in January 1758, in which he says, 'I have taken chambers in the temple.'

15. Percy has written '9' under the last figure of the date.

16. Over '100 Pd. per annum' is written, 'some pecuniary stipend.'

17. 'Thraldom' is excised, and 'situation' substituted.

18. From this point to 'and he thought it incumbt', the writing is scratched over. The bracketed portion is illegible.

19. 'And he' is inserted to make the passage read smoothly, after the excision.

20. Here two parallel lines are drawn, and seem to indicate where Goldsmith's dictation ends, and Percy's personal recollections begin.

Dr Goldsmith's Character*

THOMAS PERCY

This comedy¹ was very successful, and afterwards kept possession of the stage as a stock play. It added very much to the author's reputation, and, as was usual with Dr Goldsmith, brought down upon him a torrent of congratulatory addresses and petitions from less fortunate bards, whose indigence compelled them to solicit his bounty, and of scurrilous abuse from such of them, as being less reduced, only envied his success. We shall produce an instance of each.

* In *The Miscellaneous Works of Oliver Goldsmith, M.B.*, vol. 1 (London: T. Johnson *et al*, 1801) pp. 1–118. Editor's title.

ON DR GOLDSMITH'S COMEDY

SHE STOOPS TO CONQUER.

Quite sick in her bed Thalia was laid,
A sentiment puke had quite kill'd the sweet maid,
    Her bright eyes lost all of their fire:
When a regular Doctor, one Goldsmith by name,
Found out her disorder as soon as he came,
And has made her (for ever 'twill crown all his fame)
    As lively as one can desire.

Oh! Doctor, assist a poor bard who lies ill,
Without e'er a nurse, e'er a potion, or pill;
    From your kindness, he hopes for some ease,
You're a GOOD-NATUR'D MAN all the world does allow,
O would your good nature but shine forth just now,
In a manner – I'm sure your good sense will tell how,
    Your servant most humbly 'twould please.

The bearer is the author's wife, and an answer from Dr Goldsmith by her, will be ever gratefully acknowledged by his

Humble Servant,
JOHN OAKMAM
GRANGE COURT, SWALLOW STREET, CARNABY MARKET.

Saturday, March 27, 1773.

The other was an attempt to check our author's triumph, on the
ninth night of the representation, and was inserted in the *London
Packet* of Wednesday evening, March 24th, 1773, printed for
T. Evans, in Paternoster Row.[2] As our successful bard, we can scarcely
suppose, could be much elevated by the panegyrical strains or
addresses of his supplicatory adulators; so doubtless he would have
treated the base scurrility of his envious detractors with equal disregard or contempt, but for the officious kindness of one of those
good friends, who are so obliging as to take care that nothing disagreeable shall escape the notice of the aggrieved party. The offensive publication was very eagerly brought to him by a friend of this

stamp, who is believed to have been one of his own countrymen, an officer in the army, who thought he could not confer on him a greater favour, than by engaging him in a quarrel. Among his papers has been found the following unfinished relation of the adventure, dictated to an amanuensis; for the poor doctor's hand was too much bruised to hold a pen.

As I find the public have been informed by the newspapers of a slight fray, which happened between me and the editor of an evening paper; to prevent their being imposed upon, the account is shortly this.

A friend of mine came on Friday to inform me that a paragraph was inserted against me in the *London Packet*, which I was in honour bound to resent. I read the paper, and considered it in the same light as he did. I went to the editor, and struck him with my cane on the back. A scuffle ensued.

The editor alleged, that Dr Goldsmith came into his shop, and thus accosted him:

You have published a thing in your paper, (my name is Goldsmith,) reflecting upon a young lady. As for myself I do not mind it.

The publisher, who was probably as unconscious of the mischief to which he was instrumental, as the horse, that draws the artillery, is of the havoc it makes; stooped down to look behind his counter for the paper complained of. When our poet's friend pointed to the man's back, as presenting a fair mark for his cane, which he exercised upon it without mercy; and, as he says, a 'scuffle ensued,' wherein the Doctor himself got his share of blows, while his military friend, with great *sangfroid*, stood looking on. Nor is it easy to guess how it might have ended, when Dr Kenrick, a noted libeller, who was believed to be the author of the scurrilous letter, and was all the while in the publisher's counting-house, at length thought proper to interpose, parted the combatants, and sent the Doctor severely bruised home in a coach.

The subject of this dispute was long discussed in the public papers, which discanted on the impropriety of attacking a man in his own house; and an action was threatened for the assault; which was at length compromised, after our bard had published in the *Daily Advertiser* of March 31, 1773, the following address:

TO THE PUBLIC

Lest it should be supposed that I have been willing to correct in others an abuse of which I have been guilty myself, I beg leave to declare, that in all my life I never wrote, or dictated, a single paragraph, letter, or essay in a newspaper, except a few moral essays, under the character of a Chinese, about ten years ago, in the *Ledger*; and a letter, to which I signed my name, in the *St James's Chronicle*. If the liberty of the press, therefore, has been abused, I have had no hand in it.

I have always considered the press as the protector of our freedom, as a watchful guardian, capable of uniting the weak against the encroachments of power. What concerns the public most properly admits of a public discussion. But of late the press has turned from defending public interest, to making inroads upon private life; from combating the strong, to overwhelming the feeble. No condition is now too obscure for its abuse, and the protector is become the tyrant of the people. In this manner the freedom of the press is beginning to sow the seeds of its own dissolution; the great must oppose it from principle, and the weak from fear; till at last every rank of mankind shall be found to give up its benefits, content with security from its insults.

How to put a stop to this licentiousness, by which all are indiscriminately abused, and by which vice consequently escapes in the general censure, I am unable to tell; all I could wish is, that, as the law gives us no protection against the injury, so it should give calumniators no shelter after having provoked correction. The insults, which we receive before the public, by being more open, are the more distressing; by treating them with silent contempt, we do not pay a sufficient deference to the opinion of the world. By recurring to legal redress, we too often expose the weakness of the law, which only serves to increase our mortification by failing to relieve us. In short, every man should singly consider himself as a guardian of the liberty of the press, and, as far as his influence can extend, should endeavour to prevent its licentiousness becoming at last the grave of its freedom.

OLIVER GOLDSMITH

On the subject of this adventure, we find the following curious and amusing conversation in Boswell:

On Saturday, April 3, the day after my arrival in London this year, I went to his (Dr Johnson's) house late in the evening, and sat with Mrs Williams till he came home. I found in the *London Chronicle* Dr Goldsmith's apology to the public for beating Evans, a bookseller, on account of a paragraph in a newspaper published by him, which Goldsmith thought impertinent to him and to a lady of his acquaintance. The apology was written so much in Dr Johnson's manner, that both Mrs Williams and I supposed it to be his; but when he came home he soon undeceived us. When he said to Mrs Williams, 'Well, Dr Goldsmith's *manifesto* has got into your paper', I asked him if Dr Goldsmith had written it, with an air that made him see I suspected it was his, though subscribed by Goldsmith.

JOHNSON. Sir, Dr Goldsmith would no more have asked me to have written such a thing as that for him, than he would have asked me to feed him with a spoon, or to do any thing else that denoted his imbecility. I as much believe that he wrote it, as I had seen him do it. Sir, had he shown it to any one friend, he would not have been allowed to publish it. He has, indeed, done it very well, but it is a foolish thing well done. I suppose he has been so much elated with the success of his new comedy, that he has thought everything that concerned him must be of importance to the public.

BOSWELL. I fancy, Sir, this is the first time that he has been engaged in such an adventure.

JOHNSON. Why, Sir, I believe it is the first time he has *beat*; he may have been *beaten* before. This, Sir, is a new pleasure to him.

Dr Johnson took every opportunity that presented itself of praising the talents and genius of our author. Goldsmith's medical friend, [unidentified], by whose valuable and interesting communications we have been much obliged, has furnished us with the following anecdote:

I was dining at Sir Joshua Reynolds's, August 7, 1773, where, amongst other company, were the Archbishop of Tuam and Mr (now Lord) Eliot, when the latter making use of some sarcastical reflections on Goldsmith, Johnson broke out warmly in his defence, and, in the course of a spirited eulogium, said, 'Is there a man, Sir, now who can pen an essay with such ease and elegance as Goldsmith?'

On another occasion this great critic observed, 'Dr Goldsmith is one of the first men we now have as an author, and he is a very worthy man too. He has been loose in his principles, but he is coming right.'[4]

One of his last publications was, *An History of the Earth and Animated Nature*, in 8 vols. 8vo which was published in 1774, and which for two or three years before he had been preparing. The elegance and purity of the style, the interesting and striking reflections with which it abounds, and the powers of description which so frequently appear must atone for the want of original information on the subjects introduced, and for the occasional mistakes, which were impossible to be avoided by a writer who took all his materials on trust; and, as far as they could be supplied, chiefly from Buffon. For this work he is said to have been paid by the bookseller, 850*l.* and during the time he was engaged in this undertaking he had received the copy money for his comedy, and the profits of his third nights; so that his receipts amounted at this time to a considerable sum. He was however so liberal in his donations, and profuse in his disbursements; he was unfortunately so attached to the pernicious practice of gaming: and from his unsettled habits of life, his supplies being precarious and uncertain, he had been so little accustomed to regulate his expenses by any system of economy, that his debts far exceeded his resources; and he was obliged to take up money in advance from the managers of the two theatres, for comedies, which he engaged to furnish to each; and from the booksellers, for publications which he was to finish for the press. All these engagements he fully intended, and doubtless would have been able, to fulfil with the strictest honour, as he had done on former occasions in similar exigences; but his premature death unhappily prevented the execution of his plans, and gave occasion to malignity to impute those failures to deliberate intention, which were merely the result of inevitable mortality.

Dr Goldsmith, however, wrote by intervals about this time, his poems entitled, *The Haunch of Venison*, *Retaliation*, and some other little sportive sallies, which were not printed till after his death. He altered about this period the *Grumbler* from Sedley, which was acted at Covent Garden in the year 1772.[5] This alteration was made to serve Mr Quick at his benefit, and acted only on that night; it was never printed. But the chief publication which he was then projecting was *An Universal Dictionary of Arts and Sciences*. This he intended should be a work of general entertainment as well as instruction; in which by the graces of his style and his powers of writing, he hoped to render his account of the other sciences as interesting and amusing as he had made natural history in his book of *Animated Nature*. He had engaged all his literary friends, and the members of the club to contribute articles, each on the subject in which he excelled; so that it could not but have contained a great assemblage of excellent disquisitions. He accordingly had prepared a *Prospectus*,[6] in which, as usual, he gave a luminous view of his design; but his death unfortunately prevented the execution of the work.

He was subject to severe fits of the strangury, owing probably to the intemperate manner in which he confined himself to the desk, when he was employed in his compilations, often indeed for several weeks successively without taking exercise. On such occasions he usually hired lodgings in some farmhouse a few miles from London, and wrote without cessation till he had finished his task. He then carried his copy to the bookseller, received his compensation, and gave himself up perhaps for months without interruption, to the gaieties, amusements, and societies of London.

And here it may be observed, once for all, that his elegant and enchanting style in prose flowed from him with such facility, that in whole quires of his histories, *Animated Nature*, &c. he had seldom occasion to correct or alter a single word; but in his verses, especially his two great ethic poems,[7] nothing could exceed the patient and incessant revisal, which he bestowed upon them. To save himself the trouble of transcription, he wrote the lines in his first copy very wide, and would so fill up the intermediate space with reiterated corrections, that scarcely a word of his first effusions was left unaltered.

In the Spring of 1774, being embarrassed in his circumstances, and attacked with his usual malady, his indisposition, aggravated too by mental distress, terminated in a fever; which on 25th March had become exceedingly violent, when he called in medical assistance. Although he had then taken ipecacuanha to promote a vomit, he would proceed to the use of James's Fever Powder, contrary to the advice of the medical gentlemen, who attended him. From the application of these powders he had received the greatest benefit in a similar attack nearly two years before, but then they had been administered by Dr James himself in person. This happened in September 1772. But now the progress of the disease was as unfavourable as possible; for from the time abovementioned every symptom became more and more alarming till Monday April 4th, when he died, aged 45.

Mr Hawes, his apothecary, who had discouraged the use of these powders, in the manner Dr Goldsmith chose to apply them, published in vindication of himself, and of two eminent physicians, who had concurred with him in opposing their patient's use of them:

An account of the late Dr Goldsmith's illness, so far as relates to the exhibition of Dr James's Powders, &c. London, printed for W. Brown, &c. 1774, 4to.[8]

In reply to some positions in this pamphlet an advertisement was printed in the papers containing the depositions of the servants, who had attended their master in his illness, in which it appeared that Goldsmith had strongly intimated his opinion, that he had not received the genuine powders, from the effects being so different from what he had ever experienced of this his favourite medicine.

It was deliberated by Sir Joshua Reynolds and other friends of the poor departed bard, whether it was more expedient to give him an expensive public funeral, or to inter him privately, and reserve the expenditure for a more lasting monument in the Poets' Corner in Westminster Abbey. The latter opinion prevailed, and his remains were privately interred in the Temple burial-ground, at five o'clock on Saturday evening, April 9, attended by the Rev. Joseph Palmer, (nephew of Sir Joshua Reynolds, and now Dean of Cashel in Ireland,) Mr Hugh Kelly, the dramatic poet, Messrs John and Robert Day, Mr Etherington, and Mr (now Dr) Hawes, his apothecary.

By a subscription raised among our poet's friends, and chiefly by his brethren of the club, a marble monument was executed by Nollekens, and placed in Westminster Abbey, between that of Gay and the Duke of Argyle in the Poets' Corner; consisting of a large medallion, with a good resemblance of the Doctor in profile, embellished with appropriate ornaments; and underneath on a tablet of white marble, the following inscription written by Dr Johnson.[9]

OLIVARI GOLDSMITH,
Poetæ, Physici, Historici.
Qui nullum fere scribendi genus
Non tetigit.
Nullum quod tetigit non ornavit
Sive Risus essent movendi
Sive Lacrymæ.
Affectuum potens at lenis Dominator
Ingenio sublimia – Vividus Versatilis

Oratione grandis nitidus Venustus
Hoc Monumentum Memoriam coluit
Sodalium Amor
Amicorum Fides
Lectorum Veneratio
Natus Hibernia Forniæ Lonfordiensis
In Loco cui Nomen Pallas
Nov. xxix. MDCCXXXI.[10]
Eblanæ Literis institutus
Obiit Londini
April iv. MDCCLXXIV.[11]

In addition to this Latin epitaph Dr Johnson honoured the memory of his friend with the following Greek tetrastich:

Τὸν Τάφον ἐισοράας τον Ολιβαρίοιο, χονίην
Αφροσι μὴ σεμνην, Ξἐινε, πόδεσσι πἁΤει °
Οἴσι μέμηλε φύσις, μὲΤρων χάρις, ἑρΤα παλαιῶν
ΚλαιέΤε ποιήΤην, ιοΤόριχον, φύσιχον.

The general traits of Dr Goldsmith's character have been in a great measure delineated in the preceding pages. He was generous in the extreme, and so strongly affected by compassion, that he has been known at midnight to abandon his rest, in order to procure relief and an asylum for a poor dying object who was left destitute in the streets. Nor was there ever a mind whose general feelings were more benevolent and friendly. He is however supposed to have been often soured by jealousy or envy; and many little instances are mentioned of this tendency in his character: but whatever appeared of this kind was a mere momentary sensation, which he knew not how like other men to conceal. It was never the result of principle, or the suggestion of reflection; it never imbittered his heart, nor influenced his conduct. Nothing could be more amiable than the general features of his mind: those of his person were not perhaps so engaging.

His stature was under the middle size, his body strongly built, and his limbs more sturdy than elegant: his complexion was pale, his forehead low, his face almost round and pitted with the smallpox; but marked with strong lines of thinking. His first appearance was not captivating; but when he grew easy and cheerful in company, he relaxed into such a display of good humour, as soon removed every unfavourable impression.

Yet it must be acknowledged that in company he did not appear to so much advantage as might have been expected from his genius and talents. He was too apt to speak, without reflection, and without a sufficient knowledge of the subject; which made Johnson observe of him, 'No man was more foolish when he had not a pen in his hand, or more wise when he had.'[12] Indeed with all his defects, (to conclude nearly in the words of that great critic,) 'As a writer he was of the most distinguished abilities. Whenever he composed, he did it better than any other man could. And whether we consider him as a Poet, as a Comic Writer, or as an Historian, (so far as regards his powers of composition,) he was one of the first writers of his time, and will ever stand in the foremost class.'[13]

NOTES

Goldsmith had named his friend Reverend Thomas Percy (1729–1811), Bishop of Dromore, to be his official biographer and had provided him with materials to help him in this task.

1. *She Stoops to Conquer.*
2. We would not defile our page with this scurrilous production, so shall insert it in the margin. (Percy's note.)

FOR THE LONDON PACKET

TO DR GOLDSMITH

Vous vous nayez par vanité.

SIR,

The happy knack which you have learnt of puffing your own compositions provokes me to come forth. You have not been the editor of newspapers and magazines, not to discover the trick of literary *humbug*. But the gauze is so thin, that the very foolish part of the world see through it, and discover the doctor's monkey face and cloven foot. Your poetic vanity, is as unpardonable as your personal; would man believe it, and will woman bear it, to be told, that for hours the *great* Goldsmith will stand surveying his grotesque orang-outang figure in a pier glass? Was but the lovely H—k[3] as much enamoured, you would not sigh my gentle swain in vain. But your vanity is preposterous. How will this same bard of Bedlam ring the changes in the praise of Goldy! But what has he to be either proud or vain of? *The Traveller* is a flimsy poem, built upon false principles; principles diametrically opposite to liberty. What is the *Good natur'd Man*, but a poor, water-gruel, dramatic dose? What is the *Deserted Village*, but a *pretty* poem, of easy numbers, without fancy, dignity, genius, or fire? And pray what may be the last *speaking pantomime*, so praised by the doctor himself, but an incoherent piece of stuff, the figure of a woman, with a fish's tail, without plot, incident, or intrigue? We are made to laugh at stale, dull jokes, wherein we mistake pleasantry for wit, and grimace for humour; wherein every scene is unnatural, and inconsistent with the rules, the laws of nature and of drama, *viz.* Two gentlemen come to a man of fortune's house, eat, drink, sleep, &c. and take it for an inn. The one is intended as a lover to the daughter; he talks with her for some hours, and when he sees her again in a different dress, he treats her as a bar girl, and swears she squinted. He abuses the master of the house, and threatens to kick him out of his own doors. The Squire, whom we are told is to be a fool, proves the most sensible being of the piece; and he makes out a whole act, by bidding his mother lie close behind a bush persuading her that his father, her own husband, is a highwayman, and that he is come to cut their throats; and to give his cousin an opportunity to go off, he drives his mother over hedges, ditches, and through ponds. There is not, sweet sucking Johnson, a natural stroke in the whole play, but the young fellow's giving the stolen jewels to the mother, supposing her to be the landlady. That Mr Colman did no justice to this piece, I honestly allow; that he told all his friends it would be damned, I positively aver; and from such ungenerous insinuations, without a dramatic merit, it rose to public notice: and it is now the *ton* to go to see it; though I never saw a person that either liked it or approved it, any more than the absurd plot *of the Home's* tragedy of *Alonzo*. Mr Goldsmith, correct your arrogance! reduce your vanity; and endeavour to believe, as a man, you are of the plainest sort; and as an author, but a mortal piece of mediocrity.

> *Brise le miroir infidèle*
> *Qui vous cache la vérité.*

TOM TICKLE

3. Mary Horneck (?1750–1840), of whom Goldsmith is said to have been fond.

4. James Boswell, *The Life of Samuel Johnson, LL.D.*, vol. 1 (London: Charles Dilly, 1791) p. 367.

5. Goldsmith felt so much indebted to the actor, Quick, for ensuring the success of *She Stoops to Conquer* that for Quick's benefit-performance he adapted a three-act farce by Brueys and Palaprat, *Le Grondeur* (1693), under the title of *The Grumbler*; or to be exact, he adapted Sir Charles Sedley's translation of it, which had been produced in 1702. *The Grumbler* was presented at Covent Garden in 1773, not 1772.

6. This, with other papers and fugitive pieces, fell into the hands of Mr Bott, a gentleman in the Temple, and author of a valuable work on the Poor Laws (since dead) who had lent Dr Goldsmith large sums of money, and being his principal creditor, took possession of his effects, &c. (Percy's note).

7. *The Traveller* and *The Deserted Village*.

8. Included in this book.

9. See a humorous account of an address to Dr Johnson, in the form of a round robin, concerning this epitaph, in Boswell's *Life of Johnson*, vol. III, p. 84 (Percy's note).

10. The year of Dr Goldsmith's birth had been universally mistaken, until his family some time after his death furnished correct information of the circumstance, which they state to have happened in the year 1728. That he was born in that year is confirmed by his letter to his brother Henry, written in 1759, when he says his age was 31 (Percy's note).

11.   This Monument is raised to the Memory of
                      OLIVER GOLDSMITH,
                  Poet, Natural Philosopher, and
                             Historian,
              Who left no species of writing untouched,
                                 or
                      Unadorned by his Pen,
                     Whether to move laughter,
                          Or draw tears:
                      He was a powerful master
                        Over the affections,
                Though at the same time a gentle tyrant;
                 Of a genius at once sublime, lively, and
                        Equal to every subject:
                    In expression at once noble,
                        Pure and delicate.
                       His memory will last
                 As long as society retains affection,
                  Friendship is not void of honour,
              And reading wants not her admirers.
              He was born in the kingdom of Ireland,
                    At Fernes, in the province
                           Of Leinster,
                  Where Pallas had set her name,
                         29th Nov. 1731,
                   He was educated at Dublin,
                      And died in London,
                        4th April, 1774.

12. Boswell, *Life of Johnson*, vol. 4, p. 29.

13. *Ibid*, vol. 3, p. 273.

The Character of Goldsmith*

JAMES BOSWELL

No man had the art of displaying with more advantage as a writer, whatever literary acquisitions he made. *Nihil quod tetigit non ornavit.*[1] His mind resembled a fertile, but thin soil. There was a quick, but not a strong vegetation, of whatever chanced to be thrown upon it. No deep root could be struck. The oak of the forest did not grow there, but the elegant shrubbery, and the fragrant parterre appeared in gay succession. It has been generally believed that he was a mere fool in conversation,[2] but in truth this has been greatly exaggerated. He had, no doubt, a more than common share of that hurry of ideas which we often find in his countrymen, and which sometimes produces a laughable confusion in expressing them. He was very much what the French call *un étourdi*,[3] and from vanity and an eager desire of being conspicuous wherever he was, he frequently talked carelessly without knowledge of the subject, or even without thought. His person was short, his countenance coarse and vulgar, his deportment that of a scholar awkwardly affecting the easy gentleman. Those who were in any way distinguished, excited envy in him to so ridiculous an excess, that the instances of it are hardly credible. When accompanying two beautiful young ladies (the Miss Hornecks) with their mother, on a tour to France, he was seriously angry that more attention was paid to them than to him; and once at the exhibition of the fantoccini in London, when those who sat next him observed with what dexterity a puppet was made to toss a pike, he could not bear that it should have such praise, and exclaimed, with some warmth, 'Pshaw! I can do it better myself!'

He, I am afraid, had no settled system of any sort, so that his conduct must not be strictly scrutinised; but his affections were social and generous, and when he had money he gave it away very liberally. His desire of imaginary consequence predominated over

---

* In *The Life of Samuel Johnson, LL.D.*, vol. 1 (London: Charles Dilly, 1791) p. 377. Editor's title.

his attention to truth. When he began to rise into notice, he said he had a brother who was Dean of Durham; a fiction so easily detected, that it is wonderful how he should have been so inconsiderate as to hazard it.

NOTES

1. See Goldsmith's Epitaph in Westminster Abbey, reproduced in this book, p. 202.

2. Horace Walpole, who admired his writings, said, 'he was an inspired idiot;' and Garrick described him as one

for shortness called Noll,
Who wrote like an Angel, and talk'd like poor Poll.

3. scatterbrain; harum-scarum; a thoughtless, heedless person.

He had Many Good Qualities*

MARY HAMILTON

Dr Johnson said of the late Dr Goldsmith that he never knew a head so unfurnished; he gave him credit for being a clerical scholar so far as he had learnt at school, but that he knew very little of any subject he ever wrote upon; that his abilities were equal to any man's he ever met with, but that he had no application; upon the most common subjects he was very ignorant, of which he gave many and daily proofs; he had the habit of lying to such a degree that the Club to which he belonged and the society he lived in never scrupled to tell him they wanted faith for what he advanced. He was one of the most envious of men; he could not bear to hear the praise of anyone, nay! even the beauty of a woman being praised he could not endure. Kelly having been successful in some of his publications, it greatly

* In *Mary Hamilton, Afterwards Mrs John Dickenson, At Court and at Home, from Letters and Diaries, 1756–1816*, ed. Elizabeth and Florence Anson (London: John Murray, 1925) pp. 181–3. Editor's title.

irritated him. After talking of him one day with great acrimony he looked at himself in the glass and said, 'I am not so ugly as Kelly either'. Mrs Carter said [that] Goldsmith was a very vulgar man and vastly conceited. Mrs Garrick told us that Goldsmith had lived much at her house during Mr Garrick's lifetime, that he never was happy if he did not gain the attention of the whole company to himself, that he would sometimes utter the grossest nonsense, and talk like a man that had not common sense; the laugh against him, however, was never so painful as the not being attended to in preference to anyone else. He had many good qualities; his chief failings were: want of veracity, envy, vanity and want of economy. One striking instance of the first-mentioned, was when he was introduced to the Club of which Johnson, Burke, Reynolds, etc., were members, he told them that his brother was Dean of Durham, *thinking to impose on the company.* When this was mentioned Miss More exclaimed: 'Surely the *Red Book* would have informed him better.' 'O,' says Johnson, 'he was so ignorant of common things that he did not know there was such a book. Though he wrote the history of England he knew nothing more of it than turning over two or three English historians and abridging them; his *Natural History* was a work of the same kind taken from Buffon; would he otherwise have assured us that cows shed their horns?' He used to say when anything he wrote was not liked, that it proceeded from the envy of the public and their malice in endeavouring to mortify him. We owe his pretty novel of *The Vicar of Wakefield* to his being plunged in debt; he was so distressed that he sat down to write that book to extricate himself; as soon as it was finished he carried it to Dodsley who would only give him £20 for the copy; upon which the necessitous author withdrew his publication. He had not a farthing in his pocket and he wrote to his generous friend, Dr Johnson, for a guinea, at the same time acquainting him with his melancholy situation. Dr Johnson sent the guinea and ordering his coach as soon as he could, drove to Goldsmith's lodgings; he found him endeavouring to drown his cares with Madeira (for the first use he made of the guinea was to procure this liquor). Johnson seized the bottle of which Goldsmith had emptied half, and corking it declared he should not taste another drop; he then comforted him by an assurance that he would sell his novel to good advantage which he did a few days after and sold it for £70. After this Dr Johnson said he did not believe Goldsmith ever ran in debt.

Goldsmith's Benevolence*

GEORGE COLMAN, THE YOUNGER

Oliver Goldsmith, several years before my luckless presentation to
Johnson, proved how *'Doctors differ.'* – I was only five years old
when Goldsmith took me on his knee, while he was drinking coffee,
one evening, with my father,[1] and began to play with me; which
amiable act I return'd with the ingratitude of a peevish brat, by
giving him a very smart slap in the face, – it must have been a tingler
– for it left the marks of my little spiteful paw upon his cheek. This
infantile outrage was followed by summary justice; and I was locked
up by my indignant father, in an adjoining room, to undergo solitary
imprisonment, in the dark. Here I began to howl and scream, most
abominably; which was no bad step towards liberation, since those
who were not inclined to pity me might be likely to set me free, for
the purpose of abating a nuisance.

At length a generous friend appeared to extricate me from jeop-
ardy; and that generous friend was no other than the man I had so
wantonly molested, by assault and battery – it was the tender-hearted
Doctor himself, with a lighted candle in his hand, and a smile upon
his countenance, which was still partially red, from the effects of my
petulance – I sulked and sobbed, and he fondled and soothed – till
I began to brighten. Goldsmith, who, in regard to children, was like
the Village Preacher he has so beautifully described – for

Their welfare pleased him, and their cares distress'd,

seized the propitious moment of returning good-humour – so he put
down the candle, and began to conjure. He placed three hats, which
happened to be in the room, upon the carpet, and a shilling under
each: – the shillings, he told me, were England, France, and Spain.
'Hey, presto, cockolorum!' cried the Doctor – and, lo! on uncovering
the shillings which had been dispersed, each beneath a separate hat,

* *Random Records* (London: Henry Colburn & Richard Bentley, 1830) pp. 110-13.
Editor's title.

they were all found congregated under one. I was no politician at five years old and, therefore, might not have wondered at the sudden revolution which brought England, France, and Spain, all under one crown; but, as I was also no conjuror, it amazed me beyond measure. Astonishment might have amounted to awe for one who appeared to me gifted with the power of performing miracles, if the good-nature of the man had not obviated my dread of the magician; but, from that time, whenever the Doctor came to visit my father,

I pluck'd his gown, to share the good man's smile;

a game at romps constantly ensued, and we were always cordial friends, and merry playfellows. Our unequal companionship varied somewhat, in point of sports, as I grew older, but it did not last long – my senior playmate died, alas! in his forty fifth year, some months after I had attained my eleventh. His death, it has been thought, was hastened by 'mental inquietude' – if this supposition be true, never did the turmoils of life subdue a mind more warm with sympathy for the misfortune of our fellow-creatures – but his character is familiar to everyone who reads: in all the numerous accounts of his virtues and his foibles – his genius and absurdities, his knowledge of nature, and his ignorance of the world – his 'compassion for another's woe' was always predominant; and my trivial story, of his humouring a froward child, weighs but as a feather in the recorded scale of his benevolence.

NOTES

George Colman, the Younger (1762–1836), English dramatist.
1. George Colman, the Elder (1732–1794), English dramatist. He produced *She Stoops to Conquer*.

Bibliography

This bibliography includes the principal accounts of the life of Goldsmith, plus some additional material not represented in this book.

'Anecdotes of the Late Dr Goldsmith', *Universal Magazine*, 67 (Aug. 1780) pp. 82–5.

Anson, Elizabeth, and Anson, Florence (eds) *Mary Hamilton, afterwards Mrs John Dickenson, at Court and at Home, from Letters and Diaries 1756 to 1816* (London: John Murray, 1925) pp. 181–3.

Balderston, Katharine C., 'The Birth of Goldsmith,' *Times Literary Supplement*, 7 Mar. 1929, pp. 185–6.

——, *The History and Sources of Percy's 'Memoir of Goldsmith'* (Cambridge: University Press, 1926).

Barbauld, Anna, [a biographical sketch of Goldsmith.] in *The British Novelists, with an Essay and Prefaces, Biographical and Critical* (London: F. C. & J. Rivington *et al.*, 1810) vol. 23, pp. i–xx.

Beattie, James, *London Diary, 1773*, ed. Ralph S. Walker (Aberdeen: University Press, 1946) *passim* (includes references to Goldsmith).

Bingley, William, 'Oliver Goldsmith', in *Biographical Conversations* (London: John Sharpe, 1818) pp. 176–87 (biographical sketch in dialogue form).

Black, William, *Oliver Goldsmith*, English Men of Letters Series (London: Macmillan, 1878).

Boswell, James, *Boswell for the Defence, 1769–1774*, ed. William K. Wimsatt, Jr. and Frederick A. Pottle, Yale Editions of the Private Papers of James Boswell (New York: McGraw-Hill, 1959) *passim* (includes references to Goldsmith's death and reactions connected with it).

——, *Boswell in Search of a Wife, 1766–1769*, ed. Frank Brady and Frederick A. Pottle, Yale Editions of the Private Papers of James Boswell (New York: McGraw-Hill, 1956; London: William Heinemann, 1957) *passim* (on the relationship between Boswell and Goldsmith).

——, *Boswell on the Grand Tour: Italy, Corsica, and France, 1765–1766*, ed. Frank Brady and Frederick A. Pottle, Yale Editions of the Private Papers of James Boswell (New York: McGraw-Hill, 1955) pp. 295–7 (a London street encounter with Goldsmith).

——, *Boswell's London Journal, 1762–1763*. Now first published from the original manuscript, with an Introduction and Notes by Frederick A. Pottle, with a Preface by Christopher Morley (New York: McGraw-Hill, 1950) *passim* (Boswell's first meeting with Goldsmith).

——, *The Correspondence and Other Papers Relating to the Making of the Life of Johnson*, vol. 3, ed. with an Introduction and Notes by Marshall Waingrow (New Haven: Yale University Press, 1969) *passim* (includes anecdotes and comments on Goldsmith).

——, *The Correspondence of James Boswell with Certain Members of the Club*, ed. Charles N. Fifer (New Haven: Yale University Press, 1976) *passim*.

——, *Letters of James Boswell*, 2 vols. Collected and edited by Chauncey Brewster Tinker (Oxford: Clarendon Press, 1924) *passim* (includes some material on Goldsmith).

——, *The Life of Samuel Johnson, LL. D.*, 2 vols (London: Charles Dilly, 1791) *passim* (includes an unsympathetic portrait of Goldsmith).

Brydges, Sir S. E., *Censura Literaria*, vol. 5 (London: Longman, 1807) pp. 54–75 (biographical sketch).

Burke, Edmund, *The Correspondence of Edmund Burke*, vol. 2, ed. Dame Lucy S. Sutherland (Cambridge: University Press, 1960) pp. 535–6.

C., S. P., 'Memorials of Literary Characters, no. XVIII: Pedigree of the Poet Goldsmith', *Gentleman's Magazine* , 7 (Mar. 1837) p. 242.

Campbell, Thomas, *Diary of a Visit to England in 1775 by an Irishman* (Sidney: David Lovett Welsh, Atlas Office, 1854; rpt. with an Introduction by S. C. Roberts, ed. James L. Clifford (Cambridge: University Press, 1947) (The Rev. Campbell took over the task of writing Goldsmith's biography from Percy, but died before the manuscript was completed).

Cary, Henry Francis, *Lives of the English Poets, from Johnson to Kirke White* (London: G. H. Bohn, 1846) pp. 222–46.

Chalmers, Alexander, 'Life of Goldsmith', in *Works of the British Poets*, vol. 16 (London: J. Johnson et al., 1810) pp. 479–87.

Chapman, R. W., 'A Goldsmith Anecdote', *Times Literary Supplement*, 13 June 1929, p. 474.

——, 'Percy and Goldsmith,' *Times Literary Supplement*, 3 June 1926; reprinted in *Johnsonian and Other Essays and Reviews* (Oxford: Clarendon Press, 1953) pp. 170–3 (review article).

Church, Richard, 'Oliver Goldsmith,' *The Criterion*, 8 (Apr. 1929) pp. 437–44 (on contemporary attitudes toward Goldsmith).

Clarke, Ernest, 'The Medical Education and Qualifications of Oliver Goldsmith', *Proceedings of the Royal Society of Medicine*, 7 (1914) pp. 88–98.

——, 'Oliver Goldsmith as a Medical Man', *Nineteenth Century and After*, 75 (Apr. 1914) pp. 821–31.

Collins, A. S. *Authorship in the Days of Johnson* (London: Robert Holden, 1927) *passim* (a study of the relation between author, patron, publisher and public, 1726–80).

Colman, George the Younger, *Random Records*, vol. I (London: Henry Colburn & Richard Bentley, 1830) pp. 110–13 (includes anecdotes of Goldsmith).

Colum, Padraic, 'Young Goldsmith', *Scribner's*, 86 (Nov. 1929) pp. 555–63 (covers the years 1749–52).

Cooke, William, *Memoirs of Samuel Foote* (London: Richard Phillips, 1805) vol. I, pp. 184–6; vol. 3, pp. 77–8.

——, 'Table Talk', *European Magazine*, 21 (Feb. 1792) p. 88; 24 (Aug. 1793) pp. 91–5; (Sep. 1793) pp. 170–4; (Oct. 1793) pp. 258–64 (anecdotes of Goldsmith by a contemporary acquaintance).

Cowley, Patrick, 'The Eighteenth-Century Divine', *Theology*, 50 (Apr. 1947) pp. 258–63 (the influence of Goldsmith's father and maternal grandfather as clergymen).

Cradock, Joseph, *Literary and Miscellaneous Memoirs*, 4 vols (London: J. B. Nichols, 1826) *passim* (includes anecdotes of Goldsmith).

Crane, Ranald S., 'Oliver Goldsmith', *Philological Quarterly*, 9 (Apr. 1930) pp. 190–91 (the date of Goldsmith's birth).

——, 'Oliver Goldsmith, M.B.,' *Modern Language Notes*, 48 (Nov. 1933) pp. 463–5 (the date at which Goldsmith first made his claim to the possession of a medical degree).

Crawford, Raymond, 'Oliver Goldsmith and Medicine', *Proceedings of the Royal Society of Medicine*, 8 (1915) pp. 7–26 (there is not enough evidence that Goldsmith received a medical degree).

Cumberland, Richard, *Memoirs* (London: Lackington, Allen & Co., 1806) pp. 257–9; 267–74 (recollections of Goldsmith by a fellow dramatist).

Cunningham, Peter (ed.) *The Works of Oliver Goldsmith*, vol. I, Murray's British Classics (London: John Murray, 1854) (includes an introduction).

Davies, Thomas, *Memoirs of the Life of David Garrick*, 2 vols (London: Thomas Davies, 1780) *passim* (recollections of Goldsmith by his publisher).

Dawson, George, 'Oliver Goldsmith', in *Biographical Lectures* (London: K. Paul, Trench, 1886) pp. 172–90.

Dobson, Austin, *Life of Oliver Goldsmith*, in Great Writers Series (London: Walter Scott, 1888).

Evans, John, 'Goldsmith and William', *European Magazine*, 53 (May 1808) pp. 373–5 (William was a servant in Dr Milner's family).

——, 'Memoirs of Oliver Goldsmith', in *The Poetical Works of Oliver Goldsmith* (London: Thomas Hurst, 1804) pp. vi–xlvi (Goldsmith's teaching at Dr Milner's school).

Forster, John, *The Life and Times of Oliver Goldsmith* (London: Bradbury *et al.*, 1848).

Forsyth, William, *The Novels and Novelists of the Eighteenth Century* (London, privately printed, 1871) pp. 305–12.

Freeman, William, *Oliver Goldsmith* (London: Herbert Jenkins, 1951; New York: Philosophical Society, 1952).

Friedman, Arthur, 'The Year of Goldsmith's Birth', *Notes and Queries*, 196 (1 Sep. 1951) pp. 188–9.

Garrick, David, *The Private Correspondence of David Garrick with the Most Celebrated Persons of His Time*, 2 vols (London: Henry Colburn & Richard Bentley, 1831) *passim*.

Gaussen, Alice C. C., *Percy: Prelate and Poet* (London: Smith, Elder & Co., 1908) chap. 8 (the friendship of Percy and Goldsmith).

Giles, Henry, *Lectures and Essays*, vol. I (Boston: privately printed, 1850) pp. 218–57.

Ginger, John, *The Notable Man: The Life and Times of Oliver Goldsmith* (London: Hamish Hamilton, 1977).

G[lover, Samuel], 'Anecdotes of the Late Dr Goldsmith', *Annual Register*, 17 (July 1774) pp. 29–34.

——, 'Authentic Anecdotes of the Late Dr Goldsmith', *Universal Magazine*, 54 (May 1774) pp. 252–5 (largely the same).

——, *The Life of Dr Goldsmith Written from Personal Knowledge, Authentic Papers, and Other Indubitable Authorities* (London: P. & J. Dodsley, 1777) (largely the same).

——, 'The Life of Oliver Goldsmith', in *Poems and Plays by Oliver Goldsmith* (Dublin: Price, Sleater, Watson, *et al.*, 1777) pp. i-x (largely the same).

Goldsmith, Oliver, *The Collected Letters of Oliver Goldsmith*, ed. Katharine C. Balderston (Cambridge: University Press, 1928).

——, 'Memorandum', in Katharine C. Balderston, *The History and Sources of Percy's Memoir of Goldsmith* (Cambridge: University Press, 1926) pp. 13–16 (Goldsmith's own autobiographical notes, dictated to Bishop Percy on 28 Apr. 1773).

'Goldsmith and His Biographers', *Littell's Living Age*, 19 (Oct. 1848) pp. 145–61 (a review article).

Graham, W. H., 'Oliver Goldsmith', *Contemporary Review*, 181 (May 1952) pp. 304–8 (aspects of Goldsmith's character).

Gwynn, Stephen, *Oliver Goldsmith* (London: Butterworth; New York: Henry Holt, 1935).

Hamilton, Walter, *Parodies of the Works of English and American Authors Collected and Annotated by W. H.*, vol. 3 (London: Reeves & Turner, 1886) pp. 3–20.

Harp, Richard L., 'Thomas Percy's *Life of Oliver Goldsmith*: An Edition', Ph.D. dissertation, University of Kansas, 1974.

Hart, Paxton, 'The Presentation of Oliver Goldsmith in Boswell's *Life of Johnson*', *Re: Arts and Letters*, 3 no. 2 (1970) pp. 4–15.

Hawes, William, *An Account of the Late Dr Goldsmith's Illness* (London: W. Brown & H. Gardner, 1774) (Hawes, an apothecary, attended Goldsmith in his last illness).

Hawkins, Sir John, *The Life of Samuel Johnson, LL.D.* (London: T. Cadell, 1787) (includes anecdotes of Goldsmith).

Henderson, W. A., 'The Birthplace of Oliver Goldsmith', *Notes and Queries*, 8 (19 Oct. 1901) p. 330.

Hodson, Mrs, 'Mrs Hodson's Narrative', in *The Collected Letters of Oliver Goldsmith*, ed. Katharine C. Balderston (Cambridge: University Press, 1928) pp. 162–77 (Goldsmith's sister Catherine).

Howitt, William, *Homes and Haunts of the Most Eminent British Poets*, vol. I (London: Richard Bentley, 1857) pp. 286–336.

Hutton, Laurence, *Literary Landmarks of London* (London: Trübner, 1885) pp. 118–26.

Irving, Washington, *Life of Oliver Goldsmith, with Selections from His Writings*, 2 vols (New York: Harper, 1840).

——, *Oliver Goldsmith* (New York: G. P. Putnam, 1849) (expands and revises his previously published *Life*).

Isaacs, J. See Scott, Temple.

Jackson, R. Wyse, 'Goldsmith in Camouflage', *Dublin Magazine*, 22 (July–Sep. 1947) pp. 47–53 (much of Goldsmith's life still needs explanation).

Jeffares, A. Norman, *Oliver Goldsmith*, in Writers and Their Work Series (London: Longmans for the British Council and the National Book League, 1959) (includes a brief biographical survey).

Kalisch, M. M., *The Life and Writings of Oliver Goldsmith* (London: privately printed, 1860).

Kelly, Rev. J. J., 'The Early Haunts of Oliver Goldsmith', *Irish Monthly Magazine*, 7 (1879) pp. 194–205. Reprinted in book form as *The Early Haunts of Oliver Goldsmith* (Dublin: Sealy *et al.*, 1905).

Kent, Elizabeth E., *Goldsmith and His Booksellers* (Ithaca, N.Y.: Cornell University Press, 1933).

Kent, W. Charles, *Dreamland, with Other Poems* (London: privately printed, 1862) pp. 67–71 (Goldsmith at Edgeware).

King, Richard Ashe, *Oliver Goldsmith* (London: Methuen, 1910).

Kirk, Clara M., *Oliver Goldsmith* (New York: Twayne. 1967) (Includes some biographical material).

Kirkpatrick, T. Percy, 'Goldsmith in Trinity College, and His Connection with Medicine', *Irish Journal of Medical Science* (Apr. 1929) pp. 142–62.

Knowles, Richard Brinsley Sheridan, 'The Personality of Goldsmith,' *Dublin University Magazine*, 88 (Sep. 1876) pp. 352–67.

Krans, Horatio Sheafe, *Oliver Goldsmith* (Folcroft, Pa.: Folcroft Press, 1969) (includes biographical material).

Lautenhammer, Dr, *Oliver Goldsmith: A Biographical Sketch* (Munich: privately printed, 1874).

Lawrence, Frederick, 'Goldsmith and His Biographers', *Littell's Living Age*, 24 (Feb. 1850) pp. 337–46 (review article).

Le Breton, Maurice, 'Goldsmith et l'Italie', *Caliban*, 3 (Mar. 1967) pp. 29–56 (Goldsmith's relationship to Italy).

Leslie, Charles Robert, and Tom Taylor, *Life and Times of Sir Joshua Reynolds*, 2 vols (London: John Murray, 1865) (includes numerous anecdotes of Goldsmith).

Lucas, F. L., *The Search for Good Sense; Four Eighteenth-Century Characters: Johnson, Chesterfield, Boswell, Goldsmith* (London: Cassell, 1958) pp. 283–338.

Lytton Sells, Arthur, *Oliver Goldsmith: His Life and Works* (London: George Allen & Unwin; New York: Barnes & Noble, 1974).

McAdam, Edward L., 'Goldsmith, the Good-Natur'd Man', in *The Age of Johnson: Essays Presented to Chauncey Brewster Tinker*, ed. Frederick W. Hills. Introduction by Wilmarth S. Lewis (New Haven: Yale University Press, 1949) pp. 41–7 (a character sketch).

Malone, Edmond, 'The Life of Oliver Goldsmith', in *Oliver Goldsmith: Poems and Plays* (Dublin: Price et al., 1777) pp. iii–xi; (London: B. Newbery & T. Johnson, 1780) pp. iii–x (reprints Glover's 'Anecdotes', with corrections and additions).

Mason, William Shaw, *A Statistical Account or Parochial Survey of Ireland*, vol. 3 (Dublin: privately printed, 1849) pp. 356–66 (the Goldsmith family).

Masson, David, 'Biographical Introduction', in *The Miscellaneous Works of Oliver Goldsmith* (London: Macmillan, 1869) pp. ix–lx.

Melmoth Courtney, 'The Tears of Genius, Occasioned by the Death of Dr Goldsmith', printed for T. Becket, April 1774, pp. 1–13 (an elegy).

Milner-Barry, Alda, 'A Note on the Early Literary Relations of Oliver Goldsmith and Thomas Percy', *Review of English Studies*, 2 (Jan. 1926) pp. 51–61.

Montague, John, 'Tragic Picaresque: Oliver Goldsmith, the Biographical Aspect', *Studies: An Irish Quarterly Review*, 49 (Spring 1960) pp. 45–53.

Moore, Frank Frankfort [E. Littlemore], *The Life of Oliver Goldsmith* (London: Constable, 1910).

Morgan, Lee, 'Boswell's Portrait of Goldsmith', in *Studies in Honor of John C. Hodges and Alwin Thaler*, ed. Richard Beale Davis and John Leon Livesay

(Knoxville: University of Tennessee Press, 1961) pp. 67–76 (Boswell did not denigrate Goldsmith).

Morris, John 'Was Goldsmith a Physician?' *Journal of the American Medical Association*, 26 (16 May 1896) pp. 953–7 (there is no proof of Goldsmith's having obtained a medical degree).

Nichols, John, *Literary Anecdotes of Eighteenth Century*, 9 vols (London: Nichols, Son & Bentley, 1812–15) (includes numerous references to Goldsmith).

Northcote, James, *Memoirs of Sir Joshua Reynolds, Knt, Comprising Original Anecdotes of Many Distinguished Persons, His Contemporaries and a Brief Analysis of His Discourses* (London: Henry Colburn, 1813). Revised as *The Life of Sir Joshua Reynolds*, 2 vols (London: Henry Colburn, 1818) (includes anecdotes of Goldsmith).

Percy, Sholto (J. C. Robertson), *The Percy Anecdotes*, 20 vols (London: privately printed, 1823) (includes anecdotes of Goldsmith).

Percy, Thomas, et al., 'The Life of Dr Oliver Goldsmith', in *The Miscellaneous Works of Oliver Goldsmith, M.B.*, vol. I (London: J. Johnson et al., 1801) pp. 1–118 (the first really carefully written life of Goldsmith).

Piozzi, Hester Lynch (Thrale), *Anecdotes of the Late Samuel Johnson, LL.D. during the Last Twenty Years of His Life* (London: T. Cadell, 1786) *passim* (includes cruel anecdotes of Goldsmith).

——, *Autobiography, Letters and Literary Remains of Mrs Piozzi*, 2 vols, ed. A. Hayward (London: Longmans, 1861) *passim* (includes cruel anecdotes of Goldsmith).

Plumb, J. H., 'Oliver Goldsmith and *The Vicar of Wakefield*', in *Men and Places* (Boston: Houghton Mifflin, 1963) pp. 288–94 (Goldsmith's literary career).

Pottle, Frederick A., *James Boswell: The Earlier Years, 1740–1769* (New York: McGraw-Hill; London: Heinemann, 1966) *passim* (reference to the friendship between the two men).

Prior, [Sir] James, *The Life of Oliver Goldsmith, M.B., from a Variety of Original Sources*, 2 vols (London: John Murray, 1837) (the first full-length biography).

Quintana, Ricardo, *Oliver Goldsmith: A Georgian Study* (New York: Macmillan; London: Collier-Macmillan, 1967) (a portrait of Goldsmith).

Redding, Cyrus, 'Goldsmith's Grave', *New Monthly Magazine*, 124 (1862) pp. 426–30.

Reynolds, Sir Joshua, *Portraits*, ed. Frederick W. Hilles (London: William Heinemann; New York: McGraw-Hill, 1952) pp. 27–59 (a character sketch of Goldsmith).

Roberts, S. C., 'Oliver Goldsmith', *Times Literary Supplement*, 8 Mar. 1934, p. 162 (Boswell's attitude towards Goldsmith).

Rocher, Marg L., 'Goldsmith l'Eternel vagabond', *Revue Anglo-Américaine*, 2 (Oct. 1933) pp. 22–32 (Goldsmith's life and travels).

Rossetti, William Michael, 'Oliver Goldsmith', in *Lives of Famous Poets* (London: E. Moxon, 1878) pp. 161–75.

Ryan, Richard, *Biographical Hibernia: A Biographical Dictionary of the Worthies of Ireland*, 2 vols (London: R. Ryan, 1821) pp. 181–97.

Sands, Mollie, 'Oliver Goldsmith and Music', *Music and Letters*, 32 (Apr. 1951) pp. 147–53 (a love of music was an essential part of Goldsmith's make-up).

Saure, Heinrich, and Th. Weischer, *Biographies of English Poets* (Leipzig, privately printed, 1880) pp. 118–42.

Scott, Temple, *Oliver Goldsmith, Bibliographically and Biographically Considered* (New York: Bowling Green Press; London: Maggs Brothers, 1928) (a catalogue based on the collection in the Library of W. M. Elkins).

Scott, [Sir] Walter, *Lives of the Novelists*, vol. 2 (Paris: A. & W. Galignani, 1825) pp. 91–117.

Seitz, R. W., 'The Irish Background of Goldsmith's Social and Political Thought', *PMLA*, 52 (June 1937) pp. 405–11 (Goldsmith's admiration for the English middle class sprang from his Irish experiences).

Sells, Arthur Lytton. See Lytton Sells, Arthur.

Sherwin, Oscar, *Goldy: The Life and Times of Oliver Goldsmith* (New York: Twayne, 1961; Collier Books, 1962).

Spalding, William, 'Introductory Memoir', in *The Works of Oliver Goldsmith* (London: James Blackwood, 1858). Also in *The Complete Works of Oliver Goldsmith* (London: Blackwood, 1872) pp. 7–20.

S[tephen], [Sir] L[eslie], 'Oliver Goldsmith', in *The Dictionary of National Biography, vol. 22*, ed. Sidney Lee (London: Smith, Elder, 1890) pp. 86–95.

Taylor, John, *Records of My Life*, vol. I (London: Edward Bull, 1832) pp. 107–9.

Thrale, Hester Lynch. See Piozzi, Hester Lynch Thrale.

Vernon, G. E. Harcourt, *On the Life and Writings of Oliver Goldsmith: A Lecture* (London: J. W. Parker, 1854).

Waller, John Francis, 'Life of Oliver Goldsmith', in *The Works of Oliver Goldsmith*, with Introductions, Notes, and a Life by John F. Waller (London: Cassell, Petter & Galpin, 1864) pp. ix–xliv.

Wardle, Ralph, *Oliver Goldsmith* (Lawrence: University of Kansas Press, 1957) (the standard biography).

Watkins, John, *Characteristic Anecdotes of Men of Learning and Genius* (London: James Cundee, 1808) pp. 513–28.

Welsh, Charles, *A Bookseller of the Last Century. Being Some Account of the Life of John Newbery, etc.* (London: Griffith *et al.*, 1885) (includes accounts of Newbery's business relations with Goldsmith).

Woods, Samuel H., Jr., 'Introduction', in *Oliver Goldsmith: A Reference Guide* (Boston: G. K. Hall, 1982) pp. xiii–xx (surveys Goldsmith's biography and scholarship).

Index

(The figures in parentheses after entry numbers indicate the number of references. Works by Goldsmith are listed under Goldsmith, Oliver.)

226

INDEX

Life of Goldsmith, The (Glover), ix,
xii, 214
Life of Dr Oliver Goldsmith, The
(Percy), ix, xii, 215, 217
Life of Oliver Goldsmith (Dobson),
46, 214
Life of Oliver Goldsmith (Irving), 215
Life of Oliver Goldsmith, The (Prior),
xii, 38, 49–51, 145, 170, 217
Life of Samuel Johnson, The
(Boswell), xi(2), 8, 34, 43, 55,
175, 205, 206, 207–8
Life of Samuel Johnson, The
(Hawkins), 30, 215
Lismore, 188
Lissoy, Co. Westmeath, xiv, 131,
186
Literary and Miscellaneous Memoirs
(Cradock), 88–97
Literary Club, x, xv, 33, 80, 84, 88,
101, 124(2), 125, 126, 139, 144,
158, 180, 188
Littell's Living Age, 215, 216
Littlemore, E., 216
Lives of the Poets (Johnson), x, 187
London, 2(3), 18, 20, 24, 45, 49(2),
50(2), 82, 93(3), 98(4), 112,
114(2), 119, 126, 135(2), 136,
153, 162(4), 168(4), 172, 177(2),
181, 185, 188, 193, 199, 201(2),
207
London Chronicle, 199
London Diary (Beattie), 52–3
London Packet, 86, 87, 169, 196, 197,
204
Longford, County, xiv, 1, 10, 11, 12,
112, 131, 161, 192
Louth, Lord, 100
Louvain, 1, 134, 162
Love for Love (Congreve), 98
Love's Labour's Lost (Shakespeare),
54, 55
Lucas, F. L., 216
Ludgate Hill, xv
Ludlam, Rev. William, 90(2), 93(6)
Lumpkin, Tony (a character), 69,
94(2), 95(2), 99, 186(2)
Lyttleton, Lord, 4, 140, 152, 163
Lytton Sells, Arthur, xii, 216

Macaulay, Lord, x
Maclane, Laughlin, 1
Mainwaring, Professor, 97
Malagrida, 66
Malahide Castle, xi
Malone, Edmond, 43, 98–101, 161,
165, 190, 216
'Man in Black, The' (a character),
14, 127, 138
Marlborough, Duchess of, 166
Marlow (a character), 69(2)
Marteilhe, Jean, xv
Martinelli, Vincenzo, 31
*Mary Hamilton, Afterwards Mrs John
Dickenson* (Anson), 208–9, 212
Marylebone, 97
Marylebone Gardens, 41
Mason, William Shaw, 216
Masson, David, 167–86, 216
Mayo, Rev. Dr, 177(2)
McAdam, Edward L., 216
M'Donnell, M'Veagh, 49–51
Meade, Constance, 18, 195
Melmoth, Courtney, 216
Memoirs (Cumberland), 56–62
Memoirs of Samuel Foote (Cooke), 43,
62–3
Memoirs of Sir Joshua Reynolds
(Northcote), 152–7
Memoirs of the Life of David Garrick
(Davies), 64–73, 214
Middlesex, 79
Millamant (a character), 94(2)
Miller, Joe, 63, 64
Mills, Edward (G.'s cousin), 25, 29
Mills, Major, 59, 85, 154
Milner, Hester, 20–22
Milner, Rev. Dr Thomas, 2, 22(3),
23(2), 98, 125, 135, 136(2),
162(2), 193(2), 214
Milner-Barry, Alda, 216
Mirabel (a character), 94
*Miscellaneous Works of Oliver
Goldsmith, The*, ix, xii, 167–86,
190(2), 195–204, 216
Mitford, 37
Mitre Tavern, 39, 40, 172
Modern Language Notes, 214
Montagu, Mrs, 38

Works of Oliver Goldsmith, The, 214, 218(2)
Woty, William, 110

Yale Editions of the Private Papers of James Boswell, xi

Yates, Dick, 94(4)
Yates, Mrs (an actress), 93

Zeck, George and Luke, 3
Zobeide (Cradock), 97